THE

PANCHADASI

OF

SRIMAD VIDYARANYA SWAMI

Sri Garib Das Oriental Series No. 317

THE

PANCHADASI

OF

SRIMAD VIDYARANYA SWAMI

TRANSLATED WITH COPIOUS ANNOTATIONS

BY

NANDA LAL DHOLE

Sri Satguru Publications
A Division of
Indian Books Centre
Delhi - India

Published by
Sri Satguru Publications,
Indological and Oriental Publishers
A Division of
Indian Books Centre
40/5, Shakti Nagar,
Delhi-110007
India

Second Edition; Calcutta .1899
Third Corrected Edition : Delhi , 2008

ISBN 81-7030-871-2

Printed at Sachin Printers, Delhi.

PREFACE.

—:o:—

FOR one so deservedly reputed, as the author of the PANCHADASI, which holds a high place in the realm of Vedantic Philosophy, it is but proper, that a short notice of his life and writings should go along with its English version. But in the matter of biography, there never was a time, nor is it even now the case,—when any attention was paid to it. India boasts of a literature which is unique; every department of learning bears the stamp of genius,—originality, deep research, and profound and sublime thoughts. Unfortunately the lives, that were spent in thus enriching the Sanskrit, and opening up a world of new ideas and new philosophies, were allowed to drop in time into the gulf of eternity, without leaving any trace of their struggles and sufferings, their joys and pleasures, beyond the simple fact that they lived and died. Suppression of self or egoism was a religious principle with them; and this may to a certain extent account for the lack of authentic records of the lives of our great men and good. And, if to this be added the certain fact, that they lived quite unostentatiously, with very slender means, barely enough to satisfy the simple wants of the flesh (already reduced to starvation limits); without that artificial halo, which encircles the mushroom authors of the day: it will be evident that the incident of such lives as theirs would neither be interesting nor profitable. We had no press that could puff in those days; the art of printing was yet in the womb of distant futurity; the renown of a scholar was confined in the narrow circle of his nativity, where a solitary student would be found engaged in receiving, and he in imparting, instruction to them. His pupils, gradually spread his fame and worth ; for, after finishing their course, they turn into new pastures, and set themselves up as professors. In this way, the learned scholar draws pupils from remote places, who copy their teachers' manuscripts and writings, and, are taught in them. Under circumstances so repressive and trying it is a matter of congratulation that, what is yet left us, is a standing monument, imperishable like time itself, and undying like glory. With the paucity of materials for a suitable biography, so much of fiction has been transplanted on it that we had one time thought of giving up the idea ; but recollecting that a blind uncle is better than none, we begin our task.

Madhava, Madhavarya, Madhvacharya, and Madhavamatya were the names by which Vidyarana Swami used to pass prior to his turning into a recluse. He was born in the fourteenth century of the Christian era at Golconda. It appears that Vijayanagar was the capital of Bukkka I, whose family priest and minister our author was. Very little is known of his early life. His parents, as may naturally be expected from their connection with the reigning family, were in affluent circumstances and very highly respected. His father was, as he himself speaks of him in his commentary on Parasar's Law Book, "Narayan of good renown," and mother,—Sreemutty. He had two more brothers, called Sayan (the great Commentator of the Rig Veda)* and

* Unfortunately some Oriental scholars confound him with his brother, the subject of this memoir. Both the brothers, Sayan and Madhav, had their separate Commentaries on the Vedas.

H. D.

Somenath. They belonged to the Bharadwaj Gotra and *Bodhvayani Shakha* of the Black Yajur Veda. He wrote many works, all of which attest his learning and erudition. Next to Sankaracharya, he is everywhere recognised as an authority on the doctrine of Non-duality. He wrote on Medicine, Grammar, Astrology, besides writing Commentaries on the Four Vedas known by the name of *Madhavaprokash*; Commentaries on the *Brahma Mimansa* or *Adhikaran Mala*; Commentary on Parasar's Law Book; *Anumitiprakash Brahma Gita*, or a critical analysis of the doctrine of non-duality based on the *Sruti*, and a review of Madhava, Ramanuja and Sankar's views. Here also he has added his commentary for elucidating the text, and called *Prakashika*; *Jivanmuktiviveka*; *Drigdrishvaviveka* and the gloss of *Aparokshyanuvuti*. His *Sarvadarshan Sangraha* treats of fifteen systems as follow :—(1) Charvaka-darshna, (2) Buddha-darshana; (3) Arhata-darshna; (4) Ramanuja-darshana; (5) Puranprajna; (6) Nakulis-pasupat; (7) Shaiva; (8) Pratyabhijna; (9) Raseshavar; (10) Aulik; (11) Akshapada; (12) Jaimini; (13) Panini; (14) Sankhya; and (15) Patanjal. Among his minor works are *Jaiminya Naymala, Acharmadhava* and *Sankardigbijaya*.

It is neither profitable nor interesting to enter into details about the various anecdotes current about Madhava's snpernatural gifts. For instance, it is said, that with a view of propitiating the Gayatri Devi he had collected several learned Brahmins from various parts of the country, and on the auspicious occasion regularly commenced the Gayatripurashcharana, but he was unsuccessful in meeting her. This made him indifferent to worldly enjoyments, and ultimately turned him into a recluse. Then Gayatri insisted upon him to ask for a boon, and Madhava requested her to cause a shower of gold in the Karnatic, so that every one may become rich. This was actually fulfilled. Later in life he settled himself in the Sringeri Math founded by Sankaracharya of which he became the reputed head. Here his last work *Panchadasi* was written, but as he did not live long to finish it, the work was left to his Guru Bharatitirtha Muni, who wrote the latter nine books and thus completed the fifteen books of which the Panchadasi is made.*

N. D.

* And so it did happen that with this short Biographical Sketch of the author, the English translator of the *Panchadasi* paid his tribute of Nature. He died in his 47th year on the 14th of March, 1887 at 5-30 A. M., deeply regretted by all who knew him.

H. D.

THE PANCHADASI.

SECTION I.

SALUTATIONS be to my GURU SREE SHANKARANANDA who is non-different from the Supreme Self and who is the chief resort for the destruction of infatuity and its attendant evils derived from conceit and egoity, leading to ineffable misery every being acting under the influence of free will, like to those fearful animals—the dog, crocodile and others living in water.

2. Love and reverence to the said GURU will produce a pure heart, and enable the individual to distinguish the Real from the non-real objective world together with the elements of which it is made. This I proceed to consider.

3. To establish the identity or oneness of the Everlasting Intelligence and Bliss—PARABRAHMA—with the Individuated Self, it is necessary that the latter must also have the same everlasting intelligence and bliss. With this view, the non-difference of knowledge as helps the individual in the cognition of several objects is being cited here. We distinguish a

thing by its name, for instance a golden earring and a golden bangle are equally derived from gold, the difference in their shape determines their individuality.

4. And if this be omitted, the remaining gold is one in both, yet each has its name. In the same way, the Individual Spirit is one with the Universal:—the difference consists in their associates, which if left out, there remains only one consciousness. Hence the individual state being one of ever-lasting intelligence, it is one with the Absolute. But this requires proof and for such a purpose it is necessary, in the first instance, to establish consciousness as one and if that can be done, then it is eternal and true, for what is always one, is eternal.

5. There are three states of consciousness (*a*) waking, (*b*) dreaming, and (*c*) dreamless slumber. The first is defined as that condition when consciousness takes hold of a subject by the instrumentality of the senses. In the conciousness of the wakeful state are floating sound, touch, make, taste and smell—ether, air, fire, water and earth—(*i.e.*,) multiform subjects. What floats, is an object of cognition, subject, etc., and that in which it floats is consciousness. The respective consciousnesses which enable us to cognise an object by touch, sound, etc., may appear different and multiform, but such difference and diversity exist only in the subject or object which consciousness covers—while consciousness is one and alone; and that difference in the subject or object is easily recognisable by the individual characteristics or features presentin it.

6. For instance, a cow and horse are different from one another, a pitcher is also a separate object from a cloth; hence for variety, all objects are different from similar other objects and for oneness consciousness whether as regards sound touch, sight or in any other condition is non-different. In short, the condition which enables an individual to form an idea of an object by touch or sight, or by its sound, has reference to one

and the same consciousness, and what appears to us different *viz.*, sound quite distinct from touch, is due to the diversity of the objects. Therefore the consciousness present in the waking condition is one, but the subject or object of such consciousness is several, and for this multiformness we are apt to mistake the one and impartite consciousness as several, but if we can shake off such difference-creating-a-mistake then consciousness appears as one.

7. This intelligence is the Atma (Self) and for his being the receptacle of supreme felicity, he is full of bliss. If from extreme misery one is disgusted with his self, yet it cannot be said that self is not an object of love, for no one desires that he may be miserable, or that he may die; on the contrary every one desires that he may live long, and that he may enjoy happiness. This proves the self to be the centre of affection.

8. The affection for a son, or towards a friend is all for self, if it were otherwise, then we would have felt equally for an ascetic. But love for self is not actuated by any consideration in the way as it influences our connection in regard to a friend—for it is quite possible, and it happens so, for a rupture to take place with a son; but this is neither possible nor does it ever occur in the case of an individual's love for self. Hence the principle of individuality or self is blissfulness.

9. The individual spirit or self, having thus been shewn by the foregoing demonstrations to be eternal, intelligence, and full of bliss is expressed by the word *Twam* (Thou); the PARABRAHMA, Universal Spirit or Supreme Brahma as expressed by the word *Tat* (That) is eternal intelligence and bliss (this is self-evident.) Hence their non-difference is the object which is explained in the *Vedanta*. This will subsequently be pointed out.

10. Having thus established the Atma to be full of bliss it remains to be seen whether or not, happiness is manifested always. If it is not manifested, then Self cannot be the seat of

supreme felicity ; for unless an ojbect appear beautiful, it cannot excite our love ; moreover, even if it is manifested, Self cannot be styled to be the seat of happiness, for naturally after having derived, happiness, there is no inclination for finding out its cause, hence where is the possibility of attaching felicity to him ? And as after having tasted such supreme and ineffable happiness, there is no more hankering left for the gratification of worldly desires, therefore love for self owes its origin to no other second principle for which it is said, the semblance of bliss attached to the Atma is both manifested and its reverse.

12. As in an assembly of boys recanting the *Vedas* the voice of no one boy can be singled out plainly, though it is audible, hence it can be said to be audible and inaudible at the same time, similarly for an impediment the manifestibility of Self being full of bliss and its opposite condition are present at the same time.

13. The nature of the impediment which prevents the manifestibility of the supreme happiness of the Atma, though always present, is now being declared. That which is eternally present, but which appears to be non-eternal is called an impediment, or obstacle. In this way, the supreme felicity of the Atma is ever present but from being blinded by the poison of worldly desires, such felicity appears to be impermanent and ill defined, a result of what is called an obstacle, which prevents its manifestibility, though it is ever present.

14. What is the cause of obstacle ? As in the foregoing example of an assemblage of boys, the cause of the obstacle which prevents the voice of a single boy being heard is the combining of several voices loudly recanting, so in the present instance the cause of the obstacle which prevents the manifestibility of the supreme felicity of the Atma is *Avidya* which has neither a beginning nor end and is indescribable.

15. This *Avidya* owes its origin to *Prakriti*. *Prakriti* is the shadow of the Supreme Brahma with the three attributes

of *Satwa*, *Raja*, and *Tamas*, it is subtle. It is of two kinds, *Mâya* (Illusion) and *Avidya* (Ignorance.)

16. Though equally derived from *Prakriti* their constitution differs; for *Mâya* is made of the pure *Satwa*. The reflection of intelligence in *Mâya* after having subdued it, is called the omniscient, Iswara (the Lord).

17. The reflection of intelligence in *Avidya* and entirely subservient to it is called the *Jiva* (Life soul); purity or insentiency of Ignorance and its varying shades determine the constitution of a Deva, man, cow, horse, etc. It is likewise called the cause-body; and one having a conceit for this cause-body is called *Prâjna*.

18. Now to ascertain the Astral body (*linga sharira*) the five elements require to be considered. From the aforesaid *Prakriti* (Matter) abounding in (*Tamas*) darkness, by the command of Iswara (Lord) were derived first ether, next air, fire, water and earth for the enjoyment of *Prâjna* and others.

19. [*Prakriti*] Matter has been shown to possess the three properties, *Satwa*, *Raja*, *Tamas*, hence the elements which are derived from it, must also have them in common—for [the qualities of a cause-body are transmitted to its products.] From the satwavic particle of each of the five elements are derived in a consecutive order the several senses *viz.*, from the good particles of ether,—the ear, from air,—the skin, from fire,—eye, from water,—tongue, and from earth,—nose.

20. From the collective totality of goodness of the five elements is derived the internal organ (*antakarana*) which for a difference of its formation is divided into *Manas* (Mind) and *Booddhi* (Intellect) the first is characterised by doubts and the second by certitude.

21. From the intermediate meddlesome or active (*Raja*) quality present in each of the five elements, are derived in a serial order, speech and the five organs of action. That is to say ether is the cause of the organ of speech, air—the hands, fire—the feet, water—the anus, and earth—the genitals.

22. The collective totality of the same *Raja* as present in all the five elements is the progenitor of *Prâna* (vital air) which for a variety of function is divided into

(a) '*Prana*' the air situated at the tip of the nose.

(b) '*Apana*' the air residing in the anus.

(c) '*Samana*' which helps the digestion of food.

(d) '*Udana*' situated in the throat.

(e) '*Vyana*' which resides in all parts of the body.

23. The five senses, five organs of action, five vital airs, the mind and intellect constitute the seventeen characteristicts of the subtle body otherwise called Linga sharira. Hence to determine it, the foregoing explanation concerning the origin of ether, etc., was necessary.

24. *Prajna* associated with the impure goodness abounding in ignorance, for the conceit that he is the subtle Astral body is called *Taijas*; and *Iswara* associated with the pure goodness abounding in illusion for a similar conceit is called *Hiranyagarbha*. Here the conceit in the subtle body being identical in both, their actual difference consists in this:—that *Taijas* is the distribute segregate, and *Iswara* collective totality of all Astral bodies. That is to say Iswara or Lord has conceit that he is the collective totality of all Astral bodies while Taijas has a conceit for his individual subtle body only.

25. This *Hiranyagarbha* knows that he is non-different and inseparable from all collective subtle bodies with which he is associated. Hence he is called a collective totality. In the same way from want of knowledge *Taijas* is a distributive segregate.

26. Having thus dealt with the subtle Astral body and its associates *Taijas*, *Prajna* and *Hiranyagarbha* and *Iswara*, the origin of the gross physical body is now being considered. With this object quintuplication is to be explained. *Iswara* with a view of providing adequate food and drink for *Prajna* and other beings and their place of enjoyment, and for the production of the four varieties of gross bodies, viviparous,

oviparous, earthy and germinating, divided each of the five elements, ether and the rest, in the following wise :—

27. He divided each element into two equal parts, took the first half of each, divided it into four parts, and added to it, (one eighth), each first portion of the other elements.

28. From this quintuplication of the elements has been produced the Brahmâ's egg, and the fourteen abodes from Bhur to Patal etc., together with all the enjoyable things and the necessary bodies capable of enjoying them.* *Hiranya-garbha* for the conceit that he is present universally in the collective totality of all gross physical bodies is called *Vaiswanara*, or *Virat* [for he manifests in divers forms] *Taijas* for its presence in the distributive segregate of individual gross physical body and for the conceit that he is a *Deva*, man, cow, horse, etc., is designated *Viswa*.

29. Now the unspiritual and (ignorant) of these Devas and men for enjoying happiness and suffering woe, in this state of existence have recourse to actions which again lead to future re-births for similar enjoyment and suffering in proportion to their merits and de-merits. Thus being hurled into continual re-births, they are debarred from ever enjoying true felicity.

30. As in the instance of an insect falling into a whirlpool, pass from one whirlpool to another in an attempt to extricate itself, failing which it is prevented from attaining to happiness.

31. As the same insect for previous good actions from the kind hearted interference of an individual is rescued from

* " From the said fractional combinations of the elements have likewise been evolved, one above the other, the several abodes designated as Bhur, Bhuvar, Swar, Mahar, Janas, Tapas and Satya ; and one below the other,the nether spheres,severally called Atala, Vitala,'Sutala, Rasatala, Talatala, Mahatala, and Patala, together with Brahma's egg, the four physical (gross) bodies with their adequate food-grains and drink."—*Vide* DHOLE'S *Vedanta-sara*, p. 25.

the whirlpool and deposited under the shade of a tree on the river bank to enjoy happiness.

32. So these ignorant and unspiritually inclined *Devas* and men for previous good actions of a prior existence, having received instruction from a teacher, devoted to *Brahma*, come to differentiate the Atma from the five sheaths *Annamaya*, etc., and attain to supreme felicity (*i.e.*,) emancipation.

33. What are the five sheaths? They are the *Annamaya, Pranamaya, Manomaya* and *Anandamaya*. They cover the *Atma* like a sheath, hence they are designated *kosha* (sheaths). As the silk-worm after having woven its sac becomes confined and is subjected to much inconvenience, so these five-sheaths cover the *Atma*, render him forgetful of his real nature and hurl him into a relationship with the external world.

34. Now for an examination of these sheaths. The resulting product of quintuplication of the elements is the physical body. This is designated the *Annamayakosh* or the foodful covering. The subtle Astral body having within it the five organs of action developed from the active *Raja*, together with five vital airs constitute what is called the Life-sheath (*Pranamayakosh*).

35. The five organs of sense (eye, hearing, etc.,) the resulting product of the satwavic quality with the Mind (*Manas*) which is full of doubts represent the mental sheath. But in connection with the Spiritual Intelligence—the faculty of certitude—(*Booddhi*) the five senses form the cognitional sheath.

36. Ignorance (*Avidya*) which has been described as the cause-body has a particle of satwavic or good quality, which is impure; this with its inherent tendency for delights, pleasures, love and affection, etc., is termed the (*Anandamayakosh*) 'Blissful sheath'; in other words the *Atma* for his conceit in each of these five sheaths receives a separate appellation, that is to say in connection with food, foodful; life sheath, vital; with knowledge, cognitional; and bliss, blissful.

37. The Supreme *Atma* is to be differentiated from the five sheaths for which He has a predilection or conceit by the methods of *Anvaya* and *Vyatireka.* If by the discriminating powers of intelligence, one's own *Atma* be disintegrated or separated and rendered distinct from the five sheaths, then is discovered his condition of everlasting intelligence and bliss, consequently the condition of the finite as represented by the *Jiva* is annihilated and he merges into the indication of Brahma, with which he is one.

38. In the dreaming state, consciousness belonging to the gross physical body—the receptacle of food—(hence foodful) is absent, but the *Atma* is not wanting in manifestibility. He is present as a witness even here and such a condition is termed 'Anvaya' or connection as cause and effect. [The oft quoted example of "I knew nothing then" is a trite example. Here the phrase signifies that all consciousness is at an end, but then the knowledge of such a condition is itself an experience of a certain amount of consciousness, otherwise for one to say on waking that he knew nothing while asleep will be impossible. Now this signifies that the mind in its ordinary state is a double combination of *Atma plus* mind, we are so much in the enjoyment of this twin medley, that its least disturbance as in fits, or trance where the mind sleeps, or in the dreaming condition when the mind ceases to receive the reflection of the *Atma*,—full of intelligence,—we say we know nothing, here the literal condition of the *Atma* continues as active as ever, it is only the mind that is cut off from the influence of receiving the reflected intelligence which is its habitual wont. The *Atma* is a witness of what the mind fails to perceive and such a condition is what is meant by the term just used,] while that other condition in which the active manifestibility of the *Atma* continues in the absence of consciousness in the gross physical body [*i. e.*, the consciousness of the gross body disappears in spite of the presence of Self] is called 'Vyatireka' or dissimilitude. By these two methods

the *Atma* is clearly discernible to be quite a separate thing from the gross physical body,—the foodful sheath.

39. Carrying the same argument to the next stage, *viz.*, that of dreamless slumber the duality of Self and the subtle Astral body will be clearly established. To be more explicit, we have seen that the *Atma* is full of manifestibility and is ever so, now in the dreamless slumbering condition, the subtle Astral body is wanting in consciousness, such would not happen if it were the Atma, for the consciousness of Self never ceases so long as life lasts, hence they are twain. Therefore the two methods are simply a process of analysis. The first refers to the *Atma*, the second to the body. As in the first case, so here too, when with the absence of consciousness in the subtle Astral body, the consciousness [of Self] is not in any way affected it is his 'Anvaya'; and when with the illuminating powers of Self, the subtle Astral body loses all consciousness concerning itself, it is its 'Vyatireka.'

40. Thus therefore while the discussion of the five sheaths clearly establishes their difference from the principle Self, the introduction of the consideration of the subtle Astral body is done on purpose, for if the Atma is a distinct entity from the same Astral body, then it follows that the *Pranamaya*, *Manomaya* and the *Vijnanmaya* sheaths are also quite distinct and separate. For these sheaths are non-different from the Astral body, from which they differ only in composition and quality,—in the constituent elements of the *Satwa*, *Raja* and *Tama* qualities inherent in them, for which they have each a separate name.

41. Now are to be explained for the purpose of ascertaining the non-identity of the cause-body with the Spirit, its *Anvaya* and *Vyatrieka* in the state of the profound meditation (*Samadhi*); for such a consideration the blissful sheath or the cause-body, though it shakes of its coil of ignorance, yet the tangibility of the Spirit as a witness is of the first, while the

continuance of ignorance, notwithstanding the presence of the Spirit, is an instance of the second.

42. By the aforesaid two methods of analysis the differentiation of the Spirit from the five sheaths and its attainment of the PARABRAHMA is thus established, as in the plant *saccharum munja* the tender and new fibres covered by the firmer covering of older fibres can plainly be separated mentally by argument and reasoning, so by analysis and synthesis if the Spirit be disintegrated from its five sheaths or coverings, it attains the everlasting blissfulness and truth of the Supreme Brahma, from which it has not even the semblance of dissimilarity.

43. Now this non-duality of the individual Spirit and the Supreme Brahma is indicated by the transcendental phrase (*Tat Twam Asi*) 'That art thou.' Here if the associates be left out according to the canons of Rhetoric, of abandoning a part, 'That' refers to Parabrahma—consciousness associated with illusion (*Maya*)—while 'Thou' refers to the individual consciousness associated with ignorance, if the associates, *viz.*, illusion and ignorance, be abandoned, there remains only consciousness. This is indicated.

44. As a phrase cannot be comprehended unless the several words composing it are rightly interpreted, therefore the words 'That' and 'Thou' are being separately explained. The proximate cause of the universe,—*Maya*, abounding in darkness (*Tama Guna*) and its instrnmental cause or material agent [(*Maya*) Illusion abounding in pure goodness, with the associate Parabrahma is indicated by the word 'That.'

45. The same associate of Illusion (*Maya*) abounding in impure goodness, full of desires, is indicated by the word 'Thou.'

46. Now if the conflicting portion be left out of the signification after the canons of Rhetoric of abandoning a part

* " This term is defined in the *Vachaspatya* as " Indication abiding in one part of the expressed meaning, whilst another

of the indication, for the contradiction it implies, inasmuch as the same Illusion is characterised by the three different properties of pain, pure goodness, and impure goodness, the Impartite (remaining non-conflicting) consciousness is one in the two conditions of *Jiva* and Brahma, therefore this non-duality is indicated by the phrase.

47. [This is illustrated] :—As in the phrase, 'That' Devadatta is this, 'that' and 'this' refer to the same Devadatta with this difference in time that the first adjective pronoun refers to Devadatta seen in past time and 'this' refers to the present time, but if the contending element in the indication with reference to time past and present conveyed by 'that' and 'this' respectively, be left out, there remains only Devadatta, and that is meant by the phrase.

48. So in 'That art Thou' 'That' indicates consciousness associated with Illusion—Parabrahma, and 'Thou' consciousness associated with Ignorance—*Jiva*, if the associates Illusion and Ignorance be left out there remains only the Impartite everlasting Intelligence and Bliss—the Parabrahma.

49. So far then, having established the Parabrahma as the indication of 'That' and 'Thou' it remains to be seen whether such indication refers to the associated or unassociated condition. For if such indication refers to the associated condition then it reduces it to 'non-being' (*asat*) and therefore cannot mean the Supreme Brahma which is 'being' (*sat*). As for the unassociated condition being indicated, it is an impossibility, for neither the eye has seen nor the ear heard it, besides the attribution of signs in the indication will reduce it to the condition of an associate.

---

part of it is abandoned. As for example, in the sentence 'That is this Devadatta,' whilst the meanings expressive of past and present time are abandoned, another portion of the expressed meaning remains and conveys the idea of the one Devadatta."—*Jacob's Vedantasara*, p. 87.

50. To such an objection it may be asked whether an associate is present in an unassociated, or described as a separate entity in an associated body. For what is unassociated cannot be said to have any associate, as such a condition will reduce it to the very reverse of its actuality, then again as an associated body means a body with an associate, therefore when it becomes associated it takes up the associate, similarly the body may be associate and its associate, the body. Hence it leads to a fallacy in the premises and yields no satisfactory solution. It is called 'unactual defect.' Therefore such erroneous disquisitions are untenable on both sides.

51. Now, such a fallacy is not confined to the points at issue in the foregoing instance only, but must be admitted in all bodies which have quality, action, caste, and relation, otherwise such bodies cannot be ascertained. In other words whether a quality resides in a body with qualities, or without them. In the latter case no quality can be present and in the former the 'same unactual defect' is noticeable. Hence it is only necessary to find out the simple presence of a quality in a body and not to analyse it after the above fashion as to whether it is with or without quality, with or without an associate.

52. Therefore to attribute to the Supreme Self any associate, attribute, indication or relationship is simply the product of Ignorance, for Self is simply eternal intelligence and bliss, and without any thing else.

53. Thus to ascertain the drift of the real signification of the transcendental phrase after the method of the *Vedanta* is designated 'hearing' about the PARABRAHMA. After having ascertained it, continually to consider and reflect on it with the help of the supporting arguments is called 'consideration' (*manana*).

54. By the two methods of hearing and consideration when the mind free from all doubts and uncertainties comes

to be *en rapport* with the Supreme Self, it is called (*Nididhyasana,*) profound contemplation.

55. When such 'profound contemplation' has been ripened it is called ' meditation' (*samadhi*). In such a state when there is no recognition of subject and object, (*e. g.*, the person contemplating is the subject, and the PARABRAHMA, the object of contemplation) but the mind merges into the object of contemplation, the Supreme Self, and the function of the internal organ is unmoved like the unflickering light of a lamp it is called (*Nirvikalpa Samadhi*) 'contemplation without recognition of subject and object.'

56. In such a condition though the individual has no actual knowledge, yet on rising from his meditation he remembers that he was dwelling on the Brahma. Hence it is quite natural to suppose, that then, the mind assumed the shape of the Supreme Self, and unknowingly rested on Him.

57. If it be alleged that during such meditation the will-force is suspended, hence it is quite impossible for the mind to assume the shape of the Brahma and become one with it. For to awaken the function of an organ, exercise of individual effort is needed, without which effort no function is roused. To such a query the answer is, that at the beginning of profound contemplation there was present intense effort, which by continual exercise formed into a deep conviction, and this resulted in a continuous flow of the function moulded into the shape of the Brahma.

58. Bhagavan Sree Krishna compares the fixed condition of the mind in meditation to the light issuing from an unflickering lamp, in his discourse with Arjuna (*Vide Bhagabut Gita, Chapter* 6, *Verse* 19).

59. Such meditation enables an individual to escape the *karmaic* law which hurls a man to repeated birth and death in this transitory sphere, to reap the fruits of his deeds, good and bad, committed in a previous state of subjective existence; it destroys both good and bad actions and leads to the growth

of that pure religion which helps the individual to the knowledge of (Brahma) Supreme Self.

60. Since it rains an unceasing torrent of nectar such meditation has been termed by men learned in Yoga the 'Religion cloud.'

61. After the destruction of good and evil wishes in an infinite variety of ways and the cumulated products of good and bad actions of previous existence have been uprooted *en masse* through the instrumentality of such Religion-cloud-meditation, the transcendental phrase becomes clear and free from obstacles, at first, to help the cognition of the Brahma which was hitherto present dimly and subsequently as plainly as a thing is discovered in one's own hand.

62. The imperfect and obscure discovery of Self which follows, after hearing the discourse of an adept teacher, versed in Brahmaic lore, on such phrases as, That art Thou, etc., helps the destruction of all sins committed knowingly, like a blazing fire. In other words when one has come to know the Brahma, his wishes and actions cease.

63. The precepts of an adept teacher on the aforesaid phrase so helps the knowledge of Self as to render Him visible, then as the sun disperses darkness, so such knowledge destroys Ignorance which is the cause of this material world [and cuts of the chain of consecutive re-births.]

64. If one attached to the world will follow step by step the means of knowledge herein indicated and by close reasoning and analysis fix them in his mind, he shall then be able to cut of the chain of consecutive re-births,—soon to attain to the state of ineffable bliss.

SECTION II.

FROM the *Sruti* we gather that before the evolution of the objective world, there was present only 'existence' (*Sat*)—the secondless Reality Brahma—from which all things have been derived, hence an analysis of the several elements is necessary for the cognition of Brahma. For such a purpose, these are now being considered.

2. There are five elements:—ether, air, heat, water, and earth, distinguished by their specific properties of sound, touch, form, taste and smell. Ether and the rest are marked by the properties one, two, three, four and five in a consecutive serial order, ether has only one, the next one *plus* one, that is two, and so on till we find the last having four properties derived from the bases, together with its specific property.

3. To be more explicit, ether has only one property, sound; air, sound and touch; heat,—sound, touch and form; water,—sound, touch, form and taste; earth,—sound, touch, form, taste and smell. Hence, ether has only the property of communicating sound as evidenced in echoing, air besides emitting a peculiar sound in its passage, also communicates a sensation of heat and cold which is touch. In the same way, heat manifests itself by its crackling noise, sensation of warmth and visibility; water by its peculiar rippling or rushing sound, cold feel, white form, and mild taste; and the earth by its sound, hard feel, divers shape, variety of taste, and good or bad smell. This is evident enough.

4. [For the recognition of the said five properties, we have five especial organs of sense, to wit, the ears, skin, eyes, tongue and smell.] These organs from their separate seats becomes gradually accustomed to carry on their individual functions, and as they are very subtle,—hence cannot be seen

their presence is manifested by their functions,* by which alone they are conceivable, and they generally take hold of, or cover external objects.

5. Notwithstanding the general tendency of the several organs of sense, to cover external objects, they do at times take an inward course. For instance, if the external meatus be stopped with a piece of cotton wool, the passage of sound will find no obstruction, but will be distinctly audible, through the medium of the air situated within. In the act of drinking and eating the stomach feels a sensation of cold and warmth in the same way as the skin does; closing the eyes brings on darkness, and eructations convey taste and smell.

6. Speech, prehension, progression, excretion, and emission are the functions of the five organs of action. (Here again we find, that there are as many actions as there are organs,—an absence of the sixth function is due to the want of an organ to perform it.) Agriculture and trade &c, are carried on by means of the very same active organs, hence naturally they come within the aforesaid category of speech and the rest.

7. Mouth, hands, feet, anus, and the genitals are the five organs of action.

8. The five external organs of sensation, and five organs of action are controlled by the mind which has its seat in the lotus of the heart. It is likewise called the 'internal organ,' (Anthakarana) for its inward action is independent of them. Not so with the external, for which it has to depend entirely upon the senses.

---

* The Aryan Rishis never mistook the external organs, eyes &c., for the organs themselves, they are the external appendages merely. The seats of the sensory organs, or centres, are the several ganglia with which each especial nerve is connected and which carry the impressions to the sensorium, these are looked upon as the 'internal organ.'

9 The mind ascertains the quality or defect of an object, after it has been covered (taken possession of) by the senses. It has three qualities, the good or pleasant, the active or meddlesome, and the dark or plainful. They induce changes on it.

10. The changes induced by the good quality are indifference to earthly pursuits, forgiveness and large mindedness. Passion, anger, temptation and struggle for worldly benefits, &c., are the products of the active quality. Idleness, error, sleep (lassitude) &c., are due to darkness.

11 From the good quality of the mind arises virtue, from the active are produced the passions, anger &c., which in their turn lead to sin and other bad actions; from the third or bad are derived sloth, lassitude and sleep, hence an individual under its influence spends his time in doing nothing and keeps himself aloof from virtue and vice. What attaches personality to the individual functions of the several organs in connection with the mind is the agent or instrument. As in common parlance one who does a thing is known as the doer or subject (?) agent, or instrument, so the internal organ or mind is the agent, for it is resort of individuality.

12. The objective world can easily be determined to have derived its origin from the elements, for their specific properties sound and the rest are the attributes of ether and the other elements, thus incontestibly establishing their elementary composition, hence further consideration is not needed. Not so with the organs. Here an analysis based on reason, and the teachings of the Shastras are required to show that they are derived from the same elements.

13. Now there are five organs of sense, five organs of action, both controlled by the mind (which also must be reckoned as an organ, as it helps cognition). Whatever is known by the aid of these organs, reason, and Shastras is indicated by the word 'Edam' (all this) in the phrase "*Sadeva sonya edam*," and it means the universe

14. Before the evolution of 'all this' (universe) there was present one, secondless, existence (Sat) without a name or form. Such is laid down in the *Chandogoya Upanishad* by Udalika.

15. The three expletives 'one,' 'secondless,' and 'Existence' are used to differentiate It, from bodies similar and dissimilar. That is to say, as a tree has its branches, leaves, flowers and fruits differing from each other,—a leaf resembles not a flower, nor does a flower its fruit, nor either, a branch—thus constituting its distinguishing individuality or segregate units, for though the tree is one, yet it has its composite units different; and as such a tree is recognised from another of a different class by its family characteristics—a difference in its leaf, flower, fruit, growth, bark and stone, (its family characteristics)—and as it is easily known from other things as stone &c., it has therefore a third characteristic which serves to distinguish it from bodies dissimilar. (This may be termed contrast).

16. So in the case of the secondless Reality, no such apprehension needs be entertained as to the presence of the three aforesaid characterising traits. For such a purpose the three expletives ("Edam, Ebam, Aditiam") one, sure, and secondless are prefixed. Thus is non-duality established.

17. Moreover, it must be remembered that, as the Parabrahma is without form, and has no distinguishing individuality as noticed in the instance of the tree and its fruit &c., you cannot assign any form or name to It, for It existed prior to them.

18. Name and form are indications of creation, hence what existed prior to it cannot have a name; consequently the Supreme Self which is eternal and formless has no differentiating individual trait like the ether.

19. If there were two or more existences (Sat) then to individualise or identify them as separate entities there must exist family distinctions, but as it is secondless and one, It has

only *one* indication and not *many*, consequently there does not exist another body of Its kind. Virtually then, without the difference of Its associates in name and form, it has no distinguishing trait in Itself, therefore to describe the difference of associates and to admit them as belonging to It, is only conducive of error.

20 Nor can contrast be instituted here. For It is existence, hence contrast or dissimilarity will fix on non-existence (Asat) as dissimilar or different from It. But what is non-existent has no shape, hence the Parabrahma cannot be cleared by contrast.

21. Thus is established the oneness of Parabrahma which is eternal, Intelligence, and bliss without a second; but to establish it more firmly a consideration of the arguments adduced by the opponents of this doctrine, is now being given. Some amongst them erroneously assert that before the evolution of this universe there existed (Asat,) 'non-being' and therefore imply the non-existence of the secondless Reality which is (Sat) 'being' and essentially existent.

22. As a drowned man is bereft of his senses and loses the capacity of expressing himself, but is subject to extreme fear and hence is powerless, so these dissenters lose their senses and become bewildered when hearing the precepts and doctrines of non-duality and are overtaken by fear.

23. In the state of meditation without recognition of subject and object (worshipped) a certain dread is felt, by those persons who are given to the worship of a personal God, such is asserted by the religious teachers of Gour [Bengal] who have laid it down in their works.

24. Another name for the above variety of meditation is 'untouchable Yoga.' Because the followers of personal worship can never acquire it, in spite of the hardships enjoined for its practice, hence it is untouchable and though there is no cause for fear yet like little children evincing dread when left alone, without any substantial ground for it, these

devotees are unreasonably affected by imaginary dread, when actually there is none whatever in it, from the 'untouchable Yoga.'

25. The venerable Sankaracharya looks upon such followers of personal worship, (Madhyamic Buddhists,)—a set of controversialists who discard reason and anology from their arguments—as totally ignorant of meditation without subject and object, for the cognition of the unthinkable, essentially existent Supreme Self. [They are unacquainted with such a meditation in which the person meditating loses his personality and is unconscious of the object of his meditation, the two are blended into one—a non-dual condition]

26. They [such Buddhists] discard the *Sruti* either from Ignorance, or from want of comprehension, and drawing their inferences from possible cause and effect, they promulgate atheism and deny the existence of Self.

27. (Now the atheistic doctrine of 'non-being' is being critically examined in the way of queries and and answers.) Oh! ye Buddhists! you assert there was 'non-being' before the objective world was ushered into existence. What do ye mean by it? How can the meaning of the two words 'was' and 'none-being' be reconciled. 'Was' indicates existence, and 'non-being' non-existence, therefore two opposite conditions. Hence such an expression is full of contradiction.

28. You cannot ascribe darkness to the sun or say he is dark; to say so will be illogical and untenable, because the sun is the very opposite of darkness—light—this you know surely, and as light and darkness cannot by any means be looked upon as one or same substance, how can you possibly look upon as one and the same substance what is implied by the contradictory epithets 'was' and 'non-being' in your expression "there was non-being in the beginning"?

29. The *Vedanta* teaches the doctrine that the elements ether and the rest, potentially existed in the Parabrahma, and their separate designation and form are simply the result of

Illusion, if you attach a similar signification to your 'non-being' and fancy its existing potentially in the essentially existent Self, through the same Maya, then your 'non-being' is transformed into Self and may you live long for it.

30. If you say, that like your 'non-being' our attribution of name and form to the essentially existent Parabrahma is imaginary, for in It, we do not admit name and form and if such attribution is due to Illusion, then that Illusion must rest on something (real), for an Illusion means a mistake for something real, [as in the familiar example of a snake in a rope] and without some reality resting in the back-ground no error can arise. Hence, how can it be possible for your 'non-being' to convey a similar attribution to that of name and form

31. If you contend that our Vedantic expression in the beginning 'there was existence' is alike faulty, inasmuch as existence is twice implied by the two words 'was' and 'existence' when they are considered separate, and tautological when otherwise, and therefore though "There was nothing" is alike faulty, it is passable. No, ye Buddhists ! do not say so, for repetition of a word is sanctioned by usage :—

32. As doing right, telling a word, holding the ascertained, &c. These words have familiarised repetition to all pupils. The *Sruti* has likewise adopted the same practice in its mode of instruction when it says, 'Before the evolution of the universe there was existence.'

33. The past tense in the above passage is used to instruct a pupil, accustomed to connect a thing with notions of time. That is to say, in considering the secondless Reality, though time as a separate entity is absent, yet as the pupils are habituated to time, the past tense is purposely introduced to help their comprehension. Hence the expression cannot lead to the inference of a second thing, in any way militating against the secondless Reality—the Parabrahma.

34. In common practice, with the objective world before you, whatever questions or inferences you gather are possible,

not so with what relates to non-dual spirituality. That is to say, when there are many objects, and the knowledge relating to them many, then only questions will arise for solution in a variety of ways, but when the object of knowledge is reduced to number one as happens in the conception of non-duality, no such question or inference will cause an interruption of the subject, for then, that knowledge has assumed the impartite shape or in other words, become so modified and blended with the object, that it is one impartite whole. In such a condition (non-dual) questions, and answers, argument and analysis are out of the question, for the knowledge which enables the individual to cover an object for the purpose of framing a question, or deciding an answer for it, has become reduced to one and cannot master any thing else, besides it has become already one with the impartite Parabrahma.

35. To exclude duality from the spiritual Monad or Essence, the *Smriti* text is cited as authority wherein is mentioned, "Before the world had come into existence there was one, quite,—because inert, vast—so as not to be grasped by word or by the mind—unspeakable and unthinkable, nameless, —for it is impossible to portray an accurate description,—indescribable because the eyes and the other organs cannot take hold of It,—something—the antitype of nothing,—essentially existent. It is not fire, for it does not discover material objects, nor are they discovered by it. Neither is it darkness, as it enshrouds, nothing, for it is naturally uncovered, all-pervading, and equally present everywhere." [Now the controversy between a Buddhist and Non-dualist in reference to the inferences of their sacred writings is being given; 'you, refer to a Buddhist and 'we,' non-dualist].

36. If you ask, since the earth and its contents have all come into existence, it is very natural to conclude there was a time when they did not exist, yes not even the atoms, for all created objects are equally subject to destruction. But how do we comprehend ether also was then want-

ing, to avoid falling into the dilemma of admitting twain existences?

37. Oh ye Buddhists! If your conception of 'nothing' in that period of the history of the universe when it existed not, implies neither contradiction nor any difficulty, then why do you misapprehend us, when we say, that in that very same prior condition, there was only present the ONE EXISTENCE. The inference is very natural, for that prior condition is equally present in both the premises, in your 'nothing' and our 'existence.' They simply indicate the extreme—negative and positive poles. In the same way as your negative was present, our positive pre-existed every condition.

38. If you say ether is visible as a separate entity outside the globe in the shape of its atmosphere, so that as regards visibility it is not an inconclusive argument, we may then enquire of you, when and how do you see it without light or darkness? In the absence of that light or darkness ether is never visible, and both of them cannot exist *out* of the universe, consequently you never see the ether without it, this you are forced to admit. Besides,—according to your view, ether is not a really visible body.

39. If you say that according to the *Vedanta*, the essentially existent Parabrahma is also invisible, so here again the same difficulty crops up, which is pointed out in the preceding paragraph with regard to the visibility of ether, and the conditions are therefore equal, to such a query we reply that in the state of unconscious meditation without recognition of subject and object, we do conceive the Brahma as a (positive) existence and have no knowledge of non-existence, which by argument and analysis we do away with.

40. If you say, during such meditation, existence is not conceivable, for the separate function of the internal organ is at abeyance, and it cannot cover the Brahma. Our reply is, for discovering the Brahma the presence of *Boodhi* is not

needed. For, It is self-illuminated and requires no other extraneous aid for being discovered. Though not a subject of *Boodhi* (spiritual intelligence) yet it is duly reflected in the consciousness, as a witness, a presence not to be put by, a real existence, and not an unreal 'nothing.'

41. Therefore after the mind has been freed from its subjective modifications of determination and [error, mistake, or] indecision and has attained tranquility, as its associated consciousness is manifested in the form of a simple presence, or witness, doing nothing, but in a condition of passivity, so that prior condition when it existed before the objective world had sprung into existence through Matter (Maya) is easily conceivable and implies neither any difficulty nor contradiction.

42. The inherent force residing in the Parabrahma which is essentially existent, and which cannot be differentiated is called Maya. As the consuming flame of fire imparts an idea of its force, so the potentiality of the universal force resident in the Supreme Self is plainly seen in the (creative works) objective material world.

43. (Now this Maya cannot be said to be one with Parabrahma or as something distinct). As the consuming force of fire cannot be said to be fire, so the inherent force of the Supreme Brahma (Maya) is not the same with It, to say so is unreasonable, for, you cannot say "I am my own force," hence the inherent universal force is not the substance itself. Then again if you admit it as a separate entity, Can you describe its separate existence? [It will thus be evident that Maya and Force with which a Madhyamika Buddhist seeks to identify matter and Parabrahma, are two inseparably blended; we all know force cannot exist without matter as a separate entity, yet to say that it is the same as matter is absurd, hence the contention in the paragraph just asks an opponent of the Vedantic School to describe force as a separate entity.

But it may be urged that Parabrahma is force, and,—therefore to introduce the same force either in a separate or analogous form is no less absurd. For what is force, is always so, hence force *plus* force is equally force; under such circumstances the mind fails to comprehend the drift of the text. But no such ambiguity will remain, if we introduce matter in its undifferentiated condition,—a condition in which the difference between matter and its inherent force is nil, the boundary line so to speak, in which matter losing its grossness, assumes the subtlety of superetherial finis, when no matter is distinguishable as such, but all is spirit or force; and such an inference is derived from nature, for the boundary line between the mineral and vegetable, and between the latter and the animal creation is so gradually bevelled at the edges, that each passeses into the other by way of transition. For a long time, Science was undecided whether a certain vegetable was the last link in the scale of the animal series or a vegetable, so much do they resemble each other. If such a view be accepted, and it is the one advocated by Kapila—in his Mula Prakriti—then the difference between Prakriti and Purush on which many have stumbled from ignorance, no longer subsists for all practical purposes, but for syllogistic ends we may go on dabbling *ad-infinitum*. The Vedantist here presents to his antagonist, (a Buddhist) the sharp point of a sword which cuts both ways, inasmuch as it takes the ground from under his feet and makes the position of the assailant really invincible. Now, Maya is described as a force and it is elsewhere described as the chief factor of the universe, consequently it cannot be anything less than matter. So that we come to the same point whence we started, *e. g.*, matter and force. Otherwise the meaning is absurd. And this Maya or matter existed potentially in the Parabrahma and by an act of volition was created the objective world with the self-made Maya residing within It. Now such a doctrine is not open to the crticism that God made the world out of nothing, for nothing can create nothing. On the other hand He* created it out of matter which resided within him. If it be asked, since the Parabrahma is a pure spirit how can It have any connection with matter which is antagonistic to It? We reply, that spirit and force are convertible terms, and we have seen that force cannot exist without matter, hence wherever there is force, there must matter be. It is emphatically laid down that Maya existed in the Parabrahma, and it is this Maya which evolved or created the universe in a natural order of sequence, by undergoing change impressed upon it, through its force or Parabrahma. Without such changes being wrought upon it through the agency of its spirit or force, the universe and its stellar system could never have sprung up; change is the law of the universe, change every where and in every moment is the grand centre around which are deposited the nidus of future planets, their sattelites etc., and the gradual, slow but sure dissolution of the present existing ones. In this way there never was a time when the world was non-existent, nor will there ever be a time when such will be the case; though in truth it may be laid down that this world is not the first of the series; nor is our human race the first that has been called upon to fill or inhabit it. From close reasoning this must naturally establish itself as an axiomatic truth, for if the Parabrahma is eternal and essentially existent, and if such Parabrahma cannot exist as a separate entity without its Maya, (or out of matter) then matter and its force must by natural laws induce changes in each other which must end in works. Such then the *role*. We use purposely each other, because we find Parabrahma is one force, and we are told by Science that there are several forces attraction, repulsion, gravitation ;—centrifugal, centripetal and gravitation—synonymous with Satwa, Raja and Tama of Aryan writers.]

---

* Parabrahma is always neuter, we have purposely made use of the masculine gender to indicate the creative act, prominently.

44. If you say the nomenclature of Maya is similar to your 'nothing' then you contradict yourself, inasmuch as it was said (in the 27th para.) to be a product of Maya, thus then you are to regard Maya as something else then (*Sat*) 'existence,' and distinct from (*Asat*) 'non-existence' or 'nothing,' a condition that cannot be described, hence—indescribable: (virtually reminding the reader of Ignorance which is the same as Prakriti or matter, therefore Maya is matter.)

45. Now for the proofs of such an assertion the *Sruti* is quoted. "Prior to the world's springing into existence, there was neither present (Asat,) 'nothing' nor 'being' as a separate entity, but only Maya (an indication of darkness) the inherent force of the Supreme Self, having no independent existence but deriving its tangibility from the Parabrahma.

46. But such a consideration does not necessarily reduce the Parabrahma to the condition of a second. For the separate existence of a force outside of a substance is nowhere recognised.

47. If it be alleged, since with the decrease of strength, vitality is reduced and with its increase life is prolonged, we have an instance of the separate existence of force, it is laid down that strength or force is no cause for the prolongation of life. It is the cause of inducing cultivation, war, and other acts in which labour is concerned. Hence it has no separate existence from the body. Now, following a similar train of argument if it be asserted that since strength is the cause of cultivation, war, and the rest, we may as well attribute to the Supreme Brahma a second attribute or existence. But this cannot be done with any show of reason, for in that prior condition when the objective world was not in existence, neither war, nor cultivation was possible, therefore, to admit them is absurd, (and a duality of existence is not less so).

48. The aforesaid force (Maya) is not diffused in Parabrahma, but, pervades only a part, in the same way as every

sort of earth cannot be profitably turned into a jar or other earthen thing, but can moist earth only.

49. To this purpose the *Sruti* says, "One portion of the Parmatma is engrossed in the whole elements, the remaining three-fourth is eternal, pure, free, and self-manifested." In this way, the function of Maya is attributed to the Parabrahma in the *Sruti*.

50. Referring to this subject, Krishna in his discourse with Arjuna says, "With a small portion of the body, I pervade the universe and occupy it (*vide Gita, Chapter X.* last stanza.)

51. There are other *Sruti* texts and *Shariraka Sutras* equally corroborative of the above. "The Parabrahma by a small portion of its body pervades the whole universe, the remaining portion is eternal, pure and free."—*Sruti.* "The Parabrahma is not wholly enshrouded in change, but rests in an uncovered, unchanged and unaffected condition.—*Shariraka Sutra, Book IV. Chapter IV. Sutra 19.*

52. But it is formless, hence to say that a portion of Its body is covered, and subject to change, while the other is not, implies a contradiction. This is cleared in the following wise:—The *Sruti* attributes form, for the purpose of explanation to a pupil.

53. That inherent force Maya, abiding in the Parabrahma induces a change which finally ends in works usually called creative, but strictly speaking,—evolutional, in the same way as by a blending of the primitive colors a beautiful effect is produced.

54. Now the first product of the change induced by Maya is ether, which is void. And as this ether is a derivative product of Maya, which again is a force of the Parabrahma, its manifestibility is a manifestibility of its cause—the Self.

55. Hence though Self is essentially existent, its product ether has two attributes, *viz.*, existence and void.

56. In other words, ether has the attribute of sound which

is absent in the Parabrahma, therefore the latter has only one attribute, whereas Its derivative product ether has two, *viz.*, sound and existence.

57. That Maya which produces ether, after establishing the identity of ether with Self seeks further to draw opposite inferences, by attributing the property of the cause to the product and transmitting that property to the product, that is to say, Self is essentially existent, therefore to conclude ether is also similarly endowed, is a product of (Maya) Illusion.

58. The fact is, ether owes its existence to Self, and it is non-eternal, for it is a created product; hence the assumption of the Tarkikas or other ordinary men who hold ether to be eternal, is due to Illusion. For Maya naturally leads to error.

59. It is universally admitted that proofs establish the real nature of thing, while error has a contrary effect.

60. Now this ether and the rest are looked upon in a different light, till cleared by the analysis of the *Sruti*, therefore pause and reflect whether it is eternal or not.

61. Ether and the Supreme Sat (Being) are distinct from each other, for—etymologically their signification is different, moreover the consequence of the action of ether on air is the presence of sound which determines or establishes that air and not ether.

62. For He is all pervading, hence Self is the receptacle of ether which is an action or attribute, thus considered nothing remains of ether to claim a separate identity.

63. If you regard ether as naturally void, then it is quite different from (Sat) 'being,' in other words you admit it as 'non-being' (Asat). If you say though ether is different from 'being', yet it is not 'non-being,' then you contradict yourself, for what is not 'being' must be 'non-being' and you cannot maintain the one and discard the other with any show of reason.

64. If you argue, since the ether is plainly discernible, it cannot be non-existent, for in that case it would have been

invisible, we reply that it is the very nature of Illusion (Maya) to make 'nothing' appear as something like an object seen in a dream, which is non-existent, yet plainly discernible. This we call unreal.

65. In two co-existing objects no difference can be perceived. Therefore the difference between the words ether and existence is thus established. Caste and person, being and body, quality and object are each different from the other, and the method by which they can be distinguished will enable a differentiation of ether and existence.

66. (If you are not convinced about the mutual difference of the two even after understanding it, the subject is further explained by the following questions and their replies.) If you say that you understand the difference between ether and 'being,' but you cannot firmly believe it, then state your reasons for disbelief.

67. If carelessness be its cause, fix your attention and be earnest, if doubt, have recourse to proofs adduced in the *Shastras*, and weigh the arguments based on analogy and reason.

68. After the existing difference of ether and 'being' has been firmly established in the mind by fixed attention, *Shastra* proofs and analogy, ether is no longer mistaken for Reality, nor is Reality connected with the perquistes of ether and mistaken with unreality.

69. The Prajna always looks upon ether as non-eternal; and (Sat) 'being,'—devoid of the attributes of ether; (e. g.,) He is eternal, pure and free.

70. The 'liberated in life' with the aforesaid conception of ether and 'being' is astonished to find ignorant persons holding opposite beliefs; bent in worldly pursuits and full of desire, they are devoid of self-knowledge, hence believe the reality of ether.

71. Thus after establishing the unreality of ether and Reality of the Parabrahma, if the same line of argument be

carried in reference to the four other elements, It will be found different from them.

72. Though with 'being' and air—the resulting product of ether,—there is no relation of cause and effect, yet from their mutual connection, their identity can possible be established, hence to consider Sat from air their mutual relationship is being established. The essentially existent Parabrahma is closely situated to Maya, which again is similarly placed to ether, and ether to air, that is to say, each preceding one stands more or less in the relation of cause to its effect, which comes immediately after, and for such relation (of cause and effect) it is possible to look upon air and 'being' as identical.

73. In this way, after ascertaining the relation of identity between them, their existing difference can only be made out by a consideration of the properties of air. Now air has naturally four properties:—attraction of moisture, touch, motion, and velocity. And the respective properties of Sat, Maya and ether are also discernible in air (in the following wise):—

74. The existence of air is due to Sat, and if such existence be separated from it, then it is reduced to impermanence which is a product of Maya; and its sound is the result of ether.

75. In the 62nd verse it has been asserted that Sat is naturally present in air and the other elements, and not ether, but it is now said that sound, an effect of ether, is easily distinguished in air, this implies a contradiction.

76. [It is thus cleared]. In the 62nd verse it was said, the void of ether cannot be established in air; and now,—sound, the property of ether is discernible in air, hence they do not contradict each other.

77. If from its difference from Sat you admit air as impermanent and a product of Illusion, What prevents you to think it distinct from Maya since the indescribable Maya is a force and there is existing difference between force and air?

78. Because, that undefinable force or its expressed action is not due to Maya which is only an unreality or Illusion. Can you say both in the inexpressed and expressed forms—force and action—the same unreality is equally present?

79. In the consideration of the Real and unreal it is necessary to establish their difference, but there is no need of entering into the individual difference, existing in all things ncluded in the unreal.

80. If from air the reality of existence due to the Supreme Brahma be separated, the remaining portion which is material will be found to be unreal and impermanent. Hence you must cease to regard it as eternal and knowing.

81. A similar consideration will reduce fire, which is a product of air but less pervasive than it, to impermanence the five elements are said to cover the universe (Brahma's egg) more or less, one over the other.

82. In air, one-tenth of it is fire; a similar tenth portion in the other elements is spoken of in the *Purans*.

83. Now the nature and impermanence of fire is being determined. The individual property of fire is manifestibility, while existence, impermanence, sound and warmth proceed from its cause.

84. Sat and Maya, ether, and air, have the aforesaid four properties, if fire with its individual property of manifestibility be separated from Sat, it is reduced to impermanence.

85. The same consideration will reduce water to impermanence, which forms less than a tenth part of fire.

86. The five properties of water derived from its cause are:—existence, impermanence, sound, touch and form while its individual property is taste. Now by discriminating them from Sat, water is also reduced to impermanence.

87. And in water, less than one-tenth of its proportion is earth, which being subjected to a similar analysis will establish its difference from Sat, (*i. e.,*) impermanence.

88. In earth, impermaennce, sound, touch, form, and taste are derived from its cause, while its individual property is smell, hence differentiating them from Sat will reduce it to impermanence.

89. If the essentially existent Reality be differentiated from earth, it is reduced to impermanence, and less than a tenth part, with its included Brahmanda, is contrived to be present in earth.

90. In the Brahma's egg are included the fourteen abodes Vur and the rest with their adequate inhabitants.

91. The several species of being inhabiting the different abodes included in Brahma's egg possessed of five sorts of bodies (viviparous, oviparous, parasitic, and earthy) elementary in composition, when differentiated from Sat, are reduced to impermanence, in spite of their tangibility, which cannot in any way affect the secondless Reality.

92. After having ascertained the unreal nature of elements, elementary bodies and Maya, nothing will create any disturbance as to the non-dual conception of Sat.

93. Even after the elements and elementary bodies have been ascertained to be unreal, the wise do not discontinue using them, though unreal, because by their tangibility they are capable of being used.

94. Let Sankhya, Kanad, the Buddhists and other controversialists use their specific arguments to support the reality of the objective world, we do not strive to disappoint them, for we are one with them so far as calling into requisition the service of all useful objects, what we want is to determine the reality of spiritual existence.

95. We suffer no injury from them if they fearlessly shew no respect to the *Sruti* proofs explanatory of the secondless Reality, we in the same way, having framed our conception from *Sruti*, experience and analogy, as to the unreal nature of every thing else the besides *Atma*, disregard their duality.

96. To show such disregard of duality is not unnecessary

for us, because the more it becomes firm, the more will it lead to a just appreciation of non-duality. He is 'liberated in life' who by an utter disregard of duality has confirmed his knowledge of non-duality.

97. Such a disregard of duality and firm conception of non-duality does not lead to deliverance in life only, but helps the individual to attain emancipation (from consecutive re-incarnation or re-birth). As in the Gita (Chap. 2, V. 27.) Krishna says to Arjuna, " Such a wise individual delivered in life is never re-born. In the end he attains to that ineffable bliss in the Brahma known as *Nirvana.*"

98. " In the end" is thus explained :—In ordinary practice the scondless Reality and unreality are equally regarded. [That is to say though all material objects are non-real because impermanent, yet they are required for use, and are capable of being used, for they are tangible and taken cognition of by our senses; hence in daily use they are not thrown away for their unreality, therefore their use brings them to a condition of reality, for what is false cannot be handled, or seen, etc., hence independent of reality or unreality, both are alike dealt with]. But when with discriminating eyes the unreal are separated from the real, that is meant by the phrase " In the end."

99. Or, it means the separation of the vital air from the body, and this is its common acceptance. Even then, a theosophist no more confounds non-duality with duality.

100. No matter whatever may be his condition in his dying moments, whether with or without any disease, retaining consciousness and suffering the agonies of death, or perfectly unconscious, nothing can disturb the firm conception of non-duality which an individual liberated in life has.

101. Even if unconscious when dying, his knowledge of non-duality does not forsake him, and as in the case of an ordinary individual when dreaming or dreamlessly slumbering, his acquired learning may appear to him as if forgotten,

but no sooner be awakes he finds it all right, so in the aforesaid instance, a theosophist's knowledge of non-duality does not leave him when he parts with the body.

102. Contradicting proofs must be stronger than supporting proofs, before an established fact, can be proved to be false, hence non-duality based on Vedantic proofs, is never disturbed "in the end," because stronger proofs than them do not exist, therefore contradiction is impossible.

103. Thus the self-evident truths which the *Vedanta* expounds to differentiate the elements must inevitably lead a man to ineffable bliss in the Brahma.* [For ignorance being destroyed there is no more materiality left to subject him to re-birth and he merges in the Brahma to be in a condition of joy.

---

* According to the *Vedanta-paribhasa*, "The joy which admits of no increase is Brahma; as the Veda says, "He knew Brahma to be joy." The acquisition of Brahma whose essence is joy is *moksha*, and it is also the cessation of sorrow.

SECTION III.

On the five sacs or sheaths.

In the *Taitirya Upanishad* it is said, the wise enjoy all happiness by knowing that the secondless Reality—the Supreme Brahma—is situated in a cell. Here the word 'cell' has reference to the five sacs or sheaths, and as their consideration enables an individual to a right appreciation of the *Atma*, the five sacs are now being declared.

2. With a view to arrive at a correct signification of the word 'cell' in the aforesaid paragraph it is now being defined:—The physical body is the foodful sac, inside of it is the vital, within which is the mental, enclosing the cognitional within, and internal to it is the blissful sac, that is meant by it.

3. [Now the foodful sac and its non-identity with the Atma is being declared.] The gross physical body is called the foodful sac, because it is formed from semen and blood which are an altered condition of, and derived from food, and because it depends entirely upon food, for its growth. But the body cannot be called eternal, or indestructible, as prior to its birth and after death it is wanting, hence it does not resemble Self.

4. If you say that a derivative product is subject to death, and though non-eternal there is no harm in considering the gross body same with Self. (The reply is.)—Prior to birth the body was non-existent, and therefore simply from the law of *Karma* it is fulfilling its present phase of existence, the future birth will also be a product of accumulated actions*

* There are three kinds of works (*sanchita*) accumulated, (*prarabdha*) fructescent, and (*kriyamana*) current. 'Accumulated' are the works of previous re-births which have not yet commenced to bear fruit; 'fructescent' have began to bear fruit, and 'current' are those which will bear fruit in a future life. The *Vedanta*

in the present life, which it is not enjoying now but will have to wait for a future re-incarnation,—this life being simply a scene for the fruition of past actions.

5. The five vital airs which strengthen the gross body, and induce the several organs to perform their functions is designated the life-sac. It is not-self, for it is insentient.

6. The mistaken attribution of 'I' and 'mine' to the physical body and to worldly goods, is due to the influence of mind. This one is called the mental sac. It is not-self, because it is worked upon by the several passions which induce change.

7. The shadow or reflection of intelligence (*Boodhi*) which in the waking condition occupies every part of the body and merges in ignorance in the condition of dreamless slumber, is called the cognitional sac. But as it is subject to the laws of birth and death, hence non-eternal, it is not-self.

8. *Manas* and *Boodhi* (The animal and human souls) though for ordinary purposes are looked upon as the internal organ and non-different, yet they are differentiated into the mental and cognitional sacs, because *Boodhi*, as the internal instrument or agent, is the indication of cognitional, and *manas*, as the external agent, is the indication of the mental sheaths respectively.

9. When during the fruition of meritorious and virtuous deeds the internal function of *Boodhi* is full of reflected intelligence and bliss, and after such enjoyment is over, that function blends in *Prakriti* (un-differentiated cosmic condition of matter) it is denominated the blissful sac.

10. Because it is liable to immediate destruction, it is not-self. Besides Self is not a reflected shadow but is light, eternal, infinite, intelligence and bliss.

---

believes in the destruction of the first and last through knowledge of Brahma and one's identity with It. The fructescent can be only exhausted by actual enjoyment of their fruits during the present life.

11. If it be said, that from the gross body, to the 'blissful sac' every one of them is not-self, can be admitted, but it is impossible to regard any thing else as Self, for nothing can be conceived in that way.

12. It is indeed true that the physical body and the rest are easily conceivable and nothing beyond them can be determined as self. But what prevents you from identifying self with that eternal Intelligence through which you conceive the body etc.? That is Self.

13. If therefore Self is present as eternal Intelligence, Why is he then not cognizable? Because, he is Intelligence and not the object of cognition. [The introduction of subject will be incompatible with truth and infinity, besides it will create dualism; for that which cannot be demarcated in any way is infinite, and if it were a knowing subject (a knower) its knowledge would be limited by its object and cognition, hence not infinite. As regards dualism: if Brahma were conscious there would be objects of consciousness, thus there would be a relation,* and wherever there is relation there is dualism. Therefore Brahma or Self is knowledge, as an abstract.] From the absence of the cognitive subject and objects of cogtion it is not known, not because it does not exist.

14. As sugar imparts sweetness to a substance when mixed with it, but does not depend upon any thing else for its sweetness, because such sweet-imparting-substance there is none.

15. And as from want of such another substance imparting its sweetness to sugar, its own sweetness is self-evident, so from an absence of a subject and object of cognition, the Atma though unperceivable, is yet evidently Intelligence and eternal.

---

* Says the *Mundukya Upanishad*, "Brahma is neither internally nor externally cognitive, neither conscious nor unconscious." Verse 7.

16. [And we have *Sruti* testimony also confirming it]:—Self is self-illumined; before the evolution of all the worlds, He alone was existing, they follow the train of his illumination, and by him every thing is illumined or discovered.

17. That Intelligence which cognises the phenomenal world cannot be cognised by any other object. The several organs are powerless to cognise it, because they are prone to cover objects of cognition, and are incapable of holding the cogniser himself.

18. The proofs are:—"All objects of cognition are known to the Supreme Self, but no one can know Him. He is different from all known objects and is yet separate from unknown. He is the Supreme God, eternal and Intelligence."

19. He who fails to conceive of the Supreme Brahma after understanding Its difference from known and unknown, as knowledge itself, is merely a lump of clay in human shape, that is to say, it is impossible to make so dull-headed a person, understand the proofs cited in the *Shastras*.

20. To say "I have no knowledge of the eternal Self" is as unreasonable, as it is shameful to say "I know not whether I have a tongue," and yet a tongueless individual cannot speak, similarly He is knowledge and not to know him will amount to a perfect want of knowledge, a clear impossibility.

21. Whatever objects you come to know of, in ordinary use, leaving the the things aside, fix upon that knowledge as Brahma, and it can be termed knowledge of Brahma, for there is not another thing resembling It.

22. Though such knowledge, without the objects (as in the aforesaid paragraph) as Parabrahma, is really entitled to be called knowledge of the Supreme Self, yet a consideration of the 'five sacs' is not unnecessary, because when they are left out by close thinking, the residue of knowledge as a witness represents the Supreme Self, that is never absent. This is is explained as follows:—

23. Intelligence as indicated by the word Self can create no misapprehension with regard to one's Self, that is to say no one can be so misguided as to contend that he is not in existence, this is impossible. And who will be his antagonist in such a contention ?

24. Such a misapprehension with regard to his personality or existence never arises unless one is subject to a wild phantasy, hence the *Sruti* says "There is not one person who disbelieves his own existence."

25. He, who contends that the Supreme Self is non-existent, is himself so, for his individual intelligence is identical with self, and as that has already been pointed out to be imperceptible, then he is forced to admit his existence and with it,—Self.

26. The illumination of Self is now determined by the following queries and answers. What is the *Atma* like ? That which cannot be determined as resembling this or that, hence what is neither this nor that, is Self.

27. 'This' refers to objects visible to the eyes, and 'that'—invisible objects. But Self is not a subject of cognition by sight, nor is he invisible, for He is eternal, self-illuminated, knowledge.

Thus though unknowable, Self is determined to be eternal, and visible.

28. Therefore we find, though self is imperceptible, yet he is visible, and the same arguments will establish his self-illumination; moreover the *Sruti* indications of truth, knowledge, and infinity to Parabrahma are also applicable to Self.

29. What is not liable to destruction is called truth, hence after the dissolution of the objective world, who alone remains as a witness, is the Intelligence known as the eternal, indestructible, Supreme Self.

30. As after the dissolution of visible objects, ether (space) alone remains, so what remains after the destruction of

ether [and the rest] is knowledge, and that knowledge is called Self.

31. If it be said, nothing remains after the destruction of visible objects, and therefore we cannot call Self to be residue of destruction. [The answer is] Self is that unindicated something which you say remains *not* after destruction. Hence our difference is merely in words, the unindicated, and unascertainable residuum, left after the destruction of the world is alike admitted by both of us, (you say it to be nought, and I say it to be Self.)

32. With this object the *Sruti* seeks to differentiate the Witnessing Intelligence from all visible objects, " For even after their destruction he is indestructible, and is therefore called a residuum of destruction and eternal knowledge."

33. The *Sruti* has in the aforesaid manner established a twain condition in all impermanent objects, one of which is determinable as liable to destruction, the other undeterminable portion is the residue left after it. Now this residuary portion of destruction represents the undeterminable, eternal, infinite Supreme Self, who is imperishable.

34. In this manner is established his truth,* while that of knowledge has already been determined (*Vide Ver. 13 ante.*)

35. "He is infinite" because Self cannot be demarcated by place, time or object. He is present every where, hence it is impossible to fix a boundary line as to his locality ; as He is eternal, time cannot affect him, and as he pervades every object, it is impossible to confine him in one thing. Thus then, as He is unrestricted by place, time or object, He is infinite.

36. The *Sruti* is not alone in saying Self to be infinite, analogy alike establishes it,—for our conceptions of place,

---

* Truth is indestructible, and it is one, therefore it is Brahma, for Brahma is secondless.

time and object are illusion,* they cannot limit him, hence He is infinite.

37. It has already been shewn that the attribution of insentient material objects to Self cannot be true, inasmuch as in that case the infinite and eternal Self,—unassociated consciousness—will be reduced to the condition of the finite. Neither can he be limited by Iswara and *Jiva* for their associates are illusory, then again consciousness present in both of them is non-different from the consciousness of Brahma, hence they are powerless to distinguish it.

38. [Now the associates of Iswara and the individual are being set forth.] The force of the Supreme Brahma is centred in every object, from the 'blissful sac' to the rest, and as it controls them all, it is the associate of the Lord (Iswara.)

39. If that force were not to control the laws which govern the universe, they will act against one another and reduce every thing into chaos and disorder.

40. This force of the Supreme Brahma (which is eternal consciousness,) is intelligent, hence it is not impossible for it to exercise that sway which keeps the universe in order; combined as an associate with the Intelligence of Brahma it is called Iswara; that is to say when Intelligence is unassociated it is called the Supreme Brahma, and when associated with the force Maya, it is Iswara.

41. And Intelligence associated with the 'five sacs' (already mentioned), is designated *Jiva*. As in every-day life, we find the same man standing in the relation of a father to

---

* "Because the sense illusion is common and necessary law with all the senses,—external light and colors and sounds are all illusions, the cold in the hand, or in the ice, heat in the fire, pain in the foot, taste in the tongue, scent in the nose, is all illusory throughout and yet essential to existence."—H. G. ATKINSON, in *The Phil. Inq.* Vol. VII. p. 63.

his son and grandfather fo his grandson, [so the one Intelligence for a difference of associates is designated Iswara and *Jiva.*

42. As in the absence of a son and grandson, the same man is neither a father nor grandsire, so the one Intelligence when associated differently with Maya and the 'five sacs' is designated Iswara and Jiva, and when not associated, it is the Supreme Brahma Intelligence.

43. Thus when by the help of the aforesaid considerations about the 'five sacs,' an individual knows the Supreme Brahma, he attains the blissfulness of the Supreme Brahma, and after death is subjected to no more re-births; in other words, for one engaged in contemplating the Brahma, with fixedness of the mind, there are no more births and deaths. He is freed.

———:o:———

SECTION. IV.

Duality.

THE creatorship of Iswara and contrivance of the individual (*Jiva*) will form the subject of my present consideration. For in such a dual condition, the subjects that will have to be left out by him will be rendered apparent, the more so, that he may henceforth disregard them.

2. The *Shvetashvataro-panishad* mentions, that the force Maya is no other than *Prakriti* (Matter in its undifferentiated cosmic condition, without its three attributes) and Consciousness associated with it is Iswara. Now this Maya-associated Iswara is the creator of all these worlds.

3. Those who study the Rhika Veda, say that the Supreme Self, Iswara, was present in the beginning. He determined to create the world; and no sooner did such determination arise, than the creation of all (*lokas*) abodes followed.

4. Ether, air, fire, water, earth, medicine, food and body in due order, have sprung from him, with his determination.

5. "That with a view of occupying bodies numerous, did He create subjects and all the worlds." *Taitirya Upanishad.*

6. In the *Chhandodogya Upanishad* of the same Veda it is distinctly stated, that prior to the evolution of the world, (Sat) the One Existence alone was present. He declared with a solemn vow, let there be a variety of worlds, and at his will fire, water, and various creatures sprang into existence.

7. In the *Munduka Upanishad* of the Utharva Veda it is said that as sparks from fire do proceed, so from the imperishable Iswara proceeded various creatures sentient, and objects insentient.

8. In the *Vajasaneya Brihadanyka Upanishad* it is mentioned, that in its prior condition the earth was potentially but not perceptibly existent, at present it has assumed divers

name and form both in sentient and insentient visible objects, *viz*:—Virat, Manu, Man, Cow, Ass, Horse, Sheep, Goat, Birds, Ants, etc., both male and female.

9. The purport of the foregoing *Sruti* texts is:—The Supreme Iswara occupies in the shape of individual Intelligence all animal bodies, and for his supporting respiration He is designated *Jiva*.

10. The Universal Intelligence, with the collective aggregate of active and sensous organs, the five vital airs, mind and intellect, constituting the Astral body, together with its indwelling reflex Intelligence (individual)—all these collectively constitute, what is designated *Jiva*.

11. *Jiva* permeated with that Universal Intelligence (Brahma) is yet subject to happiness and misery, for Maya the associate of Iswara (Lord) is alike capable of creating the universe as of fascination; its force infatuates *Jiva* and subjects him to weal and woe during life.

12. From such infatuation, forgetting Self, the *Jiva* is hurled headlong into the concerns of a worldly life, and misery is his portion; thus the creation of the objective world* by Iswara is briefly declared.

13. In the *Saptanna Brahman* mention is made of the creation of various manifest objects by *Jiva*. He has produced seven different kinds of food by knowledge and works.

14. Of the above seven varieties of food, one is intended one for ordinary men inhabiting the earth, two for Devas (Superior beings), one for animals, and lastly, three for (*Atma*) Self.

They are specified as follows:—

15. The first class contains grains; the second consists

---

* Hence the manifested world is an indication of duality, the author has introduced it simply to show further on, the true aspect of the one Eternal Intelligence; the noumenal and phenomenal represent but two aspects of the One Existence.

of sacrifices done half monthly, and monthly during full moon; animals have milk; and *Atma* has Mind, speech and respiration for his portion.

16. As all of them are included in the world, naturally they come within the category of Iswara's work, and they are known so too, but as by his knowledge and act *Jiva* have admitted them into use as food, they may be looked upon as his production.

17. Now all this world, and the seven varieties of food (above mentioned) indicating it, though identically the same, yet virtually they are known separately as products of Iswara and the admitted food of *Jiva.* Every object has a similar bearing, it has two aspects though naturally it is one, as a woman begat by her father is for the enjoyment of her husband.

18. Iswara's force—a function of Maya—gave birth to the world, and his determination or volition is regarded as the cause of creation. The desire of a *Jiva* for the enjoyment of all enjoyable things—a mental function—is regarded as a means for their acquirement.

19. Though the creative products of Iswara cannot be re-created by *Jiva,* yet jewels and other precious stones, etc., (without subjecting them to any change of form) are differently used in a variety of ways, according to individual taste and intelligence or capacity of enjoying.

20. And as such enjoyment is varied, owing to a difference in the taste, inclination and knowledge of an individual, though the object may be same, yet we find that one is very much delighted with a jewel, another is much vexed in not having it, while a third is perfectly indifferent whether he gets it or not.

21. Thus in its enjoyment, we find *Jiva* creating three different forms in the jewels, (*e.g.,*) pleasure, annoyance and indifference, but as created by Iswara it is always one and knows no distinction.

22. As the same woman stands differently related to several individuals, to one she is wife, to another daughter-in-law, a sister-in-law to a third, mother to a fourth and so on according to the knowledge of her several relations, though as created by Iswara she is one, and has no such distinctions present in her.

23. If you say that in the above instance the difference in the relationship of the female is merely established, and as that does not create a particular difference in her form and features, it is inapplicable.

24. We reply, external objects are of two kinds: externally, they are elementary in composition; and internally, full of mind; so that, if there be no difference in her configuration or flesh, yet the mental function determines her relationship as a wife, daughter-in-law, etc.

25. If you say that in the conditions of error, dream, sovereignty of the mind, and memory there is possibility for the mental function overtaking an external object, but in a state of walking no such mental function appears probable.

26. The answer is:—When an external object is connected with the internal organ by means of sight, hearing and the rest, it assumes the shape of that external object, hence in the waking state for an external object, to become mental, is admissible. This has been particularly declared by the Vashykar, and Vartikkara.

27. (Vashykar's illustration is introduced as a proof.) "As copper melted in a crucible by heat assumes its shape, so the internal organ assumes the modification of an external object which it seeks to discover by taking possession of, by means of the senses."

28. "Or like the sun, whose rays of light discover an object by assuming its shape, the internal organ which is a discoverer of all objects, assumes the shape of what it takes possession, and thus helps the individual to know it."

29. [The corroborating evidence of Vartikkara is now

being cited.] "When an external object comes within the reach of eye-sight, etc., the function of the internal organ originated by the demonstrating intelligence of *Boodhi*, takes possession of it, and becomes converted into its shape, consequently as an object externally is derived from the elements, so internally it is full of mind." This can be admitted.

30. In this manner, the twain character of a pot and all similar objects is established. They are both elementary and mental; in reference to Iswara's creation a pot is externally earthy, but to the individual (*Jiva*) it is created in his internal organ, therefore mental.* The external earthy pot is cognised by sight, while the mental pot is discovered by the witnessing Intelligence of the internal organ.

31. By the methods of *Anvaya* and *Vyetrieka*† we know all mental objects cause worldly enthrallment and lead the

* We find here two different sorts of creation. External and internal, or elementary and mental. The objective world is elementary, derived from the elements ether and the rest, while as their cognition follows only by the mind assuming their shape, the senses are simply, so to speak, the channel by which the function proceeds from that organ to take possession of them and till they are thus covered, to all intents and purposes they cease to exist. But this is so quick that scarcely have we any notion of the steps involved in the process of a single act of consciousness. Then again some will have it, that it is transient too, for in the ordinary course of our every-day life we are continually forming conceptions of things and objects, which are replaced by others, and they again by others. That is to say a prior conception is re-placed by a second, and that by a third and so on, hence the supporters of the transient theory are called the *Kshanik Vadins*. They look upon the whole thing, as a current of consciousness in which the objects that are perceived follow as a current of water in a river, or as waves follow continually without any break of continuity.

† 'Anvaya' is relation of cause and effect. 'Vyetrieka' is discrimination of separate distinction.

individual to consecutive re-births:—The presence of such mental objects produces pleasure or pain; their absence, neither.

32. For instance, in the dreaming state, all knowledge of external objects is absent, but the mental function still continues busy in covering mental objects and enthralls the individual, while in dreamless slumber, trance, and profound meditation, both external and mental objects are absent and the mental function is at abeyance, hence there is no more attachment.

33. When a father is informed of the demise of an absent son residing in a distant country, by a liar, he is sure to give vent to his grief in tears and crying.

34. Or as in the absence of certain news about the death of his absent son, a father continues to live happily with a gladsome heart, though such son is dead, we therefore find mental function is the chief cause of worldly attachment everywhere in all individuals.

35. [But it may be asked.] What necessity is there for establishing the existence of the objective world when mental function is the cause of an individual's attachment?

36. The necessity lies in this:—Inasmuch as the mental function must assume the shape of the object it seeks to discover, it is essential that objects must be in a state of existence so as to lend their reflection to the internal organ. If it be affirmed that from previous conceptions gathered in former births, the earth can be realised mentally without the external objective world, so that its existence is not a prime necessity, even admitting such to be the case, you cannot do away with its exposition as altogether useless, because that which is dependent on proofs stands in necessity for the proofs of its existence, therefore in the tangible proofs of its existence the phenomenal world is not unreal.

37. If such mental world be the cause of the individual's re-birth, then the practice of abstaining the mind—a certain

form of *Yoga*—will help to stop such conception of duality that is certain enough. But what is the use of studying knowledge of Brahma?

38. Because by refraining the mind in the aforesaid manner, conception of duality is destroyed for the time being, suspended, so to speak—but no *Jiva* can be freed from successive re-incarnations unless he has attained to the knowledge of Brahma, as has been over and over repeated in the Vedanta.

39. According to the ('Avedabadi') non-dualist, simple knowledge of the unreality of the external world, without refraining the mind from it, is enough to lead to a knowledge of the Brahma, but it by no means follows that a want of the external world will produce a similar knowledge of the secondless Brahma;

40. Inasmuch as in (Pralaya) final dissolution of the universe and its contents, duality is wanting to contend against non-duality, the preceptor and *Shastras* are alike destroyed, yet no knowledge of the secondless Brahma is possible in such a condition.

41. [Therefore] Iswara's creation—the external world and the elements which constitute duality—is not antagonistic to, but a means for attaining a knowledge of non-duality, in other words without a preceptor and instruction on the *Shastras*, or a knowledge of the unreality and impermanence of the elements and elementary bodies which go to make up the objective world, non-duality can never be realised, consequently you cannot regard it unnecessary, Under such circumstances why do the other controversialists shew their spite against it?

42. [Now *Jiva's* creation of duality is declared.] The mental creation of duality proceeding from the individual is of two kinds: (*a*) Duality in conformity with the *Shastras*, and (*b*) Duality independent of them. Of them, the last is to be relinquished; and so long as non-duality is not fully realised the first is to be practised.

43. (*a*).—This is to consider upon the non-difference of Self from the Supreme Self by analysis, and argument,—cited in the Vedanta as desires pertaining to the sacred scriptures. It is to be continued so long as knowledge of truth is not acquired, when this first form of Duality is to be abandoned.

44. On this subject the *Sruti* testimony is, "When by continual study of the Vedas and the Vedanta, unreality of dualism has been firmly established, and knowledge of the secondless Reality Parabrahma, is obtained, the sacred writings are to be abandoned, (for they have served their purpose and there is no more any necessity for them) just as a torch is extinguished by one travelling in a dark night when he arrives home or when he has no further need of it.

45. When an intelligent person by studying the Vedanta and other sacred writings has obtained a clear insight into what is real and unreal, and after having ascertained their drift has acquired knowledge of the Supreme Self, he stands in no further need of them, that is to say they are abandoned just as a cultivator, desirous of reaping grains, uses the crusher so long as there are grains, and abandons it after the work is finished.

46. The quiet and tranquil-minded seeker of truth, bent on knowledge of Self, is deeply engaged on the cultivation of that knowledge and abstains from a grandiloquent discussion of the sacred writings, because that is fruitless.

47. To know the secondless Parabrahma by restraining mind and speech and abandoning other words is the advice plainly set forth in the *Sruti*.

48. (*b*.)—'Duality not pertaining to the sacred writings' is also divisible into two varieties, of which the first 'sharp' includes desire and passion; and the second 'bad' indicates mental sovereignty.

49. Both of them are to be avoided by the seeker of truth, for the *Sruti* insists on mental quietude and meditation as the means for attaining knowledge of Brahma.

50. It is not to be supposed that they are to be avoided only prior to obtaining knowledge, but they must be relinquished even subsequent to it, by one desirous of being freed in life; because passions and desires are indications of ignorance and not of deliverance in life.

51. If it be affirmed, since knowledge of truth cuts of future re-births, that is enough for my purpose, I desire not to be known as one freed in life, and no harm can follow from a continuance of passions and desires. The reply is, if you think in that way, you are sure to be re-born again, after enjoyment of heaven for a brief period. In other words you are no knower of Self, but simply a person engaged in actions sanctioned by religion.

52. If you do not desire enjoyment of heaven because it is temporary, What prevents you from abandoning passions and desires which are faulty and worthless ?

53. If after acquiring knowledge of non-duality, you still persist in keeping up your desires and passions, then you break the very sacred writings which guide you in your actions and become a follower of your own inclinations.

54. If in spite of your knowledge of truth, you act according to the bent of your desires, where is the difference between you and a dog that lives on unclean food ?*

---

* Two very extreme views pervail in regard to this subject. Yateshtacharan or acting according to a person's inclination is condemned by Suresvaracharya, an illustrious disciple of Sankararcharya. Our author holds similar views too, and the passage in the text is an appeal to that end. But it is said, the Upanishads contain several passages in which the opposite doctrine is maintained, and a Theosophist is free to act as he likes. Professor Gough in his article in the *Calcutta Review* (1878, p. 34) says " The Theosophist liberated from metempsychosis, but still in the body is untouched by merit and de-merit, absolved from all works good and evil, unsoiled by sinful works. (*Brihadaranyako-panishad*

55. In such a condition you are reduced to something worse than what you were before, inasmuch as prior to such knowledge you had to suffer from the pain of your passions and desires, while now in addition to that, people will speak ill of you. Ah how much glory then, does your knowledge bring unto you!

56. Therefore a knower of truth should not desire to follow the bent of his inclination like the swine and wild boar, but by abandoning passions and desires, he must raise himself to the dignity of a Deva and be an object of worship and reverence everywhere.

57. [Now the means for relinquishing mental defects, passions, etc., are being determined.] To find out impermanence in a desired object is an uncommon help to reduce it and the passion for it, to nihility. This has been repeatedly explained in the Vedanta. Therefore live in happiness by relinquishing desire and passion, and by regarding all things which excite your desire to be non-eternal.

58. It cannot be said, that no such ill consequence can be attributed to the sovereignty of the mind, therefore at its presence is allowable, the more so, as it enables a person to spend his time in happiness. To consider in this wise is objectionable, for though 'mental sovereignty' leads to no evil consequence directly, yet by its influence on passions and desires, it brings forth evil, hence it is to be abandoned. 'Mental sovereignty' is therefore the source of all evil. Bhagaban Sree Krishna speaks also of the injurious effects which it leads to, by its interdependence of, and influence on, desire and passion in the following manner. (*Gita*, Chap. II. V. 69.)

59. " He who contemplates on [the acquisition of] wealth, begets a predilection for it, then follows an intense desire of acquisition, baffled in it he becomes angry and stupid, loses

4. 4. 23) uninjured by what he has done and by what he has left undone. (*Ibid* 4. 4. 22).

his memory, ultimately to die." Now what can be more hurtful than 'mental sovereignty'?

60. 'Mental sovereignty' is capable of being removed by 'profound unconscious meditation,' which follows as a result of conscious meditation.*

61. And one unable to practice that meditation, but who is devoid of all passions and desires, can keep back 'mental

---

* 'Profound meditation' is of two kinds namely :—

1. *Savikalpa*, Conscious, and
2. *Nirvikalpa*, Unconscious.

1. Conscious meditation :—The subject, the perception, and the object constitute the conscious Ego. To realise the *Brahma* without a second by concentrating the mind which has assumed the shape of the Impartite, and by indivisibly resting its function there, with the distinction of knower and knowledge, that is to say, with the retention of the individual Consciousness. Then as in the instance of an earthen toy-elephant, the mind takes cognisance of the animal along with that of its composite clay, so there is the perception of the Universal Consciousness (*Brahma*) co-existent with the Conscious Ego, or non-duality. As it has been said by the subject of such contemplation "I am that Secondless Consciousness, everpresent, pervading everywhere, good, light, without a beginning (unborn), undecaying, unblended, innate, and free."

2. 'Unconscious meditation' is the resting of the Impartite mental function on the Reality *Brahma* without a second, and becoming one with it, by the destruction of the three integral constituents of the Conscious Ego—the subject, the individual perception, and the object.—Then as in a saline solution, the salt having been dissolved assumes the shape of the water, its separate existence is destroyed, but the water alone is left to be perceived, so to discover the Real *Brahma* alone by the mind after it has been moulded into the shape of the Impartite.— *Dhole's Vedantasara, p. 47.*

sovereignty' by pronouncing the mystic syllable 'OM'* with fixed attention for a lengthened period.

62. Thus the sovereignty of the mind having been subdued, it comes to rest tranquilly, having no function to distract it any more. On this subject the sage Bashishtha has given various illustrations to Ramachandra.

63. When the external objective world is shut out of the mind, by due reflection and consideration of the secondless Brahma, and that has been visibly perceived, the way for attaining Nirvana is made easy. Then after study of the Sacred Scriptures on spirituality [The soul and the Supreme soul] with particular attention to their logical inferences, frequent conversation with other persons on the same subject, and refraining the mind from the acquirement of material comforts, nothing is more proper than to commune with Self and stop speech altogether or to become silent.

64. If as a result of 'fructescent works'—actions done in a prior birth but which have commenced to bear fruit—a Theosophist be subjected to mental distraction, it is only temporary in duration, for by repeated practice he has learned how to restore tranquility, and thus he merges into Brahma.

65. And that knower of Brahma whose internal organ is

* This word is formed of A, u and m. The two first are converted into O according to the rules of Grammar. Each letter has a distinct signification. In the Mandukya Upanishad, 'OM' is said to indicate the Self-luminous Protector of all, (*i.e.*,) Brahma. Hence 'OM' is a predicate and Brahma its subject, and between them there is no distinction whatever. Literally speaking 'OM' can lay no claim to Brahma, but as in worshipping an ammonite (Saligram) a worshipper is to fix the form of Vishnu in his mind, though the stone has no likeness to him, similarly while meditating 'OM' a person is to dwell on Brahma mentally.

never liable to meet with any impediment* from mental distraction is fit to be recognised as Brahma. For it is the unanimous declaration of all devout sages "Such a person is not a knower of Brahma, but is himself a Brahma."

66. In connection with this non-difference of a Theosophist with Brahma, Bashishta says, "He who rests on Brahma with his internal organ entirely merged in It, who has no more any knowledge of what the sacred writings teach, nor that of the objective material world, is himself a Brahma. He cannot properly be styled a knower of Brahma, for it is irrational to say that Brahma knows Itself, or is Its own knower."

67. Thus after the vast desires created by *Jiva* have relinquished their hold from the internal organ, he is delivered in life, and with that purpose in view Duality has been divided into two classes of which the first form, *Jiva's* creation is treated here differently from the second—Iswara's creation.

---

* There are eight 'means' for unconscious meditation and four obstacles. The means are (*a*) Forbearance, (*b*) Minor observances, (*c*) Ascetic posture, (*d*) Regulated breathing, (*e*) Restraining the sensory organs, (*f*) Fixed attention, (*g*) Contemplation, and (*h*) Conscious meditation.

Mental inactivity, Mental distraction, Passions and desires, and Tasting of enjoyment are the four obstacles.

SECTION V.

On the consideration of Transcendental Vedic Phrases.

INDIVIDUAL Intelligence centered in *Boodhi* that helps the cognition of all objects by sight, hearing, smell and taste, and enables us to speak, is the literal signification of the word *Prajnana* in the "*Prajnanam Brahma*" cited in the Aiterya Upanishad of the *Rhigveda*. That is to say, with a view of enabling a Theosophist desirous of release to establish his non-difference with Brahma, the four forms of Vedic expressions used as a means to that end, are now being considered. The *Rhik Veda* says "Intelligence is Brahma." This is proved in the following wise:

2. Since Parabrahma is all pervading, It is equally present in Brahmâ, Indra, and other Devas as also in man, cow, horse, and animals. As an internal knower, Its pervasion is universal, consequently it is present in me too. Thus then there being one receptacle for both the Intelligences, *viz.*, *Prajnana* and Parabrahma, they are naturally identical, hence Individual Intelligence is non-different from the Intelligence of Brahma.

3. The phrase (*Aham Brahmasmi*) " I am Brahma" cited in the *Brihadaranyak Upanishad* of *Yajurveda* is thus explained:—That infinite Intelligence, the Supreme Self, residing in the body, composed of the five elements, by the inherent force of Maya, but discovered as a witness by passivity, self-control and other 'means' for attaining Self-knowledge, is the signification of 'I' (*aham.*)

4. 'Brahma' refers to the self-existent, all-pervading, Supreme Self. And 'am establishes the non-difference of the two intelligences expressed by 'I' and 'Brahma.' If, therefore, the identity of the individual and universal Intelligence be established, then the use of 'I am Brahma' by one liberated

in life necessarily implies no contradiction but an established truth.

5. In the *Chhandogya Upanishad* of Sama Veda the phrase (*Tatamasi*) "That art Thou" bears a like signification. Prior to the evolution of all this [visible objective world] there existed a secondless Reality without name or form, but all-pervading and is yet existing in a similar condition ; this is indicated by 'That.'

6. The indwelling Intelligence residing in the internal organ of every individual, but quite distinct altogether from the physical body and the organs active and sensuous, is the indication of 'Thou.' And 'art' establishes the non-difference of 'That' and 'Thou.' Hence it is but natural to conceive them as one.*

7. The *Atharva Veda* has likewise a similar phrase with an identical signification. (*Ayam Atma Brahma*) "This self is Brahma." Here the self-luminous visible Individual Intelligence is the literal signification of 'This' and as it

* It is said 'words' are construed in one of three ways :—(*a*) literal, (*b*) indicated and (*c*) suggestive. The first is that which is at once known with its pronounciation, it is due to its energy, strength, or force. Now this force sometimes fails to convey a signification, and we have then to construe according to what is called in Rhetoric cannons of Indication. There are as many as eighty Indications. But all of them do not concern us so far as construction of the transcendental phrases go. Here we have to do mainly with two varieties of them, *viz.*, Indicative Indication (lakshya lakshan bhava), and Inclusive Indication, (upadana lakshana). Indication of abandoning a part of the expressed signification (bhaga lakshana) is a composite Indication. "That art Thou" cannot be construed literally, but by abandoning the opposing elements of invisibility and visibility from the consciousness or Intelligence expressed by the words 'That' and 'Thou' respectively, the remaining non-conflicting Intelligence is meant in the same manner as "That Devadatta is this."

resides within the bodily fabric, in all its components units from the 'physical body' to 'egoism' it is spoken of as Self. Hence the two words 'This Self' indicate the individual intelligence.

8. The one cause of the phenomenal world and its substratum, *viz.*, the Universal Intelligence is indicated by 'Brahma.' It is Self-luminous too, therefore, the two Intelligences are identical.

SECTION VI.

Illustration by similitude with painting.

LIKE a price of painting four conditions are present in the Supreme Brahma.

2—3. Now in painting, the four preliminary conditions are :—(*a*) Preparation of the ground, (*b*) stretching, and rubbing the canvas, (*c*) drawing the outline, (*d*) finishing or filling it with color. Similarly in the Supreme Self we find present, (*a*) Intelligence, (*b*) Internal Knower, Thread soul, and Virat. They are explained as follows:—

4. The unassociated Intelligence of the Supreme Brahma is the first, and Iswara's Intelligence associated with Maya, the second condition. The subtle astral body [as subject of one Intellect (*Boodhi*) and called the Thread soul, for it pervades like a thread through all created beings; and as a collective aggregate it is the subjective Intelligence of Hiranyagarbha,] is the third; and Intelligence associated with gross bodies called Virat [for it is present in divers form] is the fourth condition.

5. As in a piece of painting all the figures do not rest in one position, but some are good and others badly placed, so from the Turiene column to all sentient and insentient objects—mountain, river, earth, etc.,and living beings, in short, every thing rests in due order on the Intelligence of the Supreme Brahma.

6. As the different wearing apparel of the several figures in the piece of painting are conceived to be identical with its cloth (canvas),

7. So the different Intelligence (Life soul) of individuals resting on the Universal Intelligence which is the substratum, is alike conceivable to be identical with that of Parabrahma.

Variously do they finish their sojourn here after having assumed bodily form.

8. As the wearing apparel in the painting are taken for the color of the canvas by a dull person, so the ignorant mistake an individual's career in earth for that of Brahma, and consider it so.

9. And as the painted mountains, etc., require no wearing apparel, so are insentient material objects—earth, etc.,—devoid of individual intelligence or Life soul.

10. To consider worldly existence as the supreme object of life and related to Brahma is an error called (Avidya) Ignorance. It is removed by knowledge.

11. For knowledge helps to show if Brahma were at all connected with the world then it would have been likewise eternal, but as it is otherwise, the world is merely an inheritance for the *Jiva*, who is a reflected shadow of the Supreme Self; to determine this is called knowledge, and it can only be acquired by argument and analysis.

12. This knowledge destroys ignorance; hence it is always necessary to determine the nature of the world, individual and Brahma. Because then the impermanence of the two first is clearly established, and their incompatible residue Brahma, (incompatible, because permanent) is discovered as eternal and pure.

13. Thus then to find out the transitory condition of all created objects, to ascertain that incompatible residue [of destruction] the Supreme Brahma, is knowledge, and it leads to emancipation. Now the word 'incompatible' does not refer to knowledge, in that case it will be want of knowledge, and an individual in trance and profound dreamless slumber may as well expect to be 'freed.'

14. When real knowledge of Brahma is firmly established, and the world reduced to impermanence and unreality, that is meant by 'incompatibility.' This is its proper signification,

otherwise to *forget the world* is not meant, as in that case, emancipation in life will be impossible.

15. From such a consideration arises two sorts of knowledge: invisible and visible; the former is to be continually practised till it leads to the latter, when all analysis and arguments are to cease.

16. [The 'invisible,' and 'visible' are now being explained.] Knowledge which establishes Brahma to be Secondless, Intelligence and Cause of all, is called invisible, and when it helps a person to say "I am the eternal, true, and free Brahma," it is called visible.

17. This second sort of knowledge is facilitated by enquiring into Self, hence that is imperatively needed; because by means of it, the individual freed from all fetters, abides in Intelligence (Brahma) and soon enjoys that felicity whose sole essence is joy.*

---

* 'Liberation' is the acquisition of Brahma, whose essence is joy and the cessation of misery. For we find it said in the Veda "The knower of Brahma becomes Brahma, the knower of self passes beyond all misery." Now, sensuous gratifications or abode in heaven, or any other blissful region is not *Moksha*, for they are derived from works, therefore transitory and non-eternal: The blissfulness of Brahma is not open to a similar objection, it is eternal; we are deluded into an opposite belief simply from Ignorance, hence the destruction of that Ignorance by cultivating self-knowledge. Though the 'means' prescribed for that end helps the cognition of Brahma and removes the envelopment of Ignorance, yet it cannot be said that as knowledge brings in conception of bliss and destruction of misery; prior to it, there was neither perception of felicity nor cessation of sorrow, thus blissfulness of Brahma has a beginning, and what has a beginning is open to destruction, therefore, both bliss and the cessation of misery are non-eternal.

Then again to say, that it is useless to attempt acquiring a thing already got, that is to say, since the felicity of Brahma is naturally present, cultivation of knowledge is no longer necessary.

18. (The nature of Intelligence is to be ascertained before enquiring into Self, with this view it is considered in its four aspects.) They are :—Uniform,* Brahma, Individual and Iswara Intelligences. As the same ether for a difference of its associate receives various appellations, so is one Intelligence severally called.

19. For instance. There is pitcher-ether as follows: that is to say, ether confined within and bounded by a pitcher, to distinguish it from the impartite and all-pervading ether called *Mahakas.*† Aqueous-ether or reflection of the sky with stars and cloud in the water contained in a pitcher.

20—21. Now the clouds present in the great body of (unappropriated) ether represent vapor, which is simply a transformed condition of water (for vapor is a product of evaporation of water by the sun's rays) hence the reflection of ether in cloud is easy to conceive, and as such it has a separate designation, and called cloud-ether.

22. From quintuplication of elements is produced the gross body which is likewise called the foodful sac for its dependence upon food; the three other sacs, Vital, Mental, and Blissful, are not a result of such combination, and they constitute the Astral body. Intelligence pervading it, is termed uniform, because it knows no change.

But that should not be, because we find it so happen, when a man has forgotten about a piece of gold in his hand, he recovers possession of it, as if he had not got it already, when pointed out by another. In the same way, acquisition of bliss already possessed and destruction of misery already destroyed, can only be recovered by means of knowledge, hence cultivation of knowledge is a proper object for an individual to be engaged in.

* *Kutasta chaitanya* is perpetually and universally the same, hence it is uniform.

† *Maha* means great; because it is the source of that, appropriated by a pitcher, etc., in short, it pervades everywhere, in and out.

23. The reflection of 'uniform Intelligence' on *Boodhi*,* for its supporting the vital airs,† is called *Jiva*, and he is subject to pleasure and pain.

24. With a view of ascertaining the unassociated and associated nature of the Intelligences, 'uniform' and 'individual,' they are here regarded separate, but from ignornance *Jiva* is incapable of determining the exact nature of the first, hence it can be said that he shuts such knowledge; in the same way as ether of the water contained in a pitcher displaces the pitcher-ether. In the Commentaries of Sariraka treatises it is called (*Anayanyadhyas*) 'Mutual Illusion.'

25. The cause of this mutual illusory attribution or transferring one intelligence to the other is (*Avidya*) Ignorance, or as it is otherwise called Primordial, Ignorance, without a beginning. That prevents *Jiva* from perceiving the nature of uniform Intelligence.

26. Now this Ignorance‡ has two powers.

(*a*) Concealment and (*b*) Projection.

(*a*) Concealment prevents the apprehension of the eternal, self-illuminated, uniform Intelligence, and renders it invisible.

27. Concealment or want of apprehension receives corroboration from the experience of an ignorant person, who if asked about the 'uniform Intelligence' says "I know. it not," "I cannot apprehend it," and "There is no such thing as uniform Intelligence."

28. If one is inclined to argue in the following strain: "As shadow and light cannot rest together, so Ignorance cannot exist with uniform Intelligence, whose nature is light, for they are antagonistic to one another, consequently where ignorance is wanting, concealment cannot be expected to be

---

* Intellect. Mr. Sinnet in his *Esoteric Buddhism* calls it the Spiritual Soul.

† Inspiration, expiration, etc.

‡ Nescience.

present," the experience of ignorant persons as exemplified above will remove his mistake.

29. If one would not trust to his own experience, How can a *Tarkika* determine an entity by argument? It will not help him. Because argument has no end; one person draws his inference in one way, which a man of intellect refutes and determines differently.

30. Though argument alone cannot ascertain truth, yet to help its apprehension, if probable (conformable) arguments are required, you can have recourse to them, in a manner, as will help *Boodhi* to draw natural inferences in conformity to experience, but abstain from close reasoning and ill-matched arguments in the elucidation of truth, for sophistry misleads and is a source of great evil.

31. Now the probable arguments to determine the uniform Intelligence conformable to experience, are being reiterated. While describing the power of envelopment of Ignorance the experience of a person in reference to it has already been mentioned. He says. "I know it not," etc. Therefore use conformable arguments as help the ascertainment of the uniform Intelligence and in no way bear against it.

32. If you regard the discoverer of the power of envelopment or concealment of Ignorance—uniform Intelligence—as opposed to it, How can you otherwise apprehend concealment? (This you cannot). Therefore know the indication of a wise man and look upon (*viveka*) 'discrimination' as an antagonist of (*avidya*) nescience or Ignorance.

33. (*b*) 'Projection' or 'superimposition is now being set forth. It may likewise be termed misapprehension. It is determined by the illustration of silver in nacre. That is to say as silver is mistaken in nacre from illusion, so from the force of creation or superimposition, the uniform Intelligence, enveloped in ignorance is apt to be mistaken for the physical and subtle bodies and individual intelligence. This

is called the mistaken attribution of creation, superimposition or projection.

34. When nacre is mistaken for silver, though the silver is entirely false, yet the [preceeding portion] lying in front and designated by the term, 'This nacre' is not unreal; similarly though the attribution of individual intelligence to the uniform is not real, yet its practical resemblance to Self and Reality is a fact.

35. And as during the occurrence of that mistake, its tri-angular shape and blue color cease to be present in the nacre, so the unassociated felicity, etc., of uniform Intelligence are removed, when it is mistaken for individual intelligence.

36. Thus then as in its illusion, the mistaken perception of nacre is called silver, so the superimposition of false perception on uniform Intelligence is *Jiva*.

37. Then again, as in nacre, illusion of silver occurs only when its preceeding part is visible, so the attribution of *Jiva* to uniform intelligence only follows on the parts represented by Self and Reality.

38. Though as a matter of fact, a mistake is the substitution of one thing for another, yet without a close resemblance of the two, no mistake is apt to occur; now in the case of nacre there is ordinary and particular distinction in its fore-part, and a close resemblance* with silver, hence the mistake;

---

* Two very extreme views prevail in regard to this subject amongst Hindu metaphysicians. Some hold that between a predicate and subject their does not exist any difference in the meaning. Bhadri supports the view of difference along with non-difference, while our author seeks to maintain the existence of a difference. The arguments on which each rests his opinion are being given here to enable our readers to comprehend both the views.

It is said, there is difference along with resemblance between a material cause and its product, just as there is between a quality and its receptacle, or between caste and person; between

similarly between the literal signification or predicate of the words 'self'—uniform Intelligence—and '*Jiva*' there is both

---

an instrumental cause and its resulting action, there does not exist such a relation both of difference and resemblance, but extreme difference only. For example, the instrumental cause of a jar,—a potter with his wheel and turning rod—is extremely different from that jar, which is a product of his manipulation, but between its material cause—a lump of clay—there exists both difference and resemblance, and if they were extremely different from each other, then the cause clay would alike have the property of producing oil, another substance extremely different from it; but since it is otherwise, we may with equal propriety conclude no clay shall produce a jar. Similarly if the material cause of a jar were to bear the strongest affinity, resemblance or similarity with it, no jar would result. Hence there is distinction along with resemblance between them. Now for this difference, the objections of extreme difference and of agreement or the faults of difference, do not apply to this view. Thus then it is an established fact. It likewise derives proofs from our own perception, because externally we find a jar different from clay, but on reflection, we know that every part of the jar is composed of clay, hence the two are identical.

Bhadri thus refutes his rivals who consider the predicate and subject of a word, bear only difference. He says:—If the predicate of the word 'jar' be extremely different from a jar then as it fails to convey the import of a cloth which is extremely different from it, likewise it should fail to signify a pitcher which is also extremely different from it, moreover if you regard the predicate of the word 'jar' to be different from it and admit its signification a 'jar' or a pitcher which is extremely different from it (both in shape and size) then it may with equal propriety imply such another substance as does not bear any resemblance to it; the same consideration is applicable to that other doctrine which does not admit the presence of a force, energy or desire in a term, hence it is faulty too. Because the predicate of 'jar,'—a pitcher,—and a cloth,—which is not so—both of them are equally different from 'jar,' then inasmuch as the word 'jar' has in it the force of distinction and resemblance, for which the illusory attribution of the former takes place in the latter. Therefore the words

---

conveying the signification of a pitcher, and not of another substance, consequently beyond a pitcher the word 'jar' cannot mean any other thing. Hence the strength of a word to convey its proper signification can only render that sense perceptible, and not a different sense. Thus then there is no defect in [admitting the strength of a word] regarding a predicate and subject as always different from one another. It cannot be alleged that along with that difference there is a close resemblance, (*tadatmya sambandha)*. Because 'difference' and 'resemblance' or 'non-difference' are naturally opposed to each other; similarly between a proximate cause and its product there is said to be only difference and not difference along with non-difference (resemblance). According to the view of a Nyayika or supporter of the strength theory [of words], consideration of difference only is not at all faulty, though his opponents attribute faults wherever only difference is maintained. For say they, if there be extreme difference between a cause and its resulting action, then as a lump of clay produces a jar which is extremely different from it, it may as well produduce oil which also is extremely different, and if no oil can be produced from clay, similarly a jar should not be its product. But this fault does not apply to the view held by a Nyayika, for he looks upon (*pragbhava*) 'prior condition' as the efficient cause in the production of all things. That is to say, as for a 'jar' to be produced a potter, revolving wheel, and stick are the instrumental cause, similarly the prior condition of a jar is its cause. In the same way, in reference to the production of all objects, their prior condition is a cause. Now this prior condition of a jar resides in its material cause (clay) and not elsewhere, and that of oil, in the seed bearing it, (seesamum) and not in any thing else, so on we find each and every object residing (potentially) in that prior condition in its respective material cause, and not in any thing else, hence clay produces a jar, etc., and not oil, simlarly oil seeds produce oil and not a jar and so on. Thus then as 'prior condit ion' is a cause of production, hence to regard an extreme diffe rence between a cause and its product implies neither

'self' and 'I' (expressive of *Jiva*) do not literally bear the same meaning.

39. The difference of the two words 'Self' and 'I' is now being explained. The common acceptance of 'self' and particular indication of 'I' is being illustrated by reference to ordinary usage. In ordinary practice we find 'Self' (*sayam*) used in a variety of expressions always attached to a word, as Devadatta (him) self goes, you (your) self see, I (my) self am incapable. But 'I' cannot be similarly used.

40. Moreover as an expressive antecedent is ordinarily attached almost everywhere as "this silver," "this cloth"

---

contradiction not any other defect from the standpoint of a Nyayika. The same holds true with that other view of strength. For instance, moist earth can only produce a jar, because it has that strength only, and as it has not the strength of producing oil, no oil follows, similarly in an oil-seed there is the strength of producing oil and not a jar. Hence to regard a material cause and its product as extremely different from each other is not open to any objection.

But to say that there is difference and resemblance, is objectionable. That is to say, if as Bhadri says that between a material cause and its product there is difference along with non-differece, then the objections pointed out in connection with difference and non-difference will both apply to his view. A gambler and thief are two distinct persons, yet when a person is both a thief and gambler both the defects properly belong to him, similarly in admitting a difference and agreement between property and subject, the usual objections against difference and its reverse must equally apply. But that does not affect the strength theory inasmuch as difference only is admitted. For a substance has the strength to hold qualities in it. Consequently the objection pointed out against difference do not apply. For instance if the form, capacity and its other qualities are different from a jar, so is a cloth different from a jar and it may as well be expected to be present in a jar.

similarly the word 'self' is always applicable by attaching it to another word.

41. If, therefore, 'I' (*aham*) expressive of Individual Intelligence is thus shewn to be different in its signification from (*sayam*) 'Self,' then uniform Intelligence is to be called Self.

42. And according to my view he is the Supreme Self;* because self (*sayam*) excludes the idea of another from its signification, [such exclusion determines the reality of one Supreme Self] and that is my object.

43. Now the words 'Self' and '*Atma*' are synonymous, therefore as the first excludes the idea of another, so it is natural to attribute a similar exclusion with regard to the second.

44. As then the two words last referred are identical in their signification, the use of 'self' in conditions of trance or fainting establish his existence likewise, as, "I myself was unconscious," here Self establishes his presence even in that state.

45. Though for its pervasion, uniform Intelligence must be alike present in all insentient objects, as a pot, a pitcher, etc., yet the distinction of sentiency and insentiency is not due to it, but is the work of intelligence reflected in *Boodhi* and dependent on it. In other words objects with individual Intelligence are called sentient, while those without it are insentient.

46. And as individual Intelligence is mistaken with the uniform, so is insentiency in the case of inanimate objects contrived to be present in uniform Intelligence.

---

* As in the instances quoted:—"Devadatta himself," "I myself," every where when self is added with a personal pronoun it excludes the idea of another as if by way of emphasis, and points out strongly the person concerned, so in a similar way when Self excludes the idea of other similar selves, my point is gained, and I can look upon him as the one Supreme Self.

47. If pervasion constitute Supreme Self, since he follows everywere in all objects, in that case all such other objects asfollow everwhere ;may equally be called Supreme Self, 'that' and 'this' are equally present everywhere, and used in connection with all objects, which may be said to depend on them, therefore they ought with equal propriety be regarded identically equal to him.

48. [The reply is] though the words 'that' and 'this' like Supreme Self, are plainly perceived to be attached to all objects including even the *Atma*, they are not the Supreme Self, but like other words signifying correct or proper they are merely attached everywhere, even in conditions of extreme contrariety.

49. The signification of 'that' and 'this' 'self' and 'another,' 'thou' and 'I' are antagonistic or opposed to each other.

50. Of them, the signification of 'Self' opposed to that of 'another' is expressive of the uniform intelligence and the signification of 'thou' opposed to that of 'I' can be admitted as *Jiva*.

51. As the distinction between nacre and silver is plainly perceived, so even after the perception of distinction between individual Intelligence indicated by 'I' and uniform Intelligence indicated by 'Selt' persons fascinated with the world, attribute the uureal Jiva to the true uniform Intelligence, from illusion.

52. But this illusory attribution of resemblance or identity (*tadatmadhyas*) is a product of ignorance, consequently when that is removed, the false perception of the reality of *Jiva* is also destroyed.

53. Kowledge of self destroys ignorance with its force of envelopment, and its resulting action,—false perception or mistake ; but the force of superimposition—evolution, or projection of ignorance [*i.e.*, misapprehension]—and its resulting action of mistaken attribution (*vikshepadhyas*) require for their destruction the exhaustion or consumation of fructescent works. That is to say, without the exhaustion of actions

already commenced to bear fruit, by enjoying them, there can be no removal of 'Self.'

54. Ordinarily speaking, after the destruction of a proximate or material cause, its productive action or result yet continues for a certain time, according to a Tarkika, so that to admit the continuance of illusory attribution, created by superimposition, or misapprehension, even after the destruction of (*Avidya*) Ignorance, its material cause, is possible for a certain time, depending, as it does, upon desire of enjoying fructescent works.

55. If it be urged, according to the view of a Tarkika, after the cause is destroyed its product rests for a little time only, but to admit such duration to a lengthened period, according to the Vedantin, is illogical, the answer is :—If thread, out of which a cloth is produced, be destroyed, to say that the cloth escapes destruction for a short time, be correct, according to a Tarkika,—then when the cause of error which ranges for an indefinite length of time is destroyed, for its product to rest for a lengthened period is not unnatural, because to allow adequate time to a thing according to its space of duration is clearly maintainable.

56. The above illustration is not cited by the Vedantin with the object of establishing a lengthened stay, after that of the Tarkika's momentary duration, but to shew that if he will only cite proofs which are not admissible, but imaginary, then, why are we to abstain from the testimony of *Sruti* which appeals to experience and involves no contradiction?

57. Hence there needs be no more arguing with the dishonest Tarkika, but it is proper that we should have recourse to reason, for in the aforesaid way the *Sruti* has determined the mistake of the uniform Intelligence indicated by 'self' with individual Intelligence indicated by 'I' and imagined to be one.

58. And though that identity is only being conceived in error, yet simple argument is entirely powerless to clear this

mistake of a Tarkika and others, who pretend to be wise without a due consideration of the purport of *Sruti* on the subject.

59. Some of the opposing sects, unable to study the *Sruti* regularly in a consecutive manner, misapprehend the Supreme Self in an infinite variety of ways, and, incapable of rightly interpreting the *Sruti*, cite at random such texts which they fancy support them, without considering their applicability.

60. The dullest amongst the *Lokayats** says from the

---

* *Lokayata* or *Lokayatikas* otherwise called *Sunyavadins* and *Charvakas* were a set of heretics. They condemned all ceremonial rites, including even the *Sradha* or rites performed in connection with death on the occasion of parents by a son, without which no Hindu can be said to be purified from the impurity of death. It would appear, they were materialists and atheists; looking upon the present existence as the best, they were of opinion that wealth and gratification of desire are the highest ends which a man should pursue, and there is no other existence beyond this. Their principal tenets were according to Colebrooke (1) the identity of self with the physical body, (2) rejection of ether as an element, (3) admission of perception alone as a means of proof. They were called Sunyavadins because they expounded the doctrine of 'nothing' preceeding every thing; in short, from nothing has been produced the universe; and *Charvakas* from their teacher Charvaka Muni.

A *Charvaka* calls the physical body, derived from the four elements—fire, water, air, and earth his self, and argues thus:—The subject of the perception of Egoism is self. "I am a man," "I am fat," "I am lean," "I am a Brahman," etc. Here the physical body is perceived as the subject of Egoism, and is accordingly taken for a man, or his qualities of corpulence and of Brahman, etc. Hence the body is self or what is the subject of supreme affection is self. In this way as a wife, son and the rest are conducive to the well-being of the body, and it is the seat of the highest affection, consequently the subject of the indications of that extreme love—the body, is self, and the highest aim of uniform Intelligence to the physical body, the collective aggregate of all these, is his Self.

---

humanity consists in feeding that with good things and clothing it with good dress, jewels, etc., and death is emancipation. Now this requirs no other proof than what actually follows in every individual and is plainly seen; look for instance at the appearance of a prince with all gold and jewels over, an appearance expressing supreme indications of affection for that body, the care bestowed on its feed and dress, providing all comforts for it, and contrast it with the care-worn and pinched countence of a raggamuffin,—yet even here, you will find him struggling all day long, for the maintenance of the body which regards with affection and care. All these are proofs enough and as they are everywhere visible, there can be no contention against their cogencey.

But this doctrine of *Charvakas* is clearly untenable. For if the subject of perception of Egoism ('I') would constitute self, in that case, the organs of sense and action would be so; inasmuch as they are also perceived in the same way, as in the expressions "I see," "I hear," "I speak." Thus then the organs are also perceived as the subject of Egoism, then again in regard to an individual's affection for his body, it cannot be a subject of Egoism, consequently it is a misapplication, therefore, the physical body is not self. Moreover, wealth and riches, wife and son, as they shew good deal of affection for that body, evince a similar feeling for the organs too, consequently in the absence of the highest amount of affection, the gross body is not a subject of supreme affection, and, therefore, it is not self. Further, as the body is wanting in sentiency or intelligence, it is not self, and if a *Charvaka* were to say just as a mixture of quicklime with catechu and betel leaf produces the well-known red color, so the body for its being a mixture of the four elements, derives its power of knowledge. But this is clearly impossible, for if a blending of the elements were to produce sentiency, knowledge or intelligence, we may as well expect a 'jar' which is derived from a blending of the same four elements to possess sentiency or knowledge, but that it has not; besides, in conditions of profound sleep, fainting

61. And to support it, cite the *Sruti* text which explains the foodful sac. "This foodful sac is the Supreme Self, etc.," and "I am the Supreme Self."

---

and death, the bo. is as insentient as a jar consequently insentiency is its normal condition and hence it is not self.

If the physical body were identical with self we would never have fixed our belief in the identity of the body of our manhood, with that of our youth, though they are different from each other; and when a person who had seen us in our boyhood come to see after an absence of several years, when we have attained manhood, he for the sake of recognition recalls to our memory a few leading incidents of the past, and we exclaim, "Indeed that am I." As this is a common incident, therefore, the body is not self. Further, since the body is subject to birth and death, prior to its being born or subsequent to death, it is non-existent, consequently self who is eternal cannot be same with it. Because that will imply the acknowledgment of two defects—of destruction of actions done, and the fruition of actions not done, after death; both of them are inapplicable. That is to say, if the actions performed in life, were to produce no result, in the absence of self who is no agent and instrument, a person would then cease to practise works enjoined in the Vedas, and we see the contrary to be fact. Then again, for the existing difference of self of boyhood with that of prime, when a person has read the Vedas in his youth and boyhood should enjoy no fruits subsequent to that period either in prime or old age; similarly all works done in the present life should yield him no results, thus the admission of destruction of works done already and their unproductiveness is injurious, and in a previous birth from an absence of a doer or agent no actions could be done, so that in the present life whatever a person has to enjoy or suffer should be equally the case with all, and there shall be no cause of the prevailing difference as to happiness or woe in its various shades, as we actually find to be the case,—one is happy, a second miserable, a third beset with difficulties,—so that, it is impossible to acknowledge the fruition of actions not done, and along with it, the assumption of the body being self.

62—63. Another *Lokayata* says since with the exit of the (*Jiva-Atma*) or Life-soul the body dies, and since Egoism ('I') is plainly discernible in the organs, sensory and active—and by them words and actions are produced, they, (the organs) represent Self. Thus doing away with the assertion last mentioned of the body being Self.

64. To admit this is nothing inconsistent; though in words and the rest of actions Intelligence is not clearly discernible, yet we cannot take them for insentient objects, consequently (to a certain extent) it is allowable.

[That is to say, Intelligence being the indication or sign of self, the organs as they shew signs of intelligence can justly be regarded as self. This is what another *Charvaka* says, but it is fallacious, because self is that without which the body cannot last; in the case of the organs of sense and action, we find a person may be blind or deaf yet living, he may be paralysed, his hands and feet are deprived of action, and progression, he may be dumb, yet living, consequently self is something distinct from the sensory and active organs. They cite in support, the expression "I hear," "I see," "I am blind," etc. But it is to be remembered the first personal pronoun used in connection with that hearing, sight, etc., establishes the possession of the necessary organs with which the several functions are carried on, consequently when it is said "I hear," etc, it means "I have ears to hear," or "I see

---

Now according to *Charvakas* the chief or ulterior aim of humanity consists in eating, dressing, etc., but it is not so, because a desire for a thing constitutes an ulterior aim or supreme purport, and as every one is desirous of acquiring happiness and removing misery, necessarily that desire is the supreme purport of humanity, and the highest of that felicity and extreme destruction of misery is called 'emancipation' in the *Sidhanta*. But enjoyment cannot be ranked with this ulterior aim for it is apt to take an extreme turn, and there is no limit for it; neither can death be taken in the light of emancipation.

with my eyes," and not "I am the eye," "I am the ear." Thus then the perception of (subject of Egoism) 'I' in connection with the organs of sense is quite distinct from them; then again, if their identity be sought to be proved by similar other expressions as "My sight is indifferent," "My hearing is actute," by shewing an attachment of sight, etc., with own self, it is simply a misapplication, for the cogniser is different from cognition, and self being the cogniser is different from sight, hearing, etc. Moreover, in mental abstraction, or absence of mind, a person sees not, neither does he hear, though his sight and hearing are perfect, therefore, we may lay down the insentiency of sensory organs, and what is insentient cannot be similar to self. In connection with it, in a dead body the organs of sense and action are all present, yet they are insentient.

Further, it may be enquired whether one organ is self, or whether their collective totality is so, or they are so many different selves. The first is quite untenable, for if it be said that a single organ is self, a person should die or be insentient when that is wanting; yet the fact is otherwise, similarly if the collective aggregate of organs be regarded in that light, then in the destruction of one single organ, all the rest should equally be destroyed and their should be neither life nor intelligence; moreover, if each of them were so many different selves then like ten elephants tied to one tree breaking it asunder, the body will be similarly affected by desires originating with each of these selves.]

65. A worshipper of *Hiranyagarbha* says as life continues with respiration, though the eyes and the rest of the organs may be destroyed,*

66. And as after all the organs, etc., are engrossed in sleep, respiration (vital airs) alone continue, and as its supe-

---

* *Hiranyagarbha* is collective aggregate of *Prana*.

riority over the rest, has been mentioned distinctly in several places, it is therefore his Self.

[But *Prana* is not self. Because like the absence of motion in the external air, when there is no respiratien going on, death does not follow, we find plants do not respire* like ourselves yet they continue to grow, and preserve their vitality; in regard to animated beings it cannot be said that respiration goes on during or after death, yet there are instances when it is suspended, and vitality is seen to continue; moreover, in sleep *Prana* is awake, yet if it were intelligence or self, it should show the usual civilities to a new comer related to a person when he arrives at his house while sleeping, that it does not, nor does it prevent a thief when he robs him in sleep; hence it is not self, but insentient and unconscious. It is contended by the supporters of *Prana*, that with its exit, death follows, therefore it is self. But this does not hold true. Because with the departure [cessation of the secretion] of gastric juice, a man loses his appetite, wastes and dies, and we may as well call it self. Moreover, the superiority of *Prana* mentioned in the Veda is only with a view of producing an inclination to one engaged in devotional exercises. If it be said there are *Sruti* texts which clearly denote *Prana* to be self, but inasmuch as similar texts are also found in connection with the mental sac consequently one is contradicted by the other, hence it is not meant so; but it serves to establish the non-difference of the abiding intelligence seated in them with Brahma.]

67. Mind which is more internal than *Prana* is said by its supporters to be self, after the manner of Narad's *Pancharatra*. They say, "Persons given to the exercise of

---

* We know too well that trees and plants have inspiration and expiration.

devotion regard mind in that light;" and because, *Prana* is not an agent or instrument, but mind is so.*

68. The *Sruti* texts corroborating the view of mind as self are pointed out to support them:—"Mind is either a

* Mind is not self. Because in conditions of trance and sleep, an absence of Mind is plainly discernible. Now, the *Atma* can never leave a body without causing death to it, but in the absent conditions, when a person recovers consciousness, the Mind is again restored to its original condition. Hence Mind is said to be insentient naturally, and is not self. In proof, we may cite the expression when from some cause or other, a person is under mental abstraction, on recovering from it, he says, "I was wandering in my Mind, and hence did not hear you." Though all the time, he was apparently listening to what was being said to him. Thus then, as Mind is apt to be disturbed, sometimes fixed, at others, unsettled, it is something different from self, who is always fixed. Mind is illumined by the reflection of intelligence from self, not that self imparts something of his own consciousness, of his own will, for that he has none, as he is passive, and actionless; but like a needle attracted by a magnet when placed in apposition, the two—Mind and Self—from their close proximity to one another, are similarly influenced. Hence it is an agent and instrument. Here again there is difference, for as just said, Self is actionless, and, therefore, not an agent (doer) and instrument, whereas Mind is so, and is the cause of bondage and emancipation. But it may be asked how? The reply is, in proportion as you beget a desire for material prosperity, the more are you enticed to search after it, and that subjects you to re-birth; while on the other hand, after having ascertained the unreality of the objective world, when with due deliberation, you cease to have any concern for it, and increase your spirituality by the 'means' of knowledge, your knowledge destroys the 'accumulated' and 'current works' leaving alone the 'fructescent' for your consummation in life, so that when you part with the body, you enter into that blissful state whose sole essence is joy, and which no eyes have seen, nor ears heard, and Mind can form no adequate conception of.

cause of a person's bondage or that of his release." "Situated internal to the vital sheath, self, distinct from it, is full of mind." Therefore Mind is self.

69. Some Buddhists affirm Intellect situated more internally than the mind is self. They say, intellect which is transient in duration is regarded by its supporters to be self, and establish its internal position in this manner:—because the cause of cognition by the mind is due to intellect, and that is evident.

70. If knowledge or cognition, and the predicate of the word 'mind,' namely internal organ, were one, how can there be said to exist between them a relative condition of cause and effect? Hence their difference is being described. The internal organ has two sorts of functions—Egoism and 'This;' of them, Egoism [I am I] is called cognition (*Boodhi*), and 'This,' Mind.

71. Since without the internal perception of 'Egoism' there can be no such knowledge as "This is," therefore, Intellect or cognition is called the internal and cause, while Mind is the external and effect or action.

72. Since that (Intellect) perception of Egoism [I am I] is apt to rise and disappear every moment, it is called transitory, and self-illuminated;*

---

* A Yogachara says Intellect or spiritual soul is his self:—All objects whether external or internal are moulded after knowledge. Now this knowledge resembles a flash of lightning, it appears and disappears in a moment, hence it is transient. But as it discovers itself and other objects, it is called self-illumined. It has been compared to the light of a lamp and a river current, where wave after wave keeps up the continuity; knowledge of a first object is displaced by a second, and that by a third, and so on; hence the current of intellect or knowledge is of two sorts, of which, one is local, and the other continuous; the perception of Egoism 'I am I' is an instance of the first variety and is only another form of *Boodhi*. 'This is a jar' and similar other percep-

73. And the life soul in the *Veda*; an agent subject to birth and death.

---

tions connected with 'this':—'this body,' 'this river,' 'this house,' etc., are all instances of the second; they relate to external objects. The second or continuous flow follows the first or local. Hence the local flow of *Boodhi* produces the continuous which is its action. Therefore that one is self. Now the continuous flow is no other than Mind, therefore 'emancipation' consists in dwelling upon or concentrating the mind on *Boodhi*, and to be one with it, thereby fixing the transient flow of the intellect. But this view is objectionable. For, the action of knowledge in the perception of form, taste, smell, etc., like the sensory organs, eyes and the rest, being the means for ascertaining action, Intellect is not self; but what knows it, which ascertains or cognises all objects to a certainty, is self,—and as he is naturally luminous, he is always self-illuminated. That is to say, like the sun who is the discoverer or illuminator of all objects, which are, therefore, said to be discovered or illuminated by him, we have a similar conditional difference between Self and Intellect (*Boodhi*); Self is illumination and Intellect illuminated by Self. As the light of a lamp, covers or takes possession of a jar or another object and discovers it, the two are mixed, though naturally they are distinct; similarly Self who is consciousness is blended with Intellect so as to become one, and this twin medley is the means of perception from which cognition follows, though naturally they are distinct from each other. And as from a difference in occupation, the same Brahmana may be designated separately a reader and cook, similarly the internal organ which is a product of the good quality of the non-quintuplicated elements, ether and the rest, for its certitude is called Intellect, and for its action of doubt and resolution is designated (*Mana*) Mind; consequently the division of that internal organ into Intellect and Mind for their separate functions of internal and external objects of 'I' and 'this' is not feasible.

In reference to the transient nature of knowledge the arguments adduced by its supporters do not stand a searching scrutiny. For, if Self be liable to destruction every moment, in

74. A Madhyamika Buddhist says this transient cognition is not Self, for it is very short-lived, like a flash of lightning;

---

the absence of that Self in a prior period, there can be no acquisition of wealth; or a person advancing money to another with a promise of re-payment a year hence, must naturally forget every thing about it and will cease to demand or receive payment from his debtor. Then again, a person on rising from his dinner table will never express satisfaction the next moment that he has been well satiated, as he does; a dead man may turn into a beast, a can of milk may likewise be turned into poison a moment afterwards; it cannot be aserted with any plausibility, that a second Self is produced after the first one is destroyed retaining all his conceptions, consequently the subsequent Self is capable of retaining the knowledge previously acquired by his predecessor, and this prior knowledge is said to be due to mistake. But since the transient Self is subject to destruction in a subsequent moment, necessarily in the absence of an observer and site, there can be no mistake [as in the instance of a snake in a rope, a spectator and rope are needed to create that illusion.] Moreover, as knowledge is non-particular, its conception cannot be acknowledged. Even admitting conception to be a fact, then it must have a receptacle, vehicle, or asylum; and if it be said, knowledge is the asylum, that will do away with the non-particularity of knowledge.

If Self were short-lived, a person will have not the slightest inclination for doing meritorious deeds, but will lead a life of pleasure and run headlong into sin; for his self is changing every moment, the first one gives place to a second, and that to a third, so that the doer of sin (they regard Self so) will be re-placed by a new self the next moment, and there will be no bad consequences for him, and there will be a total absence of desire of happiness. Further, on appealing to experience, we find a person say, "My intellect is dull;" another says, "My intellect is sharp;" here also the same difference is established between self and intellect; for the intelligence of self knows no fluctuation, it is permanent, and self-illuminated while Intellect is illuminated by self, consequently dependent on him, therefore not self.

but 'Nothing' is self, as without it not another thing can be perceived.

75. And cite in support the *Sruti* text. "Before the evolution of the world there was present nothing;" and knowledge, and its subject, *i. e.*, phenomena, are only illusions created on nothing.*

76. But this assertion is inadmissible. For the asserters of 'nothing' maintain the unreality of the world which they say to be a simple illusion; but illusion must abide on something real, and in the absence of that site in 'Nothing' for an illusion to arise, consequently 'nothing' cannot be admitted to be the source; moreover, 'nothing' also stands in need of Intelligence as a witness, otherwise it cannot possibly have any power or force. [To cite an apt illustration so frequently made use of in Vedantic writings, let us take the instance of 'snake in a rope.' Here the site of the snake

* A Madhyamika Buddhist calls 'Nothing;' his self, because self and things distinct from self, are like nothing, consequently for the resemblance of all objects with 'nothing,' it is the principal entity. In profound slumber, a person loses all consciousness of external objects and he experiences nothing; for, on rising from sleep he says "I knew nothing then." Moreover, to a wise person, the remnant of ignorance in the form of the Blissful sheath, is self—a semblance of nothing. But it may be asked of him whether his nothing is with or without witness? Or whether it is self-illuminated? If the first, then that witness is something different from nothing and no other than self; the second consideration—without a witness—will be a contradiction, and the third view of self-manifestability only establishes Brahma by another name and remove 'nothing' altogether. Then again the *Sruti* text cited by him from the *Chhandogya Upanishad* that "Nothing was present before the world was ushered into existence" does not apply. It does not help his position. It has been purposely introduced to do away with the assertion of 'prior condition' acknowledged by a Naiyayika, and Vaishesika Buddhist, as an efficient cause for the world.

is rope, and when a person imagines, he sees a snake, that illusion requires the presence of the rope; without seeing it there can be no mistake of snake. We have, therefore, a real rope existing on the ground, on which is projected the form of a snake through the enveloping force of ignorance; and that snake is no actual creation, but simply a superimposition, for if it were so, a light helping us to know what the thing lying in front is, dispels it; this will be clearly impossible. Hence it is said, if 'nothing' is the real entity and phenomena are illusions created on nothing, like the snake in rope, that nothing must have something resting on the background; for there can be no illusion on nothing, as there can be no snake without a rope, etc. Then again, who discovers nothing? It cannot discover itself, intelligence is needed for that purpose, hence the real entity is intelligence, and the objective world, an illusion on intelligence.]

Therefore, if Self were to be acknowledged as Intelligence what is different from the cognitional sheath and most intrinsically situtated, and existent too—the Blissful sheath—is self. This is the instruction given in the *Vedas*.

78. Thus having shewn the contention about the nature of Self, his size is now being declared to be equally disputed by the several schools of thought. Some of them say self is atomic in size, some large, and others intermediate, resting their individual assertions on *Sruti* texts and reason.

79. A set of dissenters known by the name of Madhyamikas regard self to be equal in size to an atom, because he pervades in the finest capillaries which are no bigger than a hair divided into a thousand parts.*

* But this statement of the atomic size of self is untenable; for in that case, he will be confined within a small space in one particular part of the body, consequently a person will feel no pain all over his body in the case of illness. Self is a knower, he alone has consciousness, so that to feel pain in the feet as well as in the head at one time, clearly does away with his atomic

80. Because innumerable passages to that effect occur in the *Sruti*. " Self is finer than an atom and subtler than the subtlest."

81. Here is another illustration from the *Sruti* to the purpose. "The forepart of a single hair when divided into

---

size. But then its partisans allege, as the sweet scent of a flower or musk is diffused at a distance from the spot where such flower or musk is kept; similarly in spite of his atomic size, self is diffused all over the body, hence either pain or pleasure can be equally felt in the head and feet at one time, though they are distant from each other : but this is a mistake. Because oil seeds placed in a jar will not fill it with oil, and it is in the nature of a quality to remain confined within the body, whose quality it is; hence, external to Self, there cannot be any quality of consciousness. Then again, it cannot be maintained, like a sandal paste applied to the feet producing a pleasurable feeling of coolness all over the body, the consciousness of Self confined in one particular region of the body diffuses itself all over and pervades it everywhere. Because in the case of sandal, the watery particles of the paste are absorbed into the body thus refringerating the blood and producing the sensation of coolness, so that there is no refringerating quality present in sandal, it is only the water with which it is mixed, that has it, necessarily therefore the illustration is not an apt one but extreme. Then again, they say, like the light of a lamp illuminating the interior of a room, consciousness of self illumines by diffusing or pervading all parts of the body, though he may be confined within the narrowest limit in one particular part. Even this is open to objection. For self in that case will be visible and have a form like the lamp, both of which will reduce him to the condition of an unreality, subject to destruction, which he is not. Thus then, self is not atomic in size. The *Sruti* texts cit d by the partisans of this theory, have only been misapplied, inasmuch as they were meant to impress dull persons with an idea of difficulty as to the nature of self. As atoms are difficult of comprehension, so is self difficult of perception.

hundred parts, one fractional hundredth only is an individual capable of knowing" so very subtle is self.

82. Another sect called Digambars say, self is intermediate in size, because consciousness is present in every part of the body, from head to foot. And for the *Sruti* text:—" This self occupies even the tips of nails."

83. Though medium in size, yet he is capable of pervading in the capillaries; just as in the instance of the physical body when a person has passed his two hands in the sleeves of a coat, he is said to cover his body with it, so is the pervasion in capillaries attributed to self.

84. But it may be objected, if Self were medium in size he could not enter the body of an ant which is small, and an elephant which is a big animal, from the force of fructescent works; therefore, it is said, the entry of Self in the body of a bigger or smaller animal is due to a smaller or greater particle of self entering that body according to its size, thus establishing his medium size.

85. But the attribution of form in the manner aforesaid to self will reduce him to impermanence like a jar, etc. [For name and form are indications of creation, and, therefore, non-eternal;] hence the view of a Digambar is faulty, as it implies the destruction of works without enjoying their results (of virtue and sin) and the (accidental) fruition of merit and de-merit without works being performed. Both these defects will apply to self.

86. Thus then as both the views of self in regard to his size—excessively minute like an atom or intermediate—are defective, consequently what is neither small nor medium is great, therefore, like ether he is all-pervading and formless. As the *Vedas* say, " Like ether he is pervasive; he is eternal." " He is formless and actionless."

87. Like his size, the intelligence of Self is equally a subject of contention. Some acknowledge his intelligence, others deny it, while a third say him to be both intelligent and insentient.

88. According to a *Pravakara* and *Naiyayika* self is insentient, but like ether possessing the property of sound, he is a body, with knowledge or intelligence for a quality.

89. They attribute to him other qualities as :—

Desire, spite, endeavour, virtue, vice, happiness and misery and impression.

90. As these qualities are liable to come and go, the circumstances under which they appear and disappear and their cause are now being ascertained. When self is combined with the mind, from the influence of the unseen (*adrishta*,) the qualities intelligence, etc., arise, but in the profound slumbering condition, when the connection of mind with self is cut off, they also are effaced or wiped away.

91. Thus though self is naturally insentient, yet for his quality of intelligence, he can be acknowledged as sentient knowing or intelligent; moreover, the other qualities, desire and the rest, likewise establish it; and as he is an agent,—a doer of virtue and sin—he is, therefore, distinct from Iswara.

92. As happiness and misery are sometimes produced in self from good and bad actions performed [during life], so are desire and the rest derived from similar actions in a previous life.

93. In this manner, though self is all-pervading, yet it is quite possible for him to go away with death, and be re-born in a fresh body, as is amply testified by the *Veda* when it treats of 'Works' (*Karmakanda.*)*

94. A *Prabhakara* and *Tarkika* regard the 'blissful seath' as their self, for it remains even in the profound slum-

* If it be apprehended, since Self is all-pervading he cannot be subjected to metempsychosis; therefore, it is said, the desires etc., of the present body are a product of works done in a prior state of objective life, and like the stay of Self in the present body, actions performed now will produce a future body, where to experience felicity or misery, in proportion to merit or de-merit, self has to go, to re-habilitate it.

bering condition; therefore, self is an insentient body with intelligence, desire and the rest, already cited, for his qualities.*

95. Now the followers of Bhatta (Bartikkara of the *Purva Mimansa*) or as they are called Bhat, regard this blissful sheath which is their self to be both insentient and sentient. For a person on rising from his sleep remembers that he was sleeping soundly and knew nothing then, a condition in which ignorance [insentiency] and felicity, both are experienced; but for this remembrance of felicity, a certain amouut of consciousness must necessarily have been present, hence the *Atma* is said to be both insentient and sentient.

---

* But this doctrine of theirs is clearly untenable; for to say that in profound slumber the absence of consciousness proves self to be instentient, is opposed to individual experience; for if such were a fact, a person on rising from sleep would never have expressed "I was sleeping happily, I knew nothing then," thus clearly proving a remnant of consciousness, enough to leave an impression in the mind of the sleeper as to his perception of happiness, accompanied with ignorance. Then again, in the *Sruti*, Self is said to be without attributes; therefore to attribute desire, spite, virtue, etc., which properly belong to the internal organ, is simply a delusion. Moreover, as the said qualities desire and the rest, belong to the internal organ which continues in waking and dreaming slumber—consequently present then; but in profound slumber, that organ is absent, hence there is an absence of the qualities which mark it—it will thus be found, that the natural inference of what has been mentioned establishes the internal organ, and not self, to be possessed with the qualities, desire, etc. There is yet another consideration which precludes the applicability of the view held by Naiyayikas and Prabhakars: for say they, self is all-pervading and manifold; in that case it will be difficult to connect a particular self with one body, for all selves are related to all bodies, all works, and all enjoyments and connected with all minds.

96. Thus then, the recollection "I was sleeping insensibly," which arises in the mind of a person on his first waking, can never follow without the perception of actual ignorance or insentiency in such profound slumber, hence for the presence of ignorance and experience or perception, the consciousness of Self is said to be covered with insentiency.

97. And since the *Sruti* mentions "Self is not deprived of his consciousness in that profound slumber," and as memory establishes his insentiency, therefore he is both sentient and insentient and like the fire-fly, luminous and dark.*

---

* But this is open to objections, a few of which are here worth mentioning. As light and darkness are naturally opposed to each other, so are sentiency or consciousness, and its reverse. As for instance, it cannot be said, "This man is a jar," so the above conditions cannot exist. For instance, if it be said, that the insentient part is perceivable, and the light of consciousness is not perceivable in self, so that for the same body or substance to be possessed of properties directly opposed to each other is clearly impossible. As from the sight of a stick, it cannot be said, "here is a Dundi," but there must be present an individual carrying the stick, to deserve the appellation of a Dundi; so from the knowledge of one part, insentiency, Self cannot be determined to be both insentient and sentient. Moreover, if the part representing sentiency or consciousness be deemed amenable to perception, then insentiency must fall in the back ground of illusion—a creation of fancy.—Likewise it may be asked of them who follow Bhatta, what is the relation of the two parts, insentiency and sentiency of self? Whether it is due to combination or to an identity? Or is it only a condition of subject and owner. From the first stand-point, self will be reduced to impermanence, for objects derived from a combination of two or more substances are material, hence non-eternal; if the second view be maintained, insentiency will be identical with sentiency, and sentiency with insentiency, which is absurd; the third will reduce self to impermanence, like a jar. We find, therefore, no proofs as to one half

98. After thus exposing the error of the Bhats, the view held in *Sankhya* is now being set forth. A follower of Kapila (author of *Sankhya Philosophy*) says, a body without form cannot have both insentiency and sentiency; therefore to say self is formless, would be meaningless.

99. But the attribution of a recollection of insentiency to self in spite of his intelligence, does not imply any contradiction. For the perception of insentiency is only due to (*Prakriti*) Matter, which is possessed of the three attributes good, active, and painful or dark, and subject to change, only that self may be an agent or instrument of enjoyment, and be freed from the bondage of re-births. This is its purpose.

100. Though Self and Matter, for the possession of unconditioned bliss and sentiency by the former, and insentiency by the latter are extremely different from each other, yet from an absence of perception of the difference between Matter and Spirit, matter is regarded as the cause which helps self to enjoyment and emancipation; and for allotting bondage and emancipation to Self, like the aforesaid dissenters Tartika etc., even the followers of the Sankhya School admit a distinct difference in self.*

101. As proofs confirmatory of the insentiency of Matter and the unassociated bliss and intelligence of Self, *Sruti* texts are being cited in reference to the first. " For its being the cause, the indescribable [Ignorance or *Prakriti*] is superior to *Mahat* (*Mahatatwa*)." And in support of the unconditioned or unrelated nature of Self [we find it said] " This self is unassociated or unrelated.

---

of Self being insentient and the other half sentient; for in the *Sruti*, Self is described as a mine of knowledge. It is true the *Smriti* mentions about this insentiency, but that refers only to Ignorance in the condition of profound slumber.

* Kapila regards Matter as the cause of the world, and says, it is likewise the cause of bondage and deliverance of the

102. Thus having exposed the fallacious views held by the aforesaid dissenters in regard to the nature of Self, their opposite doctrines concerning Iswara are now being declared. For this purpose, his nature is first determined. According to the followers of *Yoga*, Iswara is the controller of matter, closely engaged [occupied] in intelligence. He is superior to all individuals.

103. As in the *Sruti* "He is the lord of Matter and Jiva, and qualities." That is to say, Iswara is the Lord of the equilibrised state of matter, when its *Satwa*, *Raja* and *Tama* are evenly blended, (likewise called *Pradhan* or primary); the individual with his tenement of flesh which is called

(Purusha) Atma or Spirit; but it is open to objection. For in periods of cyclic destruction, matter is said to be in a state of equipoise, that is to say, its three properties are evenly balanced. Evolution begins only with a disturbance of this equilibrium. The first mentioned condition is spoken of as the natural (*Pradhana*), chief or primary condition, so that with evolution arises the insentient condition; now if insentiency be the primary state, the equilibrised condition will necessarily come to be secondary. Then again, from a want of association with the intelligence (self) there is no relation with the primal condition; and as without a relativity of intelligence, the subsequent evolution cannot proceed from insentiency, consequently the primal cannot create; and that primal condition is Iswara's intelligence endowed with Maya, who is the internal ruler and creator of the world. Kapila advocates the theory of the Spirit being manifold and as many in number, as there are individuals. But to say so is futile, because admission of the oneness of the all-pervading intelligence and the attribution of enjoyment, etc., to the association of the internal organ, are enough to settle the point, and the necessity for such an infinite division of *Atma* is clearly removed; otherwise to regard the eternity of matter and manifold diversity of *Atma* will land us in the region of (*sajatiya*, *vijatiya*) defects marked by similarity and dissimilarity, or in the language of Western physicists, isomorphism and disomorphism.

ground—for it is the scene of works already bearing fruit—and the three attributes just mentioned—for they are controlled by him. It is not to be imagined that this is the only mention of Iswara in the *Veda*. For the *Brihadaranyakopanishad* have texts explanatory of him, as an internal knower.

104. Resting their opinions on such *Sruti* texts, as they believe support them, and which they construe according to their lights, a marked variety of opinion prevails in regard to Iswara among these controversialists.

105. With a view of ascertaining the view held by a Yogachara, the nature of Iswara after Patanjali is being declared. He is defined as " A particular person unconnected with felicity or misery, merit or de-merit, good or bad action, their impression and composition. Like Jiva, He is unassociated (bliss) and intelligence.*

106. But it may be asked, if Iswara is thus unconditioned

* It remains to be observed that there is a marked similarity between Sankhya and Yoga in regard to Jiva ; for as the former holds him to be unrelated, self-illuminated, uniform, and intelligence, so does the latter ; and he is an enjoyer only, but no agent or instrument. Now such an experience of his enjoyment follows from want of discrimination, for happiness and misery are the attributes of the internal organ whose function is intellection, (*Boodhi*), in connection with which, he is apt to be attributed the power of enjoying, and that *Boodhi* (spiritual soul or intellection) is the agent ; from similar want of discrimination, self is practically regarded as an agent, and so long as the intellect is not cleansed by the practice of the two varieties of meditation called *samprajnata* and *asamprajnata* or better still, the conscious and unconscious varieties of the Vedantin, misery cannot be completely extirpated ; but when these medititations have thoroughly ripened, then Jiva is roused to his sense, he has now got discrimination wherewith to keep misery at bay, and this extreme destruction of misery is called emancipation in Yoga. Sankhya does not admit Iswara, but Yoga does, and that Iswara is like Jiva unrelated or unassociated [uncondioned] Intelligence.

or unassociated intelligence, how can then he be the controller? The reply is, that does not imply any contradiction, it is quite possible for his being a particular person and a controller, otherwise there will be no regulation of bondage and emancipation. [That is to say as a king rewards a person for good and punishes for bad deeds, in the absence of Iswara as such a controller, a bad man be released while a good subjected to re-birth, and thus the inevitable law of *Karma* will be set at nought].

107. And the testimony of the *Sruti* likewise goes to establish his control. As for instance. "From his fear the wind moves and the sun shines." If it be asked how is he unrelated? "This Supreme Self for an absence of pain,* works, etc., the usual atributes or perquisites of a Jiva, is likewise a controller." And there are arguments and (good) reasons for it.

108. Moreover if Jiva be likewise devoid of pain what constitutes the distinction of Iswara? So long as there is a want of discrimination, a person is apt to consider himself as subject to grief; as has already been said. (*Vide ante V. 100.*)

109. With a view of establishing a difference between Iswara and Jiva, a Tarkika (Naiyayika) says, Iswar's three qualities, intelligence, endeavour, and will are eternal, and his unassociated control is unsound and objectionable.

110. And adduce the testimony of the *Sruti* in support:—"His desire is eternal, his determination actuates him always and knows no rest." In this manner, the eternal nature of his qualities are sought to be established.†

---

* There are five sorts of pain:—

(*a*). An Identity of sight and seer, (*b*) Ardent desire for happiness and objects tending to it, (*c*) Pain produced from material objects, (*d*) Fear of death, and (*e*) Eagerness for the preservation of the body.

† In such an admission of the eternal intelligence, etc., of Iswara there will be created a discrepancy with the *Sruti* texts

111. The opinion held by the worshippers of Hiranyagarbha (Brahma) is now being cited. They say, if Iswara be regarded as eternally intelligent, etc., the work of creation will be continued for all time, hence Hiranyagarbha who is the collective totality of subtle bodies is Iswara.

112. In spite of his having the subtle body, he is not a Jiva, because he is devoid of actions; and because in the *Udgita Brahmana* his glory has been fully declared, [he is therefore Iswara.]

113. As there can be no perception of the subtle without the gross physical body, therefore a worshipper of Vishnu says:—Virat is called Iswara for the conceit that he is the collective aggregate of gross bodies and is always possessed of head, etc., [and of divers forms].

114. And cite in support "That he has thousand feet, thousand hands, and an equal number of heads and eyes." (*Sruti.*)

115. If an immense number of hands and feet were to constitute Iswara, a *centipide* may with equal propriety be called so. Therefore abstain from calling Virat to be Iswara but look upon Brahma as so; and beyond him, there is no other Iswara, for none else has the power of creating subjects.

116. Those who are desirous of issue and large progeny worship Brahma, and regard him as Iswara; for the *Sruti* says "Prajapati (Brahma) creates all subjects."

117. But a worshipper of Vishnu says since Brahma had his origin from a lotus, and that was the navel of Vishnu, consequently the latter pre-existed him, hence he is the father and therefore Iswara, and not Brahma.

---

where it is mentioned, "With the creation of the Universe, arose the intelligence of Iswara" as also such other texts which expound the view of non-duality. Hence it is easy to infer, with every show of reason, that the words 'true desire,' etc., cited by a Tarkika, mean a duration extending to cyclic periods of destruction and not to eternity.

118. A Shivite says his own deity is Iswara, because Vishnu could not ascertain where the legs of Shiva were resting.

119. A follower of Ganesa takes cbjection to the recognition of Shiva as Iswara, for he had himself to worship Ganpat for conquering Tripur to avoid disaster; therefore Ganesa is Iswara.

120. In the same way, there are others who show a bais for their own deities whom they call Iswara; by the help of the (*Mantras*) sacred formulæ used in their respective worship, they seek to establish the truth of their assertion, as also by an analysis and argument of their meaning and by a reference to *Kalpa* [a complete cycle of four *Yugas*].

121. From the internal knower to inanimate objects all are equally denominated Iswara, inasmuch as even trees for instance, the *ficus religiosa*, *aslepias gigantea*, and bamboo are objects of worship with men.

122. In order to ascertain the correctness of the several views held concerning Iswara, by the different sects of worshippers, it is said, with the help of analogy and analysis of the arguments used in the *Shastras*, a wise and tranquil person has no difficulty in differentiating Iswara from the rest and ascertaining him as secondless. This will be shewn in the sequel.

123. The testimony of the *Sruti* on this subject is to the following effect:—" Know then *Prakriti* is *Maya* and Iswara is the particular person endowed with it." " All objects which ramify the universe have sprung from him." [That is to say, Matter is the proximate cause of the universe, and the Internal Knower associated with it is the Supreme Iswara,—the instrumental cause abiding in *Maya*.] And all objects whether sentient or otherwise which fill the universe are said to be derived from Iswara, inasmuch as the same matter which forms a feature in Iswara is equally present in the rest (*Sruti*).

124. And inasmuch as all contradictions are cleared by the *Sruti* text just referred above, the different worshippers of inanimate and animate bodies can have no further cause of disagreement.

125. And as Illusion (matter) is said in the *Nirsimha Tapani* to be full of darkness, (ignorance), and experienced by all beings, such experience is a proof of its existence, as has been over and over mentioned in the *Sruti*.*

126. And its (*Maya* or *Prakriti's*) action is described in the *Sruti* to be insentient and fascinating. It likewise establishes its property of darkness as proved from individual experience, in the following wise. "The action of Maya is both insentient and fascinating." "It is infinite." Now this infinite nature of Matter establishes its universal presence, as we actually find on appealing to the experience of all persons, both young and old, men and women alike.

127. Insentiency refers to want of intelligence. As for instance a jar. Fascination is described as what cannot be grasped by intellect; that is to say, what the intellect fails to comprehend. [It is that spiritual ignorance which leads men to believe in the reality of world and to addict themselves to mundane or sensual enjoyments.]

128. If it be said, for the universal pervasion of *Maya*, and its property of darkness or ignorance being an established fact according to individual experience, it is doubtful whether it is capable of being removed or destroyed by knowledge. For such a purpose the conclusion of the *Sruti*, and an analysis of the arguments used for and against, is cited to lead to the inference of its indescribable nature. Referring to this the *Sruti* says. "It is neither being nor non-being,

---

* We are all equally ignorant of something or other, and when asked about a thing we know not, we declare our ignorance. Ignorance is universally present, and its existence needs no other proof than our individual experience. This is what is meant.

etc." And what is neither being nor non-being is indescribable.

129. It cannot be termed non-existent, for it is experienced everywhere by all alike; nor existent, as it is capable of being destroyed by knowledge; but as something worthless from the standpoint of knowledge.

130. Thus it can be described in three separate ways:—

(a) In the light of knowledge it is something worthless.*

(b) From the standard of logical inference, it is indescribable.

(c) And according to the standard of ordinary perception it is really existent.

131. And as by spreading a picture, all its figures are rendered plainly visible, so the apparent existence of the world is due to *Maya*; with its destruction by knowledge, phenomena are reduced to the condition of non-reality, just as the figures in the painting disappear when it is rolled up.

132. In the *Sruti*, *Maya* is described as both independent and dependent; but to apply such opposite conditions to one and same substance, may appear contradictory, hence it is explained in the following wise:—Since *Maya* cannot be conceived or realized as a separate entity without intelligence, consequently it is said to be dependent, and inasmuch as it affects the unassociated intelligence it is therefore free:—

133. It has the faculty of rendering the uniform unassociated intelligence of Self insentient and making him appear totally bereft of intelligence; and through the reflex intelligence it seeks to create difference between Jiva and Iswara.

134. It may be asserted, if Self who is ever uniform and knows no change be thus affected by *Maya*, then this trans-

---

* The word worthless requires to be explained. What does not exist always in all the three conditions of time is called so. The three conditions or divisions of time are waking, dreaming, and profound dreamless slumber.

formation would indicate change. The reply is, *Maya* destroys his unchangeable and uniform nature and discovers the phenomenal world in him—and this is nothing astonishing for it.

135. Like the solvent property of water, heat of fire and hardness of stone, transformation is naturally present in *Maya*.

136. So long as a person is not disenchanted of its spells, he is apt to be filled with wonder concerning it; but when he has come to know of Iswara, the controller of *Maya*, his wonders cease and he regards it as something unreal and false.

137. To a Naiyayika and others like him, who believe in the reality of the objective world, this is applicable; and not to a Vedantin, for he believes in the unreality of *Maya*.

138. And with a view of shewing the uselessness of multiplying questions, the necessity is pointed out of cultivating knowledge wherewith to destroy *Maya*, and this is what an intelligent person should do.

140. Thus then, destruction of *Maya* is proper for all persons, and there is no necessity for ascertaining its nature; but there are men who would dissent to it, and say, it is proper that one should know what *Maya* is; hence it is said, "Ascertain its indication as known to all men."

141. And that indication is what cannot be ascertained exactly, though palpably present and manifested. Like a magical performance every thing that is presented to your sight appears real while the fact is otherwise; and *Maya* is known to all men in that manner—an illusion. How then can you ascertain its nature?

142. And phenomena are said to be a product of *Maya*, for, in spite of our diligent investigations we sadly fail to ascertain the exact nature of any one thing; hence free your self from all bias and say whether it is possible to ascertain the nature of *Maya*.

143. If all the learned men were to join in investigating the nature of a single entity out of the many, which fill this universe, they are sure to declare their ignorance somehow or other, and will fail to ascertain it.

144. For instance, if you ask them how does a drop of semen produce the human body with all its organs? Whence does Intelligence come and why? What will be their reply.

145. If they were to say, it is the very nature of semen to produce a body and its organs, we may pause to enquire, How did they know it? And point out the instance of sterile women who conceive not; consequently semen is not naturally possessed with such a property.

146. So that, ultimately they come to ackowledge their ignorance; for this reason, the wise regard both ignorance and its product, the material world, in the light of a magical performance; they are so to speak a phantasm.

147. What can be more magical than human conception? A drop of semen entering the uterus, vivified by intelligence, develops hands, head, feet, etc., in due order; gradually attains to childhood, youth and old age, is subjected to various diseases, and sees, hears, smells, enjoys and progresses to and fro.

148. Nor is this confined to man alone. For in the case of the *ficus religiosa* and other gigantic trees springing from very minute and insignificant seeds, the same *Maya* is likewise displayed. Look at the tree and the seed which gave it birth, and can you cease to wonder? Therefore by constant practice inure your mind into a belief of the magical property of *Maya*, and look upon it as something equally indescribable.

149. A Naiyayika believes, he alone is capable of satisfactorily explaining phenomena and is proud of it. Let him consult the *Khandana* of Sri Harsha Acharya and he will find his position to be no longer maintainable.

150. For what is inconceivable, cannot be ascertained

by any end of argument, therefore it is improper to connect this inconceivable world with argument even in mind.

151. Consider the source of the world, which is constructed in a manner quite impossible to conceive, and of which no definite idea can be formed, to be *Maya*, which hath for its cause the Secondless, Impartite Intelligence (Brahma) experienced in profound slumber.

152. This world which is nothing else but only a condition of waking and dreaming [a day dream] merges into its source *Maya* which continues in profound slumber; just as a tree abides in its seed. Since therefore *Maya* is the source of the universe, all impressions derived from a knowledge of phenomena are centred in it.

153. Like the ether or space appropriated by cloud, there is a dim perception of reflection of intelligence in all impressions derived from knowledge and this is known inferentially. [But it may be saïd, it is possible to perceive the presence of water in cloud, for water is nothing else but drops of moisture collected in the cloud, in which again, ether is plainly conceivable, because of the ether present in a jar filled with water, which is identical with the water of the clouds; consequently the presence of the first is easily deducible as an inference from the palpable instance of the second. And it is difficult to see how can the example of cloud-ether apply to reflection of intelligence included in all impressions of phenomena. To clear it out and shew the applicability of the example, it is said that the reflex intelligence—seed of matter—is known inferentially].

154. That reflection of intelligence is subsequently transformed into intellect, hence it is plainly discerned in *Boodhi*. In other words, Ignorance endowed with reflected intelligence modified or transformed into intellect, forms the subject of the reflection of intelligence; under such circumstances, the impression of prior perceptions in the intellect, which is a subject of contention, can be reckoned as a reflection of

intelligence, and for its being a modification, form, or condition of *Boodhi*, may be likened to its function.

155. "*Maya* and reflection of intelligence in it, constitute both Jiva and Iswara"* (*Sruti*). But then it may be remarked, How can their invisibility and visibility be determined if they are thus similar. To establish that difference, it is said :—Like the difference existing between ether present in cloud and water respectively, the knowledge of the Jiva for its being enveloped in ignorance is dimly discernible; while that of Iswara for the associate of Intellect is plainly manifested. Herein consists the practical difference of the two. In other words, the one Impartite Intelligence is through Illusion differentiated into Jiva and Iswara.

156. Similitude of Iswara with cloud-ether is established in the following wise :—*Maya* resembles the cloud, for as in cloud, it is natural to expect subtle particles of rain collected in the form of moisture, so are intellect and knowledge derived from past impressions present in *Maya*; and like the presence of the reflection of ether in that water, there is reflection of intelligence in *Maya*; that is Iswara. Thus then we find, like the space or ether appropriated by cloud and water respectively, both Jiva and Iswara rest on *Maya* and

---

* Pundit Pitambarjee the author of the well-known Bombay Edition of Mr. Sheriff Mahomed, says in his notes, it is not to be construed that Jiva and Iswara are the active products of *Maya*. That is not meant here, for he says Jiva, Iswara, Intelligence *perse*, Ignorance (*Avidya*) or nescience, and the relation of the two last, together with the subsisting difference of each of the five,—these six substances are naturally uncreate and without an origin; and the statement of the Bartikkar is directly opposed to the *Sidhanta*, and the *Sruti* text "Maya with reflexion makes Jiva and Iswara."

Here the verb to make likewise establishes Maya; for its successful dependence shows or produces Jiva and Iswara. This is what is meant.

reflex Intelligence; because like water present in the cloud, there is present knowledge derived from memory in *Maya*, and like the reflection of ether in that water, Iswara rests in the form of reflex intelligence.*

---

* It would appear from the text that Vidyaranya Swami means Iswara to be the reflection [of intelligence] in past perception originatlng from or by the intellect, but doubts may be entertained as to the truth of such an assertion, and they are cleared in the following manner. In the first place, it may be enquired whether the associate of Iswara is only Ignorance, or Ignorance with knowledge of prior impressions, or the latter only. If the first point be held, then the resemblance of Iswara with the reflected shadow of intelligence in Ignorance and knowledge of past perceptions of the intellect will create a discord. Similarly the recognition of the second view will require an admission of ignorance only as the associate of Iswara. In that case, he can lay no claim to omniscience; hence it is necessary for preserving his omniscience to consider knowledge and intellect as predicates of ignorance. But to say so is quite contradictory. Because the *satavic* particle of Ignorance can only naturally have the property of all-knowingness, for *Satwa* is light, consequently if knowledge and intellect are viewed in the same light as predicates of intelligence, there will be a perfect absence of omniscience, hence their presence is quite futile and unnecessary. If we pause to enquire into the reason why, we shall find one variety of knowledge cannot possibly take cognisance of, or embrace all objects or things, but on the other hand, for the acquirement of omniscience all knowledges must be admitted as the predicate of ignorance, which again cannot be expected to disappear in any one time save that of *pralaya*, consequently it is not for establishing omniscience.

In the same way, the second view that of intellect and knowledge with ignorance as the associate of Iswara is quite untenable. Then again, those who assert knowledge only is the associate of Iswara, it may be asked of them. Whether Iswara is the reflected shadow in such individual unit of knowledge produced from memory? Or in its collective aggregate? If they maintain

157. "And that reflex intelligence dependent on *Maya* or subservient to it, full of illusion, is the Supreme Iswara, Internal Knower, Omniscient, and the Universal Cause." (*Sruti*.)

158. Beginning with the 'blissful sheath' in the state of profound slumber, the *Sruti* says "That blissful sheath is the Lord of all." Therefore the *Vedas* denote it to be Iswara.

[But objection may be taken to it, for in waking and dreaming, the predicate of the grosser condition of materiality with the reflected shadow—the internal organ—is called the cognitional sheath. The knowing or cognitional Jiva merges into a subtle condition in profound slumber (and that is the blissful) which if regarded as Iswara, then in the absence of that merging of the internal organ in waking and dreaming conditions into the state of blissfulness, there will be a corresponding want of Iswara too. Then again, there must be as many Iswaras as there are men in profound slumber, and as there are five such sheaths or sacs recognised in the human body by all authors, the admission of 'blissful' as Iswara will render the utterances concerning the rest unnecessary and futile; hence it is said, the Blissful sac is not Iswara. This is what a Prabhakar says, but it is cleared

---

the first mentioned opinion, then as knowledge originating from the individual's intellect is infinite in variety, Iswara for his being the reflected shadow in each unit of such knowledge must necessarily be infinite in number, and as each knowledge is parviscient, the reflected shadow in it will also necessarily be parviscient. Then again, in regard to the second opinion of Iswara as the reflected shadow in the collective aggregate of all knowledges it is necessary to mention, that save and during the *pralayic* period it can never be and that in proportion to the number of associates there is a similar number of reflected shadows, consequently there cannot be one reflected shadow in all knowledges. Thus then, Ignorance alone is the associate of Iswara.

thus:—If a dull person would receive no benefit from ascertaining the indication of the transcendental phrase, it is better that he should consider and ponder well on the meaning of *Om*, as laid down in the *Mandukya Upanishad*, where likewise the 'Blissful sheath' is mentioned, the Omniscient and Universal Lord. Now as the above *Upanishad* had its object in so saying, to establish non-duality, similarly our author had been actuated to establish the oneness of Jiva and Iswara. He had no desire to make the 'Blissful,' Iswara; for it will be found elsewhere in a subsequent part of the work (Sect. XI) that He terms the 'Blissful' as a particular condition of the individual. Therefore, only with the view of establishing non-duality to persons of dull intellect, that the Blissful sheath is here referred to as Iswara, otherwise there will be a contradiction between what is stated here and in the above Section.]

159. It is not impossible for the 'Blissful sheath' to have omniscience and a paramount control over all, nor is it proper that this should create any dispute or contention; for the utterances of the *Sruti* are beyond cavil and dispute, and they tend that way. Then again, concerning *Maya* it is said, every thing is possible. [That is to say, it is the nature of illusion to create unreal, real; like things shown in a performance of magic.]

160. But as the utterances of the *Sruti* in the absence of supporting arguments to establish their truth may be set at naught like the expression "a boat made of stone" they are now being cited:—Since there is no one capable of undoing the creation of Iswara He is called the Lord Paramount. That is to say, what is created by Iswara, the objective world and the rest, cannot be destroyed in any manner, hence he is the Paramount or Supreme Lord.

161. His omniscience is established in the following wise: The perception [conception] of all beings originating from their intellect rests in ignorance in the condition of profound

slumber, and by that conception makes the whole universe its subject; and for its being the associate of ignorance, the predicate of perception proceeding from intellect (the blissful sheath) is said to be all-knowing.*

162. But then it may be asked, if it is all-knowing what prevents our experiencing it? Therefore it is said:—As intellectual impressions, associate of that blissful (Iswara) are invisible, hence his all-knowingness is not perceived. How is it then known? From their presence in all intellects, conclude omniscience to be present, inasmuch as they are only a product of intellect which is their cause and whose property it is to create perception. In the same way as the property of yarn—the cause of a cloth—is present in its product, the cloth.

163. The blissful "Iswara is the internal knower." *Sruti.* Because resting inside the cognitional and other sacs, and in every other thing besides, he employs them in due order.

164. Regarding Iswara as the internal knower the *Antaryami Brahman* of *Brihadaranyaka Upanishad* says:—"Residing in the intellect, yet he is different from it, nor can he be seen by that intellect, which constitutes his physical body, and of which he is the internal controller." In this manner Iswara is mentioned in the *Vedas.*

165. Now from a fear of its lengthiness I refrain from entering into an explanation of all the indications cited in the *Antaryami Brahman*, but will content myself with "Who resides in all elements" and illustrate it by an example. As yarn constitutes the proximate or formal cause of a cloth and rests in it, so is Iswara the formal cause of all elements and rests in them.

166. But the question is, If Iswara is the formal cause why is He unseen? The reply is, what is most intrinsically

* The reader need not be reminded what the blissful sheath means after what has been said in Verse 158 and note. It refers to Iswara. Therefore, plainly speaking, it is meant here to shew Iswara is omniscient.

situated cannot be seen. As for instance, the threads of a cloth are internal, and their filaments are internal to them; so where that intrinsicality finally rests consider that to be the the Iswara.

167. Thus for His being most intrinsically situated he cannot be seen, because he is formless;—and of concentric intrinsicalities only two or three comparatively external are capable of being determined by the sight, but as he is innermost He is hence unseen, and can only be ascertained by *Sruti* texts and proofs derived from analogy.

168. "The elements form that Iswara's body" is thus explained. As after yarn has been turned into a cloth the body of yarn is the cloth, similarly for Iswara's residing everywhere in all objects, the objective world is His body.

169. "Who resides internally in all objects, controls and employs them." This passage is illustrated by example in the following manner. As by contracting or expanding the threads, [of which a cloth is made] or shaking them, etc., the cloth must of necessity be similarly affected, and there is not the slightest mark by which the cloth can show its distinction;

170. So this internal knower Iswara has been transformed according to the impulse of his desires. That is to say, this objective world, has been produced through his consciousness, and a cow, horse, man, mountain, river, and an infinite variety of objects which fill the universe are changed conditions of Him, and they are necessarily His works.

171. After having explained the *Sruti* text referring to Iswara as an internal knower, the evidence of the *Gita* is now cited. Krishna says to Arjuna "Iswara* is situated in the

* Says the Commentator of the Bombay Edition. The word 'Iswara' is a singular noun of the first declension, hence He is one and not many; consequently as an internal knower He is one and not many as asserted by the followers of Vishnu Swami.

heart of all elementary bodies, and mounted on the mechanism of that organ makes all the elements wander through illusion." [Chap. XVIII, v. 51.]

They assert that as caste is singular number, for it is a collective noun, so Iswara for His being situated inside all hearts, may be taken as a collective noun of the singular number: but this does not hold true; for Iswara is never regarded in that light either in the *Sruti*, *Smriti*, or the *Puranas*; no where is He mentioned except as one; popular experience alike tends that way. Hence it is impossible to construe Him into a collective noun. Then again, if Iswara were so many distinct as there are individuals, there will be created a discord in the harmony of nature, for each Iswara dwelling inside each individual will refuse to be acted upon by the same natural laws which may affect another person and *vice versâ*. To be more explicit, the presence of many Iswaras in one universe will create discord by a difference of desires in them, one may be actuated with a wish to create, another to destroy, and so the two will be acting in the extreme ends, consequently synchcronism, and order will be upset. But it may be alleged, like a king having several servants there needs be no discord; for several Iswaras are all particles of the secondless Supreme Iswara, a form of *Brahma* and controlled by it. It may be asked of those who entertain this view whether that Supreme Iswara is endowed with or without almightiness and omniscience? If the reply be in the affirmative, then the necessity of several Iswaras is clearly done away with; for as an internal knower, one Iswara is quite capable of controlling all beings, and almightiness gives him that power. If on the other hand, the reply be in the negative, then Jiva will be without an Iswara. Thus then Iswara is one and not many. But objection may be taken in quite another form and the authority of Vachaspaty may be cited in support of his multiformness. Now this is clearly a mistake, for Vachaspati with the view of establishing non-duality and explaining it to one desirous of release, brings in the help of illusory attribution and its recession or withdrawal in that way. He has no other object.

172. The phrase "All the elements" in the above extract from the *Gita* is thus explained. It refers to Jiva who is the cognitional sac, and which cognition resides in the lotus of the heart. With the view of explaining the reason why that cognition is to reside in the heart, it is said:—the internal knower [Iswara] is transformed into the shape of the cognitional sac, and resides in the heart; Iswara,—the Blissful sheath—is the proximate cause of Jiva, the cognitional, and in regard to the heart is modified or changed in the form of that cognitional sheath.

[If we pause to enquire in to the drift of the text we shall find, the heart regarded as the centre of life. It is likewise mentioned as an organ. Iswara being most intrinsically situated resides inside the heart where He is transformed into cognition, intelligence or life, from His original state of blissfulness. Western physiology knows nothing or next to nothing about the heart, beyond its capacity of a forcing pump drawing the blood out and distributing it into the arterial channels. Popular literature assigns affection to the heart, and the exploded dogma of an antiquated and unscientific religion looks upon it as conscience, but nowhere is the slightest mention made of its being the tabernacle of Iswara or seat of cognition or knowledge in the abstract.]

173. The words 'mounted' 'mechanism' and 'wander' are thus explained. Mechanism indicates the physical body and the conceit that it is my body is expressed by the word 'mounted'; inclination for 'lawful' or 'prohibited action' is to 'wander.'

174. Jiva when influenced by the inherent force of *Maya*, begets an inclination for works lawful or interdicted, and attributes them to Self thus changing him into an agent and instrument. This is called wandering in [the meshes of] *Maya*.

175. The world 'controller' already mentioned [*ante* V. 164), also bears a similar signification to that of wandering as

mentioned in the *Sruti.* Therefore follow the method laid down in reference to 'controller' and through the help of your intellect apply it also to the world and all its contents. [In short recognise the presence of that internal knower Iswara in the universe and all its contents.]

176. Inclination for lawful actions though they are the means of virtue I have none, nor have I abstained from prohibited works knowing them to cause the production of sin, but moved as I am by the internal knower residing within me and in the way engaged by him, so do I act.

177. But in such a consideration of dependence of inclination on Iswara, there will be a consequent uselessness of the usual incentives [endeavour] to actions good and bad; hence to avoid it, it is said, you are not to conclude that nothing depends upon the individual's endeavour as far as the doing of actions or their reverse are concerned; for Iswara is modified or changed in the shape of what a person is capable of doing, therefore everywhere the individual's endeavour is the chief cause of all works.

178. Though therefore Iswara is modified in the form of the individual's endeavour, yet it does not set aside his control, for when that control is fully realised, the unassociated blissfulness of self is easy to be conceived of, by the Jiva.

179. "That helps and brings about his emancipation" so says the *Sruti, Smriti,* etc. And these Sacred Scriptures have been set down as the commandments of Iswara.

180. Since the *Sruti* mentions "To break His commands is hurtful and injurious," it is therefore plain enough that apart from His being the internal knower, He is the Supreme Lord. The *Sruti* says the commandments of Iswara are a cause of fear "The wind moves actuated by the fear of the Lord, etc.," hence for a fear of breaking His commands which in its turn is hurtful and produces sin, it is sought here to establish a difference between the internal knower and the Supreme Lord; and that difference is marked by the source

of fear as above mentioned, which is said to constitute the characterising feature of the Supreme Lord.

181. Two examples are cited from the *Sruti* to show the control exercised by Iswara both externally and internally "By His command the sun and moon etc." "The Supreme Self (*Paramātma*) having entered inside [of all beings] controls them."

182. This "Supreme Self is the Cause" of the universe. Another passage quoted from the *Sruti* is now being explained. In regard to the source of objective world the *Shastras* say, "He is the source from which the elements take their origin and is the cause of their destruction;" consequently Iswara for His being the creator and destroyer is the cause of this material world. And this evolution and destruction are admitted to take place in a consecutive order.

183. The subject is further illustrated by reference to an example. As by spreading a picture we bring out the several figures and other objects painted there, and present them to our view, so during the periods of evolutional activity, or say creation, all material objects are produced by Iswara.

184. And as in a rolled up picture all the figures are shut out of sight, so Iswara with the view of consummating the actions of all individuals [virtually extinguishing them from bearing any more fruits] draws the objective word within Him during periods of cyclic destruction [when they continue in a state of rarefied potentiality to be reproduced when the dawn of creation approaches.]*

---

* *Pralaya* and *Mahapralaya* are made to signify partial and total destruction respectively. In regard to the latter, opinions are divided. For instance, Sankhyakar, Gautama, the author of *Naya Sutras*, alike deny total destruction which they say to be a myth. The philosophy of Cosmosgony had no where engaged abler intellects than in India. Our ancient *Rishis* had to a great extent solved the mystery more satisfactorily and scientifically than the savants of Europe, and we challenge enquiry. But the

185. Now this being and non-being or appearance and disappearance of creation and destruction of the world is

---

views they entertain have not been thoroughly explained, hence interested motives and Missionary zeal had been co-operating to class them amongst the fabulous creations of a mytholic age. Happily the position is quite altered now, and as there is a desire of accepting truth even from an enemy's camp we subjoin the following explanation. *Brahma*, the creator has a lifetime of hundred years. But that period covers an immensity of time which staggers imagination; and on comparative analysis with the evidence forthcoming from a study of the earth's crust and its strata, the facts disclosed by Aryan researches fit nicely into the blank niches left unfinished by geology. For instance, according to the *Surya Siddhanta* we find it laid down that immediately with the advent of *Brahma* on the scene, the work of creation did not commence, the fiat of a personal creator's ordering "Let the waters recede and land appear," and so on after that fashion is never allowed here. The primary period occupied *Brahma* for five millions, six hundred, sixty-six thousand years, before he was in a position to begin his work. All this time, the earth was passing through the several geological epochs, its crust was solidifying or otherwise undergoing the requisite changes to render it fit for life to appear. And if it be remembered that a day of *Brahma* is equal to 14 *Manantwaras* or *Manus*, and a night of equal length, that gives us a period covered by four thousand human *Yugas* or one thousand eighty-four Mahayugas, one of which lasts for 4,320,000. Therefore (4,321,000 × 1084)2 *Brahma's* day and night of 24 hours. This multiplied by 100 will give the period he is to live. He has passed over six Manantwaras and is in the middle of the seventh, so that if 24 Manu constitute the period of his day, he must necessarily be near 12 o'clock noon of the very first day, and after another such period there will follow night, when there will be a *pralaya*, again to disappear with the advent of dawn. This is the rule. After 100 years *Brahma* also is swallowed up in the universal destruction and Iswara and the rest are all gone, leaving the One Life, PARABRAHMA above mentioned. This is a long account of evolution as understood amongst us.

Illustrated further by comparing them to night and day, profound slumber and waking, opening and shutting of the eyelids, contentment and distraction of the mind. Like these several conditions the resemblance between destruction and creation is complete.

186. But it may be asked whether Iswara as a creative source of the world is its instrumental or modifying cause? Both these views do not apply to the conclusions which have been here maintained. For Iswara has a requisite force [in the form of *Maya*] wherewith to create and destroy, [and as He is secondless and formless He is neither an instrument nor a modifying cause of the world.] For what is formless cannot be modified into something else of a different shape and form, and what is secondless cannot be regarded as an instrument or beginner.*

---

* The word beginner requires an explanation. Its Sanskrit equivalent *'Arambhaka'* or *'Arambhakarta'* can only be satisfactorily accounted for in this manner. When from a combination of several causes, there results a product entirely different in shape and form from them, for a connection of parts with the whole, it is called *Arambhavada.* As for instance by combining either half of a pitcher, is produced a jar which is entirely different in shape from that half. Here the material cause does not leave its own shape, but a thing is produced different from that cause; or as from a combination of one filament with another of thread, a fine thread is produced out of which is produced a cloth; here also the difference between the cause and its product, cotton-thread and cloth is admitted; now such a view of beginning in regard to the origin of the world by Brahma is inapplicable, inasmuch as It is secondless and there is a want of an action or product different from It. Then again, if the theory of beginning were to hold good, subsequent to the production of an action, its cause, which is different from such product, continuing present in the same state must require in regard to one cause the beginning of several products as actions. Hence the view of a Naiyayika [*Arambhavada*] is inconsistent.

187. Now Iswara is secondless, how can then He be the natural cause of both the sentient and insentient? The reply is, His associate of *Maya* is the cause of insentient as the reflection of intelligence is that of sentient creatures.

188. Objection may be taken in regard to Iswara, who is endowed with *Maya*, as the cause of the universe. For Sureswar Acharya (Vartikkar) distinctly attributes to the Supreme Self such causation. In this way, does a dissenter speak in this and the following verse. The Supreme Self associated with *Maya* abounding in darkness or insentiency is the cause of body, while for his preponderance of intelligence, and according to the conception, knowledge and merits or de-merits of individuals which form the instrumental cause of their origin, that Self is the cause of both sentient and insentient objects. In short He is the Universal Cause.

189. In the above manner Vartikkara says, "The Supreme Self and not Iswara is the universal cause of both sentient

---

Now between the modifying cause and its resulting product there is said to be no difference. As for instance, clay modified into a jar, internal organ modified in the form of its function, and the modification of Prakriti into Mahatatwa (according to Sankhya). It is a fact well-known that phenomena are regarded only as another form of matter by Kapila and his followers. Then again, there are others who consider it to be only another modification of Brahma; but how can that be? For the world is material and Brahma immaterial; the former is insentient, the latter intelligence; the first is non-eternal and the last eternal. Thus then, if it were a modification of intelligence, that is to say, a changed form of it, intelligence will be destructible, for what is subject to change is always so.

In regard to *Vivarta Karana*, it is alleged, when a cause produces a result without undergoing any change, as for instance, silver in nacre the faults and inconsistencies of the first two methods do not apply, and it is the accepted doctrine of the *Vedanta* for a solution of the Cosmos.

and insentient." With the view of refuting it, our author says. Ye dissenters, hear what a *Siddhanti* has to say against ycur deduction.

190. With a desire of establishing the signification of "That' to include the Uniform Intelligence and things dissimilar, attributed by illusion, like the signification of its complement 'Thou' [of the phrase "That art Thou" the Supreme Self is mentioned as the Universal Cause. This is untenable and rebutted by the *Siddhanti*:—Here like Jiva and Uniform Intelligence (concerning the indication 'That') Iswara endowed with *Maya* and Brahma and their mutual illusory attribution after having been established by Him, Sureswar Acharya expounds the Supreme Self as the Universal Cause.

191. To this effect the *Sruti* mentions, "From the Supreme Brahma which is truth, knowledge and bliss, have been derived ether, air, fire, water, earth, medicine, food-grains, and the physical body."

192. But it may be asked wherein consists the allegation of mutual attribution through illusion in the passage above quoted? It is therefore said, the attribution of casuation of the universe to Brahma having the indications of truth, knowlege and the rest, and the attribution of truth to the universal cause, the reflected intelligence inherent in *Maya* (that is Iswara) is due to a want of proper discrimination arising from the illusory attribution of one to the other.

193. This mutual illusory attribution of one to the other has already been exemplified [*Vide ante* V. 1-3, Chap. VI.], but is here again illustrated by reference to the starching of a piece of cloth:—As in a cloth that has been starched, the starch appears to be one with it, through mistake; similarly the oneness of Iswara and Brahma or their mutual attribution of one another is due to illusion.

194. As a person of dull intellect fails to discriminate the difference between the space appropriated by a cloud and the

unappropriated infinite space [of which it is a part,] so do the ignorant conceive the oneness of Iswara and Brahma.

195. But that difference can only be conceived by ascertaining the purport under the six features. These are :—the beginning and the end, repetition, novelty, result, illustration by praise and by supporting argument.* If the purport of the *Sruti* be determined in the above manner under the six methods cited, it will appear that Brahma is unassociated (unconditioned) while Iswara is the reflected shadow of intelligence in *Maya*. He is the creator of universe.

196. In *Sruti*, the unconditioned nature of Brahma is plainly set forth in the beginning and end: for instance, in the beginning Brahma is described as "Truth, knowledge and infinite;" and in the conclusion, "Whom speech cannot grasp——unspeakable."

197. The nature of Iswara is now declared by referring to *Sruti* text. "*Maya* is the creative source of the universe, it likewise is the cause of the individual's enthralment." [He is subject to bondage.] Hence Iswara endowed with predicate of *Maya* is the creator, while the individual is a subject of metempsychosis.

198. The mode in which creation of Iswara took place is now being declared. [From the standpoint of knowledge.] He desired to be manifold, and thus became the collective totality of subtle bodies—Hiranyagarbha†—just as the profound slumbering condition passes into dreams.

---

* Says the *Vedantasara* :—The commencement and the conclusion repetition, novelty, the result, illustration by praise and by supporting arguments are the means for determining the purport; the reader is referred to DHOLE'S *Vedantasara*, pp. 44-45.

† The subtle astral body has one or several indications, according to the manner of observing it collectively or individually like the wood and the reservior, or the tree and water considered before; that is to say, either it is the subject of one Intellect (Spiritual Intelligence or *Boodhi*) or of several. In the former condition it is the

199. From the two views expounded in *Sruti*, in regard to creation; of consecutive serial production [as for instance, ether first, then air, fire, water, and earth] or their simultaneous beginning, not telling against one another, both of them are worth knowing; in the same manner as dreams happen in both ways, consecutively and simultaneously.

200. The nature of Hiranyagarbha is defined:—For the conceit that he is the collective aggregate of subtle bodies, and pervading like a thread through all beings (called Thread-Soul) he is the predicate of desire, action, and intelligence of all individuals.

201. As in the morning and evening twilight all objects partially covered by darkness can only be dimly perceived, so the objective world is but faintly apprehended in the Hiranyagarbha condition.

202. As the sketch on a piece of canvas duly prepared with starch can only be plainly perceived when drawn with a crayon, so is the body of Iswara marked by the subtle astral body derived from non-quintuplication of elements.

Thread-Soul or *Sutratma*, for it pervades like a thread through all created beings, and is the subjective Intelligence of *Hiranyagarbha*, thus constituting a collective totality. In the latter or individual condition it is the special or separate intelligence of every living being. Consciousness associated with the collective totality of subtle astral bodies is known by the names of *Sutratma* (Thread-Soul), for it pervades through all such bodies like a thread, and *Hiranyagarbha* or *Prana*, for the conceit of its being the five great elements in a state of simple uncombination, with knowledge, will-force, and active energy for its attributes.—It is the subtle body itself. Iswara associated with [*Maya*] illusion abounding in pure goodness and for the conceit that He is the astral body is called Hiranyagarbha. Prajna associated with Ignorance abounding in impure goodness, for a similar conceit that he is the subtle astral body, is called Taijasa.—*Vide* DHOLE's *Vedantasara*, p. 23.

203. Like the tender stalks or leaflets of a seed that has germinated, this Hiranyagarbha is the tender seedling out of which is produced the universe.

204. As in the full blaze of the sun all objects are plainly visible; as the figures and trees and plants bearing fruits or sheaths of corn are rendered manifest, in a piece of painting filled with colour, so is this material world plainly manifested in Virat's condition.

205. This Virat is mentioned in the fifth chapter of the *Second Ashtaka* of the *Yajur Veda Sanhita* and *Purush Sukta.* "From Brahma to the Turienne column all this universe is mentioned as constituting the shape and form of Virat.

206. From the unanimous testimony of the different sects of worshippers this can be gleaned concerning the nature of Iswara [mentioned in Verses 202—208]. From the internal knower to a spade every object is fit to be worshipped as Iswara. [This is pointed out in this and the two following Verses.] The internal knower, Thread-Soul, Virat, Brahma, Vishnu, Siva, Fire, Ganesa, the king of difficulties, Vairab, Myral, Marika (goddess), Yaksha, and Rakshas;

207. Brahman, Kshetrya, Vaiswa, Sudra, cow, horse, deer, bird, the *ficus religiosa* and banyan, mangoe, barley, paddy, and grass;

208. Water, stone, earth, wood, an axe and spade, all these are Iswara, and to worship them is meritorious, for they yield good fruits.

209. A person engaged in the worship of such objects derives benefit according to the mode of his worship; and in proportion to the dignity of the object worshipped will be the measure of his reward. That is to say, the worshippers of low reptiles, or inanimate objects derive the least amount of benefit, while the higher divinities worshipped as Iswara bring forth the best results.

210. But there is only one means for cutting off metempsychosis and getting emancipated, that is knowledge of

Brahma; just as to keep away dreams one must necessarily keep himself awake, so by dispelling ignorance one is freed.

211. All the phenomena which at present are discernible to us, from Iswara, Jiva, physical body, to animate and inanimate objects which go to make up the universe, all this is a dream for they are material in the light of knowledge of secondless Brahma. Brahma alone is real and the rest are impermanent, hence in regard to Brahma they are like objects seen in a dream.

212. For Iswara (the blissful sheath) and Jiva (the cognitional sheath) are both contrived in *Maya* and from these two have been produced this universe.

213. Of them which portion of creation is Iswara's and which belongs to Jiva is now being set forth according to the citation of *Sruti*. "From determination to entrance is Iswara's, and from the waking condition, etc., to emancipation is Jiva's." "The Supreme Iswara observed, certainly I have made the several abodes (with their adequate inhabitants food and drink) and have made my entrance in the body of the individual through the cranial aperture in the center."

214. From a want of knowledge of non-duality about the oneness of Brahma and individual self, established in the *Sruti*, persons opposed to that doctrine or unacquainted with it are found engaged in disputing about Jiva and Iswara who are endowed with *Maya*—and in vain.

215. The sight of an emancipated person gives me pleasure, that of a worldly-minded person enquiring after self-knowledge excites my sympathy and makes me feel pity for him, but with those dull* dissenters who are ever entangled in

* There are three grades of dullness, hence such persons are classified as either good, indifferent or bad. Those who have no faith in the teachings of the Shastras though they have a conception of their purport belong to the first class. Those having neither faith in, nor knowledge of, the Shastras and following the

the meshes of error and know not the unassociated intelligence of the PARABRAHMA, I need not engage in any more wrangling about the real nature of Iswara and Jiva.

216. From the worshippers of grass, trees, bricks to Yogachars, all of them are in error concerning the real nature of Iswara; from the followers of Sankhya to those of Charvak (Lokayats) all are in error concerning the nature of Jiva.

217. For so long as there is no adequte knowledge of the Supreme Brahma, they are all entangled in error, and where is their happiness and deliverance?

218. Though according to the dignity of their objects of worship, there is an appreciable difference amongst them, but of what benefit is it? Or as a kingdom obtained in a dream, or wealth acquired by begging in that condition is of not the slightest use when the dream is dispersed and the person awakes; so do their respective devotion bring forth neither bliss nor emancipation from future re-births.

219. Thus then, it is incumbent upon one desirous of release instead of engaging in fruitless disputes about Iswara, to ascertain the nature of Brahma, and to acquire that knowledge (which would procure deliverance to him.)

220. If as a means of acquiring that knowledge [of self] it be necessary to begin with the nethermost rung of the ladder, with Jiva and Iswara, by all means do adopt that method, but beware of being entangled in endless disputes in your preliminary enquiry, and do not allow yourselves to lose sight of that one object, Brahma.

221. If you contend that according to *Sankhya* Jiva is unassociated, pure intelligence, and Iswara is similarly men-

---

bent of their wishes are indifferent; while the third class include those who have a faith in the Shastras, but from ignorance act as they choose. With persons of above description, the author writes, all disputes are useless.

tioned in *Yoga*, or that the indication of 'That' and 'Thou' of the transcendental phrase "That art Thou," cited in *Yoga-Shastra* can be clearly ascertained to indicate Jiva and Iswara. The reply is, in spite of the oneness of properties both in Iswara and Jiva, *Yoga Philosophy* maintains an actual existing difference between the two, which is not the conclusion of our *Vedanta*. Do therefore listen :—

222. We (Vedantins) do sometimes avail ourselves of the indication of the two words 'That' and 'Thou' as a step for facilitating the comprehension of non-duality, otherwise they are not for establishing actually a difference in their signification. In other words, when they are spoken of separately as conveying each a separate signification, it is only for the purpose of establishing an identity of indication, which refers to the one and same thing, *viz.*, the Individual Self and the Universal Self are one.

223. One entranced in the meshes of *Maya* which is without a beginning, is apt to conceive of a difference between Jiva and Iswara ; and for preventing such an erroneous notion of subsisting difference, the signification of those words are cleared of all inconsistencies and made to indicate non-duality.

224. That can be done in the same way as in the instances already cited before :—Of the space appropriated by a jar, having no difference whatever with the infinite space of which it is a mere unit, or as between the ether of water and that of cloud the difference is nil.

225. As in the instance of the ether of water and cloud a difference in their associates [water and cloud respectively] constitutes the difference of the two, which is far from real ; and their receptacles, the ether present in a jar, and that infinite body which fills all space are pure for they are un-associated :

226. So the blissful sac (Iswara) and the cognitional (Jiva) are dependent on the associates of Illusion (*Maya*) and In-

tellect (*Boodhi*) respectively; and their occupation or seat, Brahma and Uniform Intelligence are ever pure [and unrelated.]

227. If it be said, in order to arrive at a proper understanding, in regard to the indication of the words 'That' and 'Thou' no harm can result in the admission of the views of *Sankhya* and *Yoga*, for they help to establish the meaning clearly; the reply is, we may as well take the help of the doctrines of a Charvaka for comprehending the indication of the 'foodful sac' and that [the physical body] is fit to be considered [by the help of this borrowed interpretation] as self.

228. Since between the doctrines of the *Vedanta* and those of *Sankhya* and *Yoga* there is marked difference, it is impossible to expect any agreement. This the author shews in the following manner:—According to *Sankhya* and *Yoga* there is a difference in Self; and the world is real, and Iswara is something distinct from the world and Jiva (*Yoga*). Unless they set aside these doctrines, there can be no agreement between them and a Vedantin.

229. If the question be asked what necessity is there for ascertaining non-duality, since a knowledge of the unrelated condition of *Jivatma* is enough to procure release? The reply is, in that case an individual may fix his belief on the reality of sensuous enjoyment as garland and sandal, and considering them to be ever-lasting, attain his release.

230. That is to say, as it is impossible to regard a garland, sandal, etc., in the light of real and eternal substances, so it is impossible to separate the Jiva from his relationship with Iswara and the universe.

231. Why? Because he is material in constitution; and Matter (*Prakriti*, *Ajnana* or *Maya*) has always the property of creating real, unreal; moreover, Iswara is his controller; how then can he get rid of future re-incarnations when he is thus placed between Matter and Iswara, deluded by the first and controlled by the last?

232. But want of a right discrimination is alone the

source of creating the above named conditions of relation and control; when they are destroyed, by the advent of knowledge, or say, discrimination, the chance of creating the relationship and control is alike destroyed; on this ground an antagonist may take his stand. In that case, he is one with a follower of *Sankhya.* [For indiscrimination is either want of discrimination, or something else; or something opposed to it. Now these are the three forms; of them the first is untenable, for, want implies an absence or nothing, and that cannot act as a productive cause of something, hence want or absence of discrimination cannot account for a cause of relation and and control. Neither the second form holds good; for we do not find that 'something else;' as for instance, a jar, to be such cause; and the third form as it maintains something opposed to discrimination, clearly establishes ignorance which is the same with *Prakriti* of *Sankhya.* Thus then, it upholds *Sankhya.*

233. If for the purpose of attributing bondage and release, Self be declared to be manifold, even that is not possible, for *Maya* is quite capable of doing that.

234. How? Like things created in a magical performance, (as the creation of a tree bearing mangoes or other fruits,) what is difficult of being produced is easily created by (*Maya*) Illusion and for its being naturally endowed with opposite or antagonistic properties [*i. e.*, unreal], creates bondage and release or emancipation. Now it cannot be contended that as the first is an action of ignorance, consequently emancipation must be admitted as a necessity; as that will be against *Sruti*, for nowhere does *Sruti* suffer the actualitity of emancipation, like that of bondage, to prevail.

235. As for instance in reference to his actual condition Jiva is said to be truly "Without destruction, and origin, neither subject to bondage nor emancipation, without the means (hearing and the rest) and any desire of release, and in whom has ceased ignorance.

236. But the milch cow *Maya* has two calves, Jiva and Iswara, who, according to their inclination, drink the milk of duality, but that does not affect non-duality anyhow, nor can cause it any injury.

237. Except a difference in name, there is no difference really present between the Uniform Intelligence and Brahma, just as there is none whatever between the space appropriated by a jar and the great body of it outside, infinite ether (*Mahakas*).

238. That Non-dual Principle or Entity [Secondless Brahma] which was present prior to the creation of the universe, (as is said in the *Sruti*) is even present now, and will so continue in the future *i. e.*, during emancipation; there is no doubt about that, but it is true. Then why are people generally so fond of creating a difference? Ignorance or Illusion alone leads people astray and that is the reason why the generality of mankind are fond of creating a difference between the Individual Self and Brahma.

239. But the question is, if the unreality of the universe and reality of the secondless Entity or Principle, Brahma, which form the subject under consideration, be an established conviction with the wise, why are they found to behave like a man of the world [ignorant]? Where then is the necessity of acquiring knowledge of self. Therefore it is said, from the force of fructescent works, many wise persons are found to have, the same inclination for using material objects as they were accustomed to, prior to the rising of knowledge, but as they are free from illusion they are never ensnared in its meshes as ignorant persons are.

240. To show that the wise are free from error, the opposite condition of the ignorant is being first cited here. The ignorant have a firm belief in their mind as to the reality of enjoyment or suffering, both in the present sphere as well in the next [heaven, etc.,] and there is neither room for the secondless Brahma, nor is It discernible in their mind.

241. The wise have an exactly opposite belief ; hence according to their individual perception and conviction, people create either bondage or release.

242. [Arguments for establishing the reality of Brahma and unreality of the universe are now being given.] The manifestibility of the secondless Brahma is derived from the *Shastras* and not from experience. It may be contended, as the secodless Brahma is not visible, hence it is impossible to ascertain It with any definite precision. But this assertion is untenable, inasmuch as Brahma in the form of intelligence is everywhere manifest and is clearly the subject of perception and experience in every individual. Then again, if it be said, this manifestibility of intelligence can be admitted, but as its entireness cannot be perceived, the universe also in its entirety is not perceived, therefore you are constrained to admit an equality between non-dual Brahma and the dual objective world, so far as an absence of complete perception goes ; and if in regard to the latter that does not stand in the way of your conception, why is Brahma to remain unmanifested then ?

243. Thus then, the manifestibility or perception of both the phenomenal and noumenal in the same province being equal, if that does not prevent you from enquiring into the reality of the former, what objection can there be to hold a similar view with regard to the secondless Brahma ?*

244. Now the Vedantin's opponent adopts a different line of argument to do away with non-duality. He says—the

* As in a pot of boiled rice, by feeling one rice, the whole of its contents are known to have been well cooked, so by the faculty of ascertainment residing inside the physical body, in intelligence, 'felicity, fulness, eternal freedom, unassociation,' etc., which Brahma is endowed with, are easily perceived in every individual self after the destruction of ignorance has ceased to produce any more illusion.

'secondless' is without a duality. Hence non-duality and its reverse, are naturally opposed to each other; and from a perception of the phenomenal, no noumenal can be made out. Adopting a similar course, the Vedantin may as well exclaim, from their natural antagonism, when the secondless Brahma (noumenal) is manifested, the phenomenal must cease. Thus then both of us are equally placed so to speak; but his opponent replies to this:—The perception of intelligence is not opposed to the phenomenal, hence we are not in the same position. In other words from an absence of antagonism between your perception of the non-dual Brahma in intelligence, and our duality, there is no similarity with the question raised by you and me.

245. But inasmuch as the phenomenal is unreal though it is manifested, its reality (apparent) is not opposed to that of the secondless Brahma, and a *Siddhanti* says in reference to it:—If you say so, then listen to me: the phenomenal is in a condition of non-being, impermanence or non-existence (*asat*) but full of illusion; and that Brahma is the only Reality which no *pralaya* can affect, but continues to the end fully manifested.

246. "To the end" is being illustrated:—These unthinkable worlds are full of illusion and created out of it, hence they are unreal. Having thus ascertained them, it is natural to consider Brahma as the only Reality. ['Unthinkable' signifies what is not fit for thinking; these worlds for their being material are unreal, and for the matter of that 'indescribable.' Therefore having found out the unreality of the phenomenal, to regard the secondless Brahma as the only Reality is but natural.]

247. If subsequently, the reality of phenomena reasserts again in your mind after having known them to be unreal, you are again to have recourse to arguments and analysis over and over, till that error ceases to exist, [and for such

repetition there is the authority of Vyas as laid down in the *Sariraka Sutras*, Chap. iv.]

248. But it may be enquired how long is that necessary to be practised? Hence it is said, arguments for discriminating the secondless Reality, or the means 'hearing' and the rest to that end, are not attended with pain and as they are beneficial, inasmuch as they destroy every thing else which is harmful to such knowledge of non-duality, they can be had recourse to *ad libitum*. In this respect, they differ from the supporting arguments of duality, for they are painful, as they cost an effort on the part of the individual seeking to establish it.

249. Moreover, it may be argued that a person even with his knowledge of Brahma, is subject to hunger and thirst, in short,—of the same worldly pursuits as he used to be before, in his state of ignorance; now whether the declaration "I am hungry," "I am thirsty," indicates self? Or the first personal pronoun has reference mainly to the Intelligence which is self? To such a question, a Vedantin admits the first view, so that the principle of egoism or individuality, you may well see, and no one asks you to do otherwise [not to see.] It may as well be mentioned here, that the second view is inapplicable, because self is unrelated and unassociated, and he can have no concern with hunger, thirst and the rest.

250. But this discussion does not stop here: a dissenter is apt to maintain, though hunger and thirst may not properly be the subjects of self, yet through illusion or mistake one is apt so to perceive;—and says a Vedantin, in such a circumstance [of attributing hunger and thirst to self through illusion] the best plan is to destroy that illusion, and to practise discrimination always.

251. For, illusion comes from interminable desire which has no beginnning; and for its removal, the repeated practice of discrimination [from things real and unreal] is very proper.

252. That unreality of the phenomenal world, and its

illusory nature can only be found out by argument, analysis and deduction, and not by experience. But objection may be taken to it, for the experience of the exquisitely beautiful composition of the universe, which is quite unthinkable* and for its being a subject of cognition for the witness, it cannot be maintained that its unreality is alone capable of being determined by arguments and not experience. And that is now being removed as follows:—It is not to be said, that the discrimination of unreality proceeds from argument only, where the witness has an experience of the unthinkable composition [of the phenomenal.]

253. That unthinkable (composition) is an indication or sign of the falsity of an object; but a dissenter seeks to connect it with the pervasion of intelligence of self, and says, intelligence is endowed with it. To this, the reply is, from a want of prior contact or combination, the unthinkable composition, is one indication or sign of non-duality; and the Vedantin admits the unthinkable source of self, because he must be either that or its reverse; in the latter contingency, his origin must be capable of being conceived with ease, which is not a fact, because eternal; hence there is no other alternative but to call him (*Achintyarachana*) unthinkable, etc.

254. How can intelligence said to be eternal? Because nothing can be conceived anteceding it. If any one were to say, intelligence has a prior condition; he is to be asked, What it is? Whether it is conceived by intelligence or by insentiency? Now then of the two prior conditions either of intelligence or insentiency, insentiency cannot be the instrument of discovering intelligence, and hence cannot precede it;

---

* Literal construction of *achintyarachana* is what has been given here, that would signify either the worthlessness of thinking about the source of the world, for being outside of self and a duality; or what cannot be accurately surmised from thinking—so vast and unknown.

with reference to the first view, the question is whether intelligence is perceived by the same intelligence or by another intelligence to constitute a prior condition; of them, if it be said in reply, that the prior condition of intelligence is quite distinct from the same intelligence, it will then amount to an admission of two intelligences,—a duality—and as non-duality does not recognise another intelligence, and even for argument's sake admitting its existence, there will yet be wanting a co-operation (*pratiyogi*) of that intelligence, without which its knowledge or perception will be clearly impossible. Then again, with that perception by another (prior) intelligence this one (intelligence) will be reduced to the condition of insentiency like that of a jar, etc. Thus then, there remains that other consideration which sets forth intelligence being manifested by the same intelligence. Even that is untenable, for want or absence of a thing cannot be perceived by itself. Moreover, in regard to phenomena, owing to a difference in the demonstrator—the internal organ and the rest,—and for an utter impossibility of perceiving an absence of that duality (the world) by itself, and for an absence of another instrument,—a prior agent of that duality—it may as well be said that like the want of prior condition of intelligence, the phenomenal has also no prior condition, of another substance preceding it. Therefore it is said, the prior condition of duality is conceived by intelligence.

255. The phenomenal with a prior condition [in intelligence] is merely a product just as a jar is, yet its composition is unthinkable, and for the matter of that, false and unreal like phantasmagoria.

256. Thus then, having shewn [*ante* 242-254] the manifestibility of intelligence in the beginning, it is consequently eternal and visibly perceptible; save and beyond it, every other thing is unreal, and that unreality is perceived through the same intelligence. But then objection may be taken as to the tangibility or visibility of the non-dual secondless Reality,

Brahma. Hence the author proceeds to clear it away. Intelligence is visible, and through it unreality of phenomena is conceived, consequently the assertion that the secondless entity Brahma is not visible, would imply contradiction.

257. If it be said, notwithstanding the explanation above given after the *Vedanta*, there are yet many Vedantins who have no faith in it, and why so? The reply is not difficult to find: for in the case of *Charvaks* many of whom are well versed in logic and sound reasoning, yet are they found mistaking self with the physical body, and why is this?

258. If you say from want of a clear intellect they are unable to discriminate properly, then I may as well conclude from a want of proper study or right interpretation of the *Shastras*, those Vedantins shew no faith in the explanation about the visibility of the secondless Reality.

259. When by a proper ascertainment of the secondless Reality, desires seated in the mind and passions are all destroyed, then an individual attains deliverance in life; and in his present life he enjoys supreme felicity. This effect of self-knowledge is mentioned in the *Sruti*, and it is impossible to deny it, for it is a visible result.

260. As for instance—"When knowledge of self arrives maturity, the joints of the heart are all destroyed" *Sruti*. 'Joints' refer to desires and passions.

261. But here 'desires,' refer to the mistaken identity of egoism (*Ahankara*) and intelligence, as instanced in the use of the first personal pronoun I and its deflections, mine, etc.

262. Though the above 'desires' are sources of evil, yet in reference to egoism, if intelligence be kept apart and separate and not mixed up with it, and in that condition of alienation of intelligence kept distinctly in view, millions and tens of millions of desires, will not be prejudicial to knowledge [of self]; for the maturity of knowledge has already destroyed the 'joints' of the heart [as has been mentioned already].

263. As for a preponderance of de-merits in you, the

perception of the secondless Reality brings you no satisfaction and comfort, so even with the destruction of the desires and passions [joints of the heart], if as a result of fructescent works—works which have already began to bear fruit—desires do come afterwards.*

264. They [desires originating with egoism or belonging to it] cannot in any way affect the Supreme Self who is intelligence; just as a disease of the physical body or the growth and decay or destruction of a tree cannot affect self, for he is quite unrelated, similarly after the destruction of illusory attribution of egoism to self, any desire originating in the first is quite incapable of distressing, causing pain or affecting him in any way.

---

* With reflex intelligence, physical body, and self, egoism is apt to be mistaken by a gradual consecutive difference of which there are three varieties, *viz.*, ordinary, active, and erroneous. The identity or oneness of egoism with the reflex intelligence is ordinary or natural, for it comes and goes with reflection of intelligence; then again, identity of egoism with the physical body is called active [*Karma*] as it is a result of fructescent works, because the conception or experience "I am a man," etc., of all individuals lasts so long as fructescent works continue; with their destruction there is no more any attachment or conceit for the physical body. And the mistaken identity of egoism with the witnessing intelligence which is quite unrelated is called erroneous, as it is conceived in ignorance,—because with the destruction of ignorance a wise person destroys that identity, and he is never found to say "I am an agent," "I am a doer, an eater, happy or miserable." Sankaracharya has in this way, illustrated the mistaken identity of egoism. In regard to the first and the second, they are seldom found to be the subject of perception in the wise: from a destruction of ignorance and error or mistake, the wise are exempt from the third variety, so that the property of egoism in the shape of reflex intelligence and desires, cannot militate against the Witnessing Intelligence, so far as a theosophist is concerned.

265. If you say, prior to the destruction of desires and passions of the heart, there is no possibility of any connection of desires with the unrelated blissfulness of the Supreme Self, hence there will be no more forgetfulness about it, for it means the same thing as destruction of the heart's joints, and that shall constitute your success.

266. If you say ignorant persons know it not, hence it is the name for a heart's joint, for the difference between a wise and ignorant is known by the presence or absence of those joints (desires).*

267. Between the ignorant and wise there is no difference whatever, so far as an attachment or its reverse, for the physical body, organ, and intellect is concerned.

268. As for example, between one who has the sacred thread, and one who has it not—though belonging to the same caste, there is no difference so far as the rules of food are concerned, but their actual difference consists in the qualification of the former for the study of the *Vedas* to which the latter is dis-entitled.

269. Destructions of passions and desires in the heart of the wise is proved by a reference to the *Gita* (Chap. XIV. v. 22) as follows:—"They neither shew an aversion for miseries already befallen, nor evidence a desire for happiness, but like a person quite unaffected by them, allow things to take their usual course," and this is called destruction of the heart's malady.

270. But the text quoted from the *Gita* may be construed as a piece of counsel for the wise; it asks them to be quite unaffected either by pleasure or its reverse, and is therefore

* The Sanskrit word '*Granthi*' means a joint, but the heart has no joint, it likewise means a knot, which even it has not, therefore it signifies crookedness, a malady, etc.; as there can hardly be any grievous mistake about it, I have allowed it to remain and this explanation is hardly called for.

no proof of destruction of the heart's malady, passions and desires. If a dissenter would argue in this strain, the significance of the word *'like'* in the verse would be rendered futile; and if it be alleged that from want of the requisite strength in the body, the wise are prevented from works, [so that virtually they cannot be said to have destroyed their desires, hence they abstain from actions,] then as a necessary deduction, it would follow that the wise are ill and suffering.

271. If you regard a knower of self, perfectly passive and indifferent to pleasure or pain, as a sick man, how very creditable is that to your intellect, and how clear is your knowledge. What next?

272. If you support your assertion by citing the *Purans* as a testimony, where it is said "Bharat and others were alike supremely indifferent, but they were sick;" What prevents you from taking note of the *Sruti* text which mentions "Even in eating, playing, and sexual intercourse, a theosophist acts like one indifferent."

273. Bharat and others did not live without eating, like wood and stone fixed in one place, but from fear of company they lived supremely indifferent to pleasure and pain.

274. And that avoidance of company owed its origin to the following reason. People who mix much in company are often found addicted to harmful works, and those without it, enjoy felicity; hence for a person desirous of happiness avoidance of company is always essential.

275. Dull and ignorant persons unacquainted with the drift of the Sacred Writings attribute de-merit to a theosophist, who has no inward longing for company, but to all appearances externally, engaged in the practice of playing on a musical instrument, or accompanying it vocally; let them do it, as it can bring forth no evil, for the unassociated condition of self is a natural inference to us [and a matter of fact].

276. Indifference, knowledge, and material abstinence

are helpmates of each other; in many instances they are present together in the same person, and sometimes separately in different.

277. But their cause, nature, and action (result) are different and are never of one and the same shape, hence, for a theosophist, it is proper to discriminate their difference.

278. To pry into the defects of all subjects is the source*

---

* If we take a little pain to enquire into the usual phases of an earthly existence we shall find everywhere we are subjected to pain varying in intensity and character. For instance, in intra-uterine life the fœtus is surrounded by and encompassed on all sides with the uterus, it floats in a quantity of fluid, and lives entirely on the mother's blood; from her rough movements, it is indeed protected by the fluid, but yet it has to change position before delivery takes place, and that is attended with pain alike to the mother as to her offspring. Its nurture and growth are attended with the same anxiety and costs a deal of trouble. So on till old age, when the limbs refuse to carry the weight of the body, the spine is doubled up, sight and hearing are almost gone, teeth have left the jaws, allowing an incessant dribbling of the saliva,—a source of nuisance both to the person and with whom he speaks,—he loses control over his excrements, and they escape sometimes quite unnoticed for which his relatives are not charitable enough to overlook. He is reprimanded as an old useless dog, his dissolution is prayed for by the family when he is confined in a bed of sickness, and if it happens to be a chronic malady, many are the curses showered upon his head. He has grown old and useless, none cares for him,—not even his children. Under such circumstances who is there that should not cultivate an aversion to life and its repeated re-incarnation? Hence it is said, a man of indifference should always take things at their natural light or real worth and attribute faults glaringly, in relief as it were, to intensify his aversion for the world.

Now the nature of indifference is to cast away every thing or shew any aversion for it. But as there are several degrees of indifference, it is classified under two varieties with several sub-

or cause of indifference, and to have an aversion for all things is its nature, and not to desire what is already discarded is its result.

279. 'Hearing,' 'consideration,' and 'profound contemplation' are the source, 'discrimination' of self the nature, and to prevent desires and passions from rising in the subjugated mind,—the result of knowledge or perception.*

---

divisions. For instance we have (1) *Par*, and (2) *Apar Vyragya*. The first is said to signify an aversion for wealth and prosperity already got, and altogether to discard or abandon it. The second is sub-divided into four varieties named respectively (*a*) struggling (*Yataman*), (*b*) distinguishing (*Vytireka*), (*c*) earnestness (*eka-indriya*), and (*d*) subjugated. They are defined in the following wise :—The 'Struggling' is an indifferent variety and consists in regarding the defective nature of things. 'Distinguishing' consists in improving the good qualities of a person, deriving satisfaction therefrom. 'Earnestness' is to ābstain the external organs of sense from internal desires; and when they have been so far subdued that they no more trouble the mind, it is called subjugated.

Of this last we have three more sub-divisions to speak of, they are called dull, sharp, and very sharp. When with the demise of a wife, child, or loss of property one feels disgusted with the world, and desires to abandon it, that is called dull. Then again, when a person incessantly prays not to have a wife, wealth, or son in his present life, with a tranquil intellect, that is called sharp indifference; and in regard to a future state when he wishes not even for the blissful abode of Brahma, it is an instance of the last variety.

* Yajnavalka addressing his wife Maitreyi says, "Self is sure worthy of being seen, he is fit to be heard [from the precepts of the wise] considered and meditated upon." Thus then in regard to the perception of self visibly by the mind the above are the several means, and as such they are sources of knowledge. Moreover, 'discrimination of self,' has reference to the ascertainment of the existing difference between the uniform intelligence and

280. 'Forbearance' and the rest* are the cause—earnest attention, the nature—and the slackening of the usual practices of people,—the result of mental abstinence.

281. Of them—'Indifference,' 'knowledge,' and 'actual abstinence,'—knowledge is the principal for its bringing in emancipation, while indifference and abstinence are merely the means of knowledge and helpful to it.

282. For all three to continue in equal force, in the same individual, can only happen to a person as a result of his superior devotion; but from some obstacles or other, it often happens for one or two of them to get reduced.

---

egoism, but this need not necessarily excite any misgiving as telling prejudicially against the doctrine of non-duality. For the uniform intelligence is something other than the physical body; organs sensory and active, vital airs, etc., etc., and to look upon it as Self or Brahma is the height of knowledge and the acme of discrimination; but then to connect desire with egoism as 'my house,' 'my son,' 'my money, mine eyes,' are conceived in error, hence the ascertainment of difference is insisted upon; but for one, who has no mistake of self as an agent or instrument, his egoism has already merged into the Absolute, the Infinite, Supreme Self, and his discrimination is matured. Similarly the concluding portion has reference to keep the mind free from being disturbed with other illusions in regard to self after it has been thoroughly subjugated and restrained from the disturbing influence of the senses.

* They include :

(1) Forbearance *(yama)*
(2) Canons to be observed *(niyama)*,
(3) Posture *(asana)*,
(4) Regulating the vital air *(pranayama)*,
(5) Restraining the organs of sense *(pratyahara)*,
(6) Fixed attention *(dharana)*,
(7) Contemplation *(dhyana)*,
(8) Conscious meditation *(savikalpa samadhi)*.

283. One whose knowledge is diminished by an increase of 'indifference' and 'mental abstinence' never attains emancipation at once, but is entitled to enjoy the felicity of the liberated in life, as a result of his pious devotions.

284. On the other hand, one who has a preponderance of knowledge with less of 'indifference' and 'abstinence' is sure to enjoy the supreme felicity of *Nirvan*, and not that destruction of visible misery which forms the happiness of the liberated in life.

285. It is the nature of indifference to regard everything as worthless, hence even the several abodes from Bhur to Brahma are looked upon as no better than straw, that is its highest limit; but knowledge has its finality in producing a steady or firm foothold of affection for all creatures, equally with one's own self.

286. As in the state of profound (dreamless) slumber all external objects are forgotten, so is forgetfulness of enjoyment [of sensuous objects] in the state of wakefulness said to be the final point of abstinence (*Upariti*).* In this mannner, the shades of difference present in indifference and the two others, are fit to be ascertained, [so that one may know which is superior or the best, and which less so—and may follow accordingly.

287. Though for a presence or continuance of fructescent works of various kinds, even a theosophist is at times infested with desires, yet that need not stand as a plea for construing the *Shastras* in a contrary light.

288. From a force of fructescent works, whatever condition a theosophist may be circumstanced to fill, it can create

* 'Abstinence' is continually to keep the external senses aloof from sensuous objects, after they have been turned away from them, thereby to keep the mind engaged in hearing the precepts on the *Brahma*; otherwise to abandon all acts enjoined in the Shastras, in the prescribed order [by turning a *Sannayasi*].

no difference, his knowledge suffers not the least, consequently his emancipation is certain.*

289. To sum up then:—As in a piece of painting several figures are duly represented, so is this exquisite objective world,—a duality—through the force of illusion attributed to the intelligence of the Supreme Self; and it is essentially requisite for that illusion to be shaken off and intelligence alone particularized (as the secondless, non-dual Reality.)

290. The fruit of reading the present treatise is enjoined in the following words:—Those of clear intellect who incessantly study it to find out its profound signification, shall cease to be enchanted with the sight of this unreal world like the ignorant, or as they used to be, in a prior stage (when wanting in knowledge).

END OF VOL. I.

---

* For with the destruction of ignorance the material of which the future body is to be built is destroyed and he is freed.

THE PANCHADASI.

SECTION VII.

On the Discovery of Felicity.

In beginning this treatise, the author BHARATITIRTHA GURU, opens with a recital of the main subject of the *Brihadaranyaka Upanishad*:—" A person who knows self,—his individual self to be one with Brahma,—has no more desire left in him, for whose enjoyment he is to hunt after."

2. The purport of the above *Sruti* text will be fully declared in the present chapter, and by that means the acquisition of felicity by one liberated in life will be thoroughly set forth.

3. With the view of explaining the signification of the word 'person' in the aforesaid passage, the mode of creation is now being determined. It is said "*Maya** through the reflection of intelligence creates (Jiva) individual and Iswara" (*Sruti*).

* Here the word *Maya* refers to the reflected shadow of Brahma, which is intelligence and bliss. The material cause of phenomena with its three attributes *satwa, raja* and *tama* is called *Prakriti*; from a difference in composition *viz.*, a preponderance of the pure good, and impure good *Prakriti* is respectively transformed into *Maya* and *Avidya*. Now the reflected shadow of intelligence of (Brahma) in Maya is Iswara, while the same reflection in *Avidya* is called Jiva. Thus then we find reflected

Hence it is natural to infer that by Jiva and Iswara the whole universe has been contrived or fabricated.

4. The question naturally arises how much of the world is created by Jiva and Iswara respectively? From determination to entrance belongs to Iswara; and from waking to emancipation, Jiva. That is to say, "Iswara for the desire that he should multiply and manifest himself in diverse forms" (*Sruti*) constitutes the beginning of the creative process indicated by the word determination; and, his entrance in the form of the Spirit or self (*Atma*) in all beings indicated by the word 'entrance' is the finality of that process. In regard to Jiva's creation the explanation is, one whose origin is the condition of wakefulness, that is to say the world, and emancipation, the final destination, for his conceit in them, they are said to be his contrivance. Now Jiva for the conceit about his body, etc., and constant occupation in works, and enjoyment of happiness, with wife, food and drink while awake, enjoys felicity in profound slumber; and in dreaming slumber, he is an agent for experiencing felicity or its reverse, and when he realizes self to be the discoverer of all the three above named conditions, and no other than Brahma, he is emancipated and has no more re-births in store for him.

5. The signification of the word 'person' is now being set forth. [He is] "that changeless, unrelated intelligence,

---

shadow of Brahma with the three attributes good, active and bad forms *Prakriti*, which for a preponderance of pure good or impure good is differentiated into illusion and ignorance or nescience. Iswara is the reflection of intelligence in *Maya*, which is entirely subservient to him, and he is called all-knowing; while Jiva is subject of ignorance (*Avidya*) it forms his cause-body, and for his conceit in it he is called Jiva; *Prajna*, etc.; and as this ignorance is varied, so are beings of diverse kinds; this is the reason why Jiva and Iswara are said to be made by reflection. *Maya* and *Avidya* are formed from *Prakriti*.

the supreme self,—subject of error and illusion which attribute the physical body, sensory and active organs, etc., to him (in short through mistake these are confounded with self). He is unrelated naturally, yet from mutual illusory attribution is said to be present in (*Boodhi*) spiritual soul, though that has no connection with him; and this (the attribute of the word 'Jiva'), is here meant by the word "person."

6. Jiva who is only a reflection of intelligence is qualified for emancipation with the uniform intelligence and not alone, because that uniform intelligence is the abiding place or seat [of reflex], and without the actuality of such site no one can be the seer of an illusion [as for instance in the case of a snake in rope, the rope is the abiding place or site of the snake but without it that illusion cannot possibly occur].

7. "That reflex with its abiding seat, the uniform intelligence is subject to bondage, etc." This is now being pointed out in the two following paragraphs. When combined with the abiding uniform intelligence, the reflex intelligence of the Jiva takes shelter of the particle of error, (the reflected shadow of intelligence is called a particle of error, for all reflections are false,) and acknowledges self to be the body, etc., and says "I am worldly."

8. And when freeing himself from error, conceives self to be no other than the uniform intelligence then he says "I am the unrelated intelligence," and is gratified with that knowledge.

9. If it be said, to attribute individuality, *i.e.*, connect the first personal pronoun 'I' with that unrelated intelligence [Supreme Self] is not possible, so as to make one exclaim "I am the unrelated intelligence," and it cannot be perceived so. The reply is, egoism or individuality has three different significations of which one is primary and two secondary.

10. Mistaken attribution of an identity of the uniform and reflex intelligences on one another is said to be the primary

indication of the word (*aham*) "I am;" for ordinarily people use it in that sense.

11. Now then for the two subordinate or secondary significations. The reflex and uniform intelligences are both of them separately looked upon as *aham*. Both in common parlance and *Vedic* illustration, all wise persons have ever been in the habit of using it in that sense.*

12. In the ordinary phrase "I do go" a wise person disconnects the uniform from the reflex intelligence, and acknowledges the former to be the literal signification of the personal pronoun 'I.'

13. In the *Vedic* expression used by way of illustration as for instance "I am the unrelated intelligence," 'I' refer to the uniform intelligence according to the light of the *Shastras*.

14. If it be alleged, knowledge and its reverse are only the attributes of the reflex intelligence, and never that of the

* The primary import of 'I am' is the predicated intelligence of the internal organ with reflection of intelligence, and it does not indicate intelligence pure *et* simple, hence its subject neither; but then by the indication of abandoning a part from the reflex of the internal organ and intelligence according to the usual practice amongst men and in the Vedas, the remaining unabandoned part implies (*Aham*) 'I am' or the principle of individuality, and this is its 'indicative indication,' but that is also its secondary or subordinate import. From the function of that indicative indication, the pure intelligence is a subject of egoism ('I am'), and as the subject of function is dependent or subject of this world, necessarily therefore from indication, intelligence is also called subject of function. Now the subject of function signifies the disappearance of envelopment from intelligence which then produces an aversion for the world; and that indifference when strengthened leads a person to discard it altogether as an unreality but existing apparently from illusion, and seek the company of a Guru for acquiring knowledge of Self.

uniform, hence how it is possible, for the reflex intelligence of the individual to perceive and acknowledge "I am the uniform intelligence?"

15. The reply is:—such a declaration is not at all faulty; for both the intelligences are identical in nature, and reflex is merely a false name; with its removal or disappearance the uniform alone remains.

16. If you say the perception "I am the eternal uniform intelligence" to be false too, I do not deny it. Just as the illusion of snake in a rope is false, and that snake has no more the power of moving or holding its head up, so the connection of egoism with either the reflex or uniform intelligence can alike be admitted to be unreal.

17. Though the perception "I am the eternal uniform intelligence" be false, and from that it is quite natural to expect the destruction of the world, for it is well-known that the offering given to a Deva is according to his dignity: therefore according to the nature of the ignorance which determines the reality of phenomena, is its destruction possible by the light of knowledge proportionately.

18. In the aforesaid manner, by regarding the reflex intelligence (Jiva) to be identical with the uniform intelligence, there follows the perception "I am the uniform intelligence," for without this knowledge of their oneness, cognition of non-duality can never accrue, as is over and over said in the *Sruti*.

19. As in the instance of the body considered to be self, men generally fix their belief without any reserve or doubt, so in the case of the finite intelligence of the Jiva regarded one with the uniform and all-knowing intelligence [of Brahma] one should alike consider it without doubt and reservation.*

---

* When a person says "I am a Brahmana" he has no more doubts nor any conflicting ideas about his being one belonging to

20. Sankaracharya in his *Upadesha Sahasri* expresses also the same opinion that such a perception is a means to emancipation: "Like the knowledge of the physical body being self, one who gets that refuting knowledge which hinders the conception or perception of the body being self, is released though he may desire it not."

21. If any one were to say that the word 'this' has reference to the visibility of self [as for instance "This jar," "This book," "This cloth." Here 'this' is used to identify the several articles in connection with which it is used; so in the phrase "This am I" the visibility of self indicated by the first personal pronoun is established by 'this'] and that visibility is full well-apprehended by us [Vedantins], for he is self-manifested intelligence, and as such, always visible.*

22. And as in the case of the visible "tenth person," ignorance can be attributed, so with regard to intelligence (self) visibility and invisibility, knowledge and imperception are alike attributable in spite of his visibility.

23. The ignorance of the tenth person, is now being declared. Ten persons collected in a certain spot to cross a river; on alighting at the opposite bank they count them-

---

the Brahman caste, and the connecting of 'I' with that caste connects Self with it; in the same way, similar knowledge in respect to each individual self is fit to be used as a means for attaining emancipation, for as in the next verse, by transplanting self from the physical body, caste, etc., on account of contradiction they imply when he comes to exclaim "I am Brahma" his emancipation is an accomplished fact, for the ignorance and the materials for future re-birth are all destroyed by knowledge. And for such a purpose the *Sruti* has used the word 'this' (*ayam.*)

* Intelligence stands in no need of discovery by any extraneous means, hence always manifested. Then again, the instrument of 'envelopment' is also wanting for which it is always visible. If intelligence were to have 'envelopment' [ignorance has it only] it will be reduced to the condition of insentiency.

selves, but strange to say, whoever counts, forgets always to include himself, and comes to stop at number nine, though the tenth (himself) is visibly present to all. Thus bewildered,

24. They exclaim that their 'tenth' is missing, and virtually he must have perished by drowning. This force of ignorance is called its 'envelopment' (*avarana*).

25. Fully believing that their "tenth person" has perished in the river, and is now no more, they bewail his loss, and vent to tears. This is due to the creating or superimposition (*Vikshep*) of ignorance.

26. At this juncture, a stranger came up—he had not been similarly affected by ignorance—and said, your tenth person has not perished; on hearing his word they got invisible knowledge of the tenth, resembling men's knowledge of *Swarga* and the several abodes.

27. Then when he shewed them their tenth by counting over, and pointed out the mistake and how it did occur, they left off crying and were very glad to find their missing number.

28. As in the previous illustration, we have the several conditions of ignorance, to wit:—envelopment, creation, invisible knowledge, visible knowledge, joy and dissipation of grief, so how self, is to be considered by attaching these seven conditions consecutively to him is shewn in the following manner.

29. Engrossed in their usual avocations and worldly concerns, when men are unable to know the real nature of self, it is called ignorance;

30. And the absence or want of manifestibility of self in that condition is called envelopment; as to regard him as an agent and instrument is akin to the creating power of the same ignorance. And they exclaim "There is no uniform intelligence." "It is not manifested," etc. [The attribution of the reflected shadow of intelligence together with the subtle and gross bodies to self, *i.e.*, to mistake them with him has for its cause the same (*Vikshep*) projecting force of ignorance.]

31. When there follows an invisible knowledge of the uniform intelligence as for instance, "It exists," from the self-evident postulates of the *Shastras*, and subsequently by due consideration, profound thinking and discrimination, an individual perceives that he is no other than the same uniform intelligence, it is called visible knowledge.

32. Then again, when by casting aside the ideas of agent and instrument with regard to that intelligence, a person is freed from experiencing delight or pain, and finally as a successful result of that knowledge experiences blissfulness, that is called dissipation of pain and satiety.

33. These conditions of 'ignorance,' 'concealment,' 'creation,' 'invisible' and 'visible knowledge,' 'dissipation of grief,' and 'delight in the form of satiety' are conditions of the individual only, and not of the uniform intelligence.

34. They are the ordinary cause of bondage and emancipation. Of them, ignorance with its powers of envelopment and creation, super-imposition, or projection are the cause of bondage: while the rest are the source of emancipation.

35. With the view of determining the nature of ignorance and its two powers, ignorance is now being declared. Wise persons* in their prior conditions had always comported themselves like persons quite indifferent; for instance they would say "we know nothing,"—which is another name for ignorance.

36. The nature of envelopment and its actions is thus set forth:—To throw aside the method of the *Shastras* and depending entirely upon arguments to say "There is no uniform intelligence and it is never manifested"—in short to act in opposition to what conduces to its knowledge or perception is a result of 'envelopment.'

---

* '*Vikshep*' signifies projection, superimposition, creation, or want of apprehension.

37 Creation or projection (*Vikshep*) is thus illustrated. To attribute the physical and subtle bodies, with the reflex intelligence (*Jiva*), to the abiding uniform intelligence is a result of this force of ignorance. It is the source of bondage; and belief concerning self as an agent or instrument (a doer of action) is its result.

38. But as prior to its arising, the force of creation or projection was absent, it may be said to speak of ignorance and envelopment as conditions of that projection is improper; it is therefore cleared :—Though it may be wanting in that prior state yet as its impress (*sanskara*) is present, therefore to look upon ignorance and its envelopment as conditions of *Vikshep* [reflex intelligence] imply no contradiction.

39. Ignorance and envelopment for their priority of continuance to *Vikshep* cannot be regarded as a condition of self [because he is unrelated and is therefore subject to no condition (unconditioned), hence ultimately it comes to this, that ignorance and envelopment are simply conditions of the reflex intelligence.

40. If it be said, instead of admitting the impress of projection (which is uncertain and not well-known) for regarding ignorance and envelopment as its condition, they can be attributed to the Supreme Brahma, and looked in the light of Its condition; the reply is, such an admission is clearly untenable for all objects are merely raised on the Parabrahma—hence their source—and they are conditions of the Jiva.

41. If it be said, the conditions which follow subsequent to the origin of 'projection' as for instance, "I am a doer," "I am a theosophist," "I am free from grief," "I am content," are found to belong to the individual and are not dependent on Brahma.

42. To that I do not disagree; for "I am ignorant, and the presence, being and manifestibility of the Supreme Brahma are not conceivable to me." In this way, the two prior

conditions of ignorance and envelopment are clearly rendered apparent to belong to the individual; hence they are his conditions.

43. Ignorance is not a condition of the Supreme Brahma and what previous professors have said regarding It, as the source or refuge of ignorance, has been only for the purpose of describing the abiding seat of Brahma. And for the conceit of all men in ignorance, it has been admitted as the condition of the Individual; this is particularly declared here.

44. Thus then having done with a description of the three conditions, ignorance, envelopment and projection—the source of bondage—it is proposed now to enter into a consideration of the sources of 'emancipation,' *viz.*, invisible and visible knowledge. By these two varieties of knowledge when ignorance is dispelled, the two varieties of envelopment which enshroud the perception and existence of Parabrahma, "It is not manifested," "There is no Parabrahma," are also destroyed.

45. The nature of that knowledge which destroys each particular kind of envelopment is now being defined. By the invisible knowledge is removed the envelopment of non-existence [of the Parabrahma] with its cause ignorance; and by the visible is destroyed want of perception together with its cause ignorance. (Invisible knowledge produces the perception "Brahma is" and this affirmation destroys the negation "There is no Brahma." Visible knowledge, on the other hand, brings in the perception "I am Brahma," consequently as no one can say that he sees not himself, therefore the want of manifestibility is removed too].

46. With the destruction of want of manifestibility,—the first form of envelopment—illusory attribution of the conditions of a Jiva to the supreme self—He is an agent, a doer of action, etc.,—are all destroyed and grief and infatuation cease altogether to affect [the theosophist].

47. With the destruction of the bonds which hurl an

individual to re-incarnation, all grief and enchantment lose their hold, and the theosophist then enjoys contentment and supreme felicity.

48. The *Sruti* likewise says concerning the realisation of content both from a removal of grief and from visible knowledge as a condition of the individual—"He who knows Self to be eternal, free, and no other than the Supreme Brahma has no more desire left in him, which to accomplish, he must wish to inherit a fresh body.—He acquires supreme contentment."

49. It has been previously mentioned that visible knowledge is divided into two varieties, of which the self-manifestibility of the subject [of that knowledge] is the first, and the visible perception by intellect, the second variety.

50. As in that first variety—self-manifestibility of the subject—so during invisible knowledge too, the self-manifestibility is equal, therefore in both of them, the existence of the self-manifested Parabrahma is established.

51. Instead of declaring "I am the Supreme Brahma," to say "Brahma is" signifies invisible knowledge; from an absence of contradiction it cannot be regarded as an error.

52. If the subject of the undisputable nature of visible knowledge be proved untrue, "There is no Brahma," then the visible knowledge is refuted or made to disappear; but since there are no forcible proofs to that end, hence visible knowledge is never subjected to refutation.

53. But there are others who raise objections to the reliability of visible knowledge. They deny its freedom from error; for say they, from an absence of form in Brahma, visible knowledge is a modification of error. But this may equally apply to knowledge pertaining to the blissful abode of heaven. [Hence it is said] if for an absence of bringing in particular knowledge, the 'visible' be regarded to be a form of error, then since no particular knowledge can be produced of *Swarga*, but only its existence can ordinarily be made

known, that should also be erroneous. That is to say, it cannot be pointed out definitely as "This is the Heaven," but there is a perception of its existence as "Heaven is," therefore this ordinary knowledge or perception of the existence of Heaven will alike be fallacious.

54. A third form of error takes this shape. "Brahma is properly to be known by the invisible knowledge, hence the application of visible knowledge is fallacious." But that is not the case. That is to say, the subject of Brahma and Its non-difference with each individual self which is fit to form the subject of visible knowledge, stands not in the least chance of error like the 'invisible.' And why is visible knowledge of Brahma free from error or mistake? Because "Brahma is invisible." In this way, for a want of Its adequacy for being visible, the invisible knowledge of Brahma is free from fallacy. But why is that knowledge invisible? Because there is a want of that definite perception as "This is Brahma."

55. A fourth form of error may arise, and one may say, "From a want of accepting a part of the visible is fallacious. In other words, notwithstanding the accepting of the parts of Brahma, the non-accepting of each witnessing part, from the visible knowledge is erroneous. It amounts to this then, that the presence of ignorance in any part of knowledge concerning an object is a source of error. If this were to hold true, knowledge of a jar, a piece of cloth, [formed bodies,] etc., must alike be erroneous, inasmuch as that knowledge cannot occupy all the parts of the jar, etc., [its interior for instance]. Thus then bodies with form are necessarily revealed partly, while another part remains unknown; but in the case of Brahma which is formless, how can it be said that Its parts are not discovered? [The reply is] to impute parts to Brahma and reduce it to a presonality is not fit for consideration. From distinction or difference in the parts which are fit for being interdicted and are unfit for being entertained,

Brahma though formless will be reduced to the condition of one with parts.

56. What are the two parts fit for interdiction? They are non-existence and want of manifestibility [imperceptibility]. The first is removed by the invisible and the last by visible knowledge.

57. That the invisible knowledge of a subject that is fit to be known visibly is not erroneous [the third form of error] is established from the following example. As in the instance of the "tenth person." "Tenth is," can be called clear invisible knowledge. Similarly "Brahma is," an instance of clear invisible knowledge, and in both, the envelopment of ignorance is alike. (It need hardly be said that as in the case of the missing 'tenth person' the assertion of a trustworthy person who comes to the spot and says the tenth is [living] produces invisible knowledge to his comrades (invisible, because he has not pointed out the person yet, and said "This is the tenth," or "here is your tenth,") and as that is clear or free from error—similarly the knowledge produced by the expression '[Brahma is [existent'] is clear and free from error; because the envelopment of non-being removed by ignorance is equal in both of them.

58. If words bring forth invisible knowledge what produces the visible? From the same source with proper discrimination; as "Self is Brahma." A person who full well understands the signification of the phrase has a visible perception of Brahma. Just as in the case of the tenth person "you are the tenth" brings him the visible perception of the tenth.*

---

* According to the deductions of works treating on Non-duality 'means' for the acquisition of the knowledge differ according to the *status* of the qualified individual; that is to say, if he has advanced a good way and belongs to the first class of qualified persons, hearing, consideration and profound contemplation are the means of his knowledge. In the case of a person tolerably

59. Or as in reply to the question who is the tenth person? if you say "you are the tenth," and subsequently counting over the number and reckoning yourself you come to recollect it, similarly by analysing the phrase, "Self is Brahma," Parabrahma becomes visibly perceptible to the mind.

60. Knowledge produced from due analysis and argument is subject neither to inconsistent idea nor doubts. This is now being shewn. In regard to the "tenth person" the knowledge that "I am the tenth" is to be admitted as free from conflicting ideas or doubts; for if a new person were to come and place himself in their middle he will never get confounded and fail to recognise himself as the tenth, leaving aside the stranger. [Similarly in regard to self, knowledge produced by the phrase "Self is Brahma" brings in the clear perception that his *Atma* is Brahma, and when this is firmly seated in his intellect, he is said to perceive it visibly.

61. In the first place then the phrase "Brahma is" helps knowledge of Its existence, and that is 'the invisible.' Subsequently the expression "you are the Supreme Brahma," the introduction of person* tends to produce the visible perception of Brahma as non-distinct from him.

62. In this manner, knowledge of Parabrama can never be confounded, when it is once visibly perceived or seated in the intellect, either with the five sheaths, foodful and the rest, or any thing else.

63. From the indication of birth, etc., the sage Vrigu first obtained an insight of the invisible Brahma; and

---

qualified, worship of the Impersonal Brahma without any attributes is the means of knowledge. In both instances, keeping up a continuous current of the mental function is an uncommon cause for knowledge.

* 'Vyakti' literally means a person; and as non-duality holds every one to be non-distinct from Brahma, hence each non-distinct Brahma refers to the individual.

subsequently by discrimination and direct reference, a clear perception, in the following manner. "From Whom these elements have been derived, to whom all things owe their life, etc, is Brahma." Now then, hearing brought forth invisible perception of Brahma as the cause of the origin and destruc- of the universe; subsequently by analysis he discriminated It to be distinct from the foodful and the rest of the sacs, so that each individual self is Brahma, and accordingly came to realize it clearly.

64. He had received instruction from his father on the invisible knowledge of the Supreme Brahma only, and though Its visible perception in the form of "Thou art Brahma" was never given him, yet by the first method he had been taught to hold It to be distinct from the foodful sac, etc.;

65. So that, by ascertaining the unreality of these sacs over and over, he was led to conclude self to be non-distinct from Brahma by Its indications of blissfulness, and realized It accordingly.

66. "Brahma is truth, knowledge and infinite." In this manner, after having spoken of the indications, It is further described as present in each individual (in the form of Self); for It is situate inside the five sacs (and he who knows that, has no more duality in him).

67. The two last verses quoted from the *Taitirya Upanishad* render it clear, how in the case of the sage Vrigu, knowledge marked by invisibility ultimately led to the visible perception of Brahma. It is further corroborated by the evidence of the *Chhandogya Upanithad* "Indra derived this invisible knowledge by the indications of self, in the following manner:—What is unrelated to the body and action, undecaying, eternal, and devoid of grief is Self. Actuated with the desire of obtaining visible perception, or clear insight of the Supreme Brahma, he repaired to *Guru* four mes with

the usual bundle of fire-wood as a present." (*Chhandogya Upanishad*, Chapter VIII).

68. The *Aitariya Upanishad* is also to the same purpose. "In the beginning, there was the secondless Parabrahma." Now this is an indication of the invisible, for it simply establishes the existence, and does not particularize It either with one thing or another. Hence the subsequent attribution of illusion and its withdrawal helps to bring forth the visible perception by the indications of that visibility, *viz.*, truth, knowledge and infinite.

69. Other *Sruti* utterances help the visible knowledge of Brahma, as the transcendental phrase does the 'visible.'*

---

* It is worth enquiring whether our sense, perception or the non-distinction of the intelligence of a subject, and that of function of the internal organ is visible knowledge? Or whether the knowledge of a subject having a present relation with one who gives evidence [*pramata*] is so called? Carrying the enquiry further we may multiply instances:—it may be asked whether knowledge produced by proper proofs concerning an adequate subject having a present relation with the demonstration (*pramata*) or the uncaused knowledge of improper and worthless proofs of a proper subject with a present relation, of the demonstrating intelligence (*pramana chaitanya*) is 'visible'? Or whether that visible knowledge has for its indication that which is conformable to the practise of self, non-different from the subject of uncovered intelligence [wanting in envelopment]? That clever Vedantin Nischal Dass Swami, the author of *Vritti Parvakar*, has entered into an examination of this indication, but this is hardly the place to introduce his metaphysical disquisitions; suffice it to say, that visible knowledge is of two sorts, (*a*) ascertaining (*avijna*) and (*b*) recognition (*pratyavijna*). When from prior impressions and connection of sense, a thing is known, it is called recognition (*pratyavijna*). It is of this form "That is this." Here even, modification [of the mental function produced by the relation] of sensory organ pervades the subject, for which non-distinction is produced between the two intelligences, *viz.*,—of the mental

70. Therefore, for a knowledge of the visibility of Brahma, one should always ascertain the significations of the transcendental phrase ; and there can be no contention about it.

71. The indication of the transcendental phrase 'That art Thou' is now being set forth :—Intelligence associated with the internal organ sustaining* the perception of Self or

---

modification and of the subject. Knowledge proceeding from the sensory organ takes the form "This is" it is called (*avijna pratkshya*) known before. But in the principal *Siddhanta*, prior impression of a thing known before as for instance, the knowledge conveyed by the expression "That is this," "That," the portion represented by 'that' is in the form of recollection, hence invisible, and 'this' visible ; for which 'that is this' is a mixture of invisible with visible perception and not the latter only. For its being external and internal, each variety of visible knowledge is either external or internal. Now the former has five more sub-divisions from the organ through which that knowledge is brought about :—aural, cuticular, ocular, palatal, and olfactory. The internal, on the other hand, has two sub-divisions, *atmogochara* and *anatmogochara*. The first for its being predicate of self is sub-divided into two and the last is into three varieties, on account of indicating the perception of Thou, and That, and their non-difference.

* We have seen it mentioned three different forms of indications implied by a word. They require a passing notice, for intance, "A jar." Here the jar is said to be the subject of both its function (a water carrying vessel, etc.,) and the word itself. Now the function is situated in the internal organ and the word is situated in the tongue and the jar itself rests on the ground, so that the three are different ; similarly the function of self (*aham*) and the subject of the word, is intelligence of the internal organ Jiva, and here "self" (function) is situated in the internal organ, the word has for its site the tongue, and the subject—the endowed intelligence of the internal organ rests on its own dignity, so that, the function is distinct from the word self. Though for that function being subordinate to the mind, it is non-distinct from Jiva, yet as there is difference between a jar and its ether,

individuality and manifested by becoming the subject of that word ['Self'],is indicated by the word 'Thou.' In other words, consciousness manifested in the form of "I am I"—the intellectual soul associated with the internal organ—and forming the subject of that word [*aham* or egoity] is the predicate of 'Thou.'

72. The literal signification of 'That' is now being defined. The associated intelligence of Maya which is the cause of the Universe, the indication of omniscience, the property of invisibility—which is existent, intelligence, and bliss is the predicate of the word 'That.'

73. When the same Parabrahma is said to be visible and invisible, finite and infinite, limited and whole, that is to say with properties naturally opposed to each other, it therefore can be ascertained by recourse to Indication [of abondaning the conflicting portion].

74. As in the phrase "That Devadatta is this," 'that' refers to past time and 'this' to the present time, both have reference to the same person, but by omitting the conflicting element according to the canons of the indication of abandoning a part, Devadatta alone is meant. Similarly by abandoning the conflicting part from the signification of the transcendental phrase "That art Thou" there remains the non-conflicting Intelligence which is meant* hence the indication of abandoning a part is easily admissible.

---

on account of distinction in their nature and properties, similarly for the qualification of the mind and the property of its intelligence being distinct, for all practical purposes a difference between Jiva and the mind or internal organ is maintained, consequently there is distinction between the function of self and the word. Then again the indicative indication of the word self is the illumination of function, *viz.*, the uniform intelligence, which is entirely different from that function. This is what is meant.

* 'That' and 'Thou' are marked by the qualities of invisibility and visibility, a result of associ ate, so if from intelligence,

75. It is not possible to include the relative and predicated signification in the meaning of the phrase 'That art Thou' but as to their referring to one Impartite, there can be no question and that has been admitted by all learned men. [For instance, in the ordinary phrase "Bring the cow." It is said that the verb 'to bring' reminds a person of the desire* of the speaker; in short the servant is asked to obey

---

which is common to them both, the conflicting element of invisibility and visibility be abandoned, there remains only intelligence.

That is to say :—

Intelligence + Invisibility = Intelligence + Visibility; striking off invisibility and visibility we have Intelligence = Intelligence.

* In Logic the source of the sense of a word depends either upon the property of its force or that of its indication. But there are four other varieties of sense (1) desire; (2) fitness; (3) purport; and (4) proximity, connection or relation between two proximate terms and the sense they convey; for instance, "Bring the cow." Here a desire is expressed; when there is a relation between the sense of one word with another, it is called fitness, as the relation of 'cow' with the verb 'bring,' here the relation is that of a subject and predicate; for the person who has been asked to bring the cow is the subject of the verb 'bring' which is the predicate of that person. Desire of a speaker is called purport, when the speaker addressing another orders him to bring the *Gam*, it expresses that desire, in a variety of ways according to the time of the day: for example, if it be the time of cooking, it should signify fire; if during bathing it should convey the sense of water, and during milking time it would signify a cow, etc. Thus then, as ordinary words are construed according to the time and other incidents connnected with the speaker, so is the purport of *Vedic* phrases to be ascertained from the commentaries in the form of 'the commencement' and 'termination' 'result,' novelty, etc.; and as in human speech the desire of the speaker is ascertained, so in the Vedic utterances the purport is Iswara's desire. The contiguity of words is called proximity. Strength of a fit term and the relation of the property of indication, creat-

his master's wish by bringing the cow, consequently a relation is acknowledged between the words 'bring' and 'cow,' and this is the relative signification. Now for the predicate "A blue and fragrant lotus." Here the lotus is marked by the qualities 'blue' and 'fragrant.' The transcendental phrase 'That art Thou'* is not to be construed like the 'Blue lotus' and that is not allowable; but as one Impartite and pervad-

---

ing no impediment to remember its sense, is also likewise called proximity. In the illustration the two terms 'cow' and 'bring' are contiguously placed, likewise the strength creates no impediment in recollecting the sense to bring the cow, hence it is proximate. Thus then, we find the source or cause of ascertaining the purport of a term, depends upon desire, fitness, purport and contiguity which are so many causes, and no term can be construed without them. This stands true in the case of all words.

* As for instance, "you bring the cow." Here there is a close connection or say relation between the subject 'you,' the object, 'cow' and the predicate 'bring'; and the sense is plain enough, as it asks another to fulfil the speaker's desire; and this sense with the relative connection is the purport. It is an example of proximity. So in the construction of a transcendental phrase, it is quite inapplicable, for if it be said let the word 'That' indicate the meaning of the word 'Thou' and *vice versa* by relation and proximity, then it will tell against other *Sruti* texts where it has been laid down. "That is unassociated, unconditioned." 'That' is marked by invisibility and 'Thou' refers to intelligence marked by visibility, hence the one is incompatible with the other.

Neither can the sentence be construed literally as 'the lotus is blue,' for here the literal sense suits, inasmuch as between the words 'blue' and 'lotus' there is the relation of subject and predicate, as blue excludes other colors as white, green, red, etc., and lotus, such other substances as cloth, jar, etc. Thus then, we see the necessity, why in construing the necessity, why in construing the sentence 'That art Thou' the use of a subject and relation does not apply, and therefore it is to be construed after the canons of Indication.

ing everywhere in all things is the purport admitted by all learned men, hence to have recourse to indication is proper.

76. The meaning of Impartite is thus set forth. Who is discovered in the form of each individual intelligence, is secondless and blissful; and who is secondles and blissful and discovered in the form of individuated intellect. In other words the intellectual soul present in each individual and manifested in the form of Witnessing Intelligence is the Secondless Supreme Self and full of bliss. And that Supreme Self is non-different from, but one with, the individuated Self, Intelligence, Intellect, or Perception (*Bodha*).

77. When the identity or oneness of Brahma and Individnated Self is thoroughly ascertained [without any lingering trace of doubt], then only the meaning of the word 'Thou' referring to individuated Self ceases to impart the idea that it does not signify Brahma.

78. And there is likewise a similar cessation of invisibility in the signification of 'That.' That is to say, mistake lands the individual into the disbelief of his oneness with Brahma, and Brahma is the subject of invisible knowledge. Both of them cease when non-duality has been firmly established as a result of ascertaining the meaning of Impartite. And if it be asked of what use are they? To make the individuated Self occupied in the fullness of bliss.

79. Thus then, the visibility of the Supreme Brahma follows as a result of knowledge of 'That art Thou' and this has been clearly established in the aforesaid manner; if any one were to say it is otherwise, and no visible knowledge follows, he surely is ignorant of the purport of the inferences derived from the *Shastras*.

80. If it be said, let the *Shastras* draw their conclusions and build upon them the visible knowledge from the indication of 'That art Thou,' but the fact is otherwise and it is possible for obtaining invisible knowledge in the same way as one knows the blissful abode of heaven, but to say so

is unjust, as already mentioned in the case of the "tenth person."

81. If you attribute invisible knowledge to result from 'That art Thou,' it will do away with your visibility and you who are engaged in ascertaining the nature of Brahma will be invisible. What a fallacy, and how very unnatural your inferences are.

82. As in ordinary usage, it is said, "For increasing it one loses his capital," that exactly applies in your case, and we have an instance of its truth exemplified in your reasoning.

83. If you say, intelligence of Jiva for its associate of the internal organ may properly be regarded as visible, but as Brahma is unassociated It cannot be so regarded (visible):

84. But Brahma is not so unassociated, because without the associated condition, it is impossible to form a conception of Its principle or nature, and so long as a person does not merge into the Non-dual after death, the associated cannot be done away with.

85. But this need not necessarily indicate there is difference in the associates of Jiva and Brahma. The presence or absence of the internal organ constitutes that difference in associate.*

86. Just as the presence of the internal organ, [its conditional relationship] forms the associate why is the absence or want of that organ to prevent a similar associate? Now here we have an 'admission' and 'exclusion.' The first associated existence [the conditional relationship of the internal organ] comes under admission, while its want is exclusion; and though both of them are associates, yet there is a difference between them of being and not being, existence and non-existence, and for this difference they are fit to be

* Says Madhusudan Swami. So long as actions continue the associate creates the difference in the condition of [Jiva and Brahma] and this is said to be the indication of an associate.

disregarded; in the same way, as a chain made of gold or iron though different so far as the metals are concerned but in the matter of inflicting punishment and confining a person's motion, they have no difference whatever and therefore no attention paid to it.

87. Professors of Self-knowledge have ascertained both 'admission' and 'exclusion' as means to that end. For instance, by the exclusion of phenomena [material Universe which is non-real and non-existent except in our senses—illusion] and admission of noumena, [Brahma which alone is real hence 'being,'] the *Vedanta* seeks to expound Brahma with a view of obtaining self-knowledge.*

88. But objection may be taken to this view, for it may be asked since the *Vedanta* seeks to expound 'That' (Brahma) by the exclusion of 'Not-That' [phenomena]; similarly for a community of reference between the words '*aham*' indicating the Uniform Intelligence, and Brahma, introduction of the Indication of abandoning a part, will fail to establish the perception "I am Brahma." And the reply is,—The indication of abandoning in regard to individuality applies only to the part marked by insentiency, as for instance the physical

---

* 'That' refers to Brahma. 'Not-That' signifies the objective world. Therefore 'That' is not 'Not-that,' and 'Not-that' is not 'That.' This is the method used in expounding the Reality of Brahma, and Its eternity, knowledge, and infinity. In other words, what is not Brahma, is this vast material expanse, therefore this vast expanse is not Brahma. And this is non-existent, it exists relatively to our senses, which is an illusion. For in sleep, we have no more relation with it, and it apparently ceases to exist; so in *pralaya* it exists not, hence it naturally follows, that as it does not exist in all time, it is impermanent, but this does not apply to Brahma, for it is 'Not-That' and the properties of 'Not-that' cannot be attributed to 'That' which is its extreme reverse. Hence Brahma is eternal, etc. In this manner, the Vedantin seeks to expound Brahma.

body, etc., and not to the Uniform Intelligence. [That is to say, if the gross body, organs, sensory and active, vital airs, mind, and thinking, be excluded from 'I am I' the remaining Intelligence is one with Brahma, hence the perception 'I am Brahma' is a natural result.

89. By abandoning the internal organ from the signification of the word (*Aham*) egoism or individuality, the remaining Witness Intelligence is rendered visible by the expression "I am Brahma."

90. Though this witness Intelligence is self-illumined, yet it is a subject of pervasion by intellect like other insentient subjects, a jar, etc., but the authors of the *Shastras* have interdicted the employment of the pervasion of result to determine it. [For, the result refers to the reflected shadow of intelligence, and that cannot be required in the case of perceiving what is self-illumined].

91. In the case of an insentient object, both the intellect and reflected shadow of intelligence situated there, pervade that 'jar'; and the necessity consists in this, that ignorance which envelops a jar is removed by intellect, and reflection of intelligence renders its visible.

92. With regard to Brahma the pervasion of intellect—function of the internal organ—is admitted for the destruction of ignorance which rests there, and as it is self-illumined, it manifests without the pervasion of the reflected shadow of intelligence, a resulting product of intellect.

93. As for finding out a jar in a dark room, the eyes and light of a lamp are both needed, and for that lamp, eyes simply are enough; similarly for the destruction of ignorance which envelops it, and for rendering it visible, both the pervasion of function and its reflection of intelligence are requisite; but for the cognition or discovery of Brahma, the pervasion of function is alone necessary.

94. Though this 'reflex' is situated in function, yet it is one with Brahma, and does not produce any increased results

in it, like what happens in the case of a jar, etc. To be more explicit:—If, as in function moulded after the shape of a jar, there is a reflection of intelligence too in the function moulded after Brahma, yet that reflex is not manifested as distinct from Brahma, but like the light of lamp overpowered by the mid-day sun, it is one with It, hence not a source of increasing Its manifestibility.*

95. In support of the pervasion of function and absence of pervasion of the resul,t the evidence of the *Vedas* is now being adduced. "Undemonstrable and unborn." "Brahma is only to be perceived by the mind." "An Intelligent person, knows Brahma to be changeless, infinite, uncaused, and undemonstrable (*i. e.*, not capable of being cognised by the sensory organs), unexampled, and unborn, is freed from re-births." (*Sruti*). Regarding it, the *Amritabindu Upanishad* says the word undemonstrable is meant to convey the exclusion of the pervasion of result.†

* Subsequent to knowledge, the individual Intelligence merges into the Supreme Brahma and becomes one, but that does not produce any increase of results like what follows in the case of an insentient object after ignorance has been removed from it by that function, and we come to view its several parts both in and out, by the reflex intelligence.

† "Brahma is only to be perceived by the mind." And "Which the mind cannot conceive" imply no contradiction. Because the mental function can only destroy the Ignorance concerning the Brahma, it cannot discover the absolute; [thus fulfilling the first condition] and because the reflected Intelligence is powerless to discover It (this has already been explained) [necessarily, therefore, the mind in such a case cannot conceive of it]. On this subject the authors of the Shastras "have interdicted the use of the reflected Intelligence, but have advised to dispel the ignorance which rests on It, by the agency of the mental function, for discovering the Supreme Brahma," because "It is light itself and therefore for any other object to illuminate

96. In the opening verse of the present treatise it has already been said :—" He who knows his individuated self to be one with Brahma, has no more desire left in him, to gratify which, he is to follow a physical body and grow old." Now this perception is called visible knowledge.

97. 'Visible knowledge' is produced by a right understanding of the transcendental phrase 'That art Thou.' But to make it firm, it is necessary again to have recourse to 'hearing' 'consideration' and 'profound contemplation.' This is the firm conviction of all professors of Self-knowledge.

98. As for instance, "Till the knowledge of 'I am Brahma' is firmly fixed in the perception of an individual, he should practise passivity, self-control, and the rest along with hearing, consideration, and profound contemplation."

99. In that firmness of visible knowledge there are obstacles such as 'impossible ideas' and 'inconsistent or antagonistic ideas.'

---

or discover It, is impossible," [what is light cannot be discovered by another object].

"Between the cognition of an inanimate object, as a jar, a cloth, etc., and the cognition of Brahma there is this difference. In the first instance (this jar, etc., the mental function assumes the shape of, or pervades through, the unknown jar and dispels the Ignorance which rests there ; by its reflected Intelligence, it then discovers or renders it visible. As is mentioned in the *Shastras* :—"The mental perception and its indwelling reflex Intelligence both occupy the jar, the first dispels the ignorance about it, the second brings it out to view, *i.e.*, renders it visible." As the light of a lamp taking possession of such articles, 'a jar,' 'a cloth,' etc., as occupy a dark corner, dispels the surrounding darkness and brings them out to view by its own brilliance, so the mental function after dispelling the Ignorance which occupies an unknown jar, brings it out or renders it cognisable to the senses by its indwelling reflex Intelligence."—DHOLE's *Vedantasara*, p. 43.

100. If from a difference of desire, and difference in the branches* of the *Vedas*, works and sacrifices enjoined in several varieties should cause any embarassment or obstruction to the firmness of visible knowledge, it is therefore necessary that one should repeatedly, over and over, have recourse to the means, 'hearing' and the 'rest.'

101. But what is hearing? The purport of the *Vedanta* in the beginning, middle and end, deals exclusively on the oneness of individual self and Brahma; to know this for certain is called 'hearing.'†

---

* The Sanskrit word '*shakha*' has been converted into 'branch'; of it *Rig Veda* has 21, *Sam* 1,000, *Yajur* 109, and *Atharva* 50 branches. Vyas divided one Veda into four parts and subdivided them into branches as above; each branch has had its representative or follower, then it is difficult to say if it is yet so. But this much is certain that the practices enjoined in the several branches are not indiscriminately adopted by all alike, but by the particular sect who is a follower of that branch, and each branch has one *Upanishad*: generally the names of the branch and its corresponding *Upanishad* are identical, and we have altogether 1180 Branches and *Upanishads*, of which 840 *Upanishads* deal on works and are called *Karmakanda*. and 232 treat on the worship of Brahma for which they are called *Upasanakanda*. But authors include devotional exercise in works therefore all the above are classed under the *Karmakānda* leaving 108 which help the cognition of Brahma; and as these are the concluding portions of the Vedas, or contain the essence of their doctrines, they are called Vedanta or *Jnanakanda*.

† The means for ascertaining Brahma are:—

1. In the beginning and the end.
2. Repetition.
3. Novelty.
4. Result.
5. Illustration by praise.
6. Illustrating by supporting arguments.

102. In the first chapter of the *Shariraka Sutras*, Vyas defines 'hearing' in the manner just mentioned. What prevents to stem away impossible ideas concerning the oneness of individual self and Brahma, that is to be demonstrated, is termed consideration in the second chapter of the same work.

103. The method by which uncomformable ideas regarding non-duality are removed or destroyed is now being declared :—from settled convictions [impressions] of several prior births, and from a consciousness of the physical and subtle bodies being none other but self, the reality of objective world is apt to arise in the perception over and over.

104. This is called an uncomformable, inconsistent or antagonistic idea, and is removed by an earnestness of the mind, *i.e.*, profound contemplation which is produced by devotional exercises on the Brahma with attributes [Personal] from the precepts of a professor concerning It.

105. Since from the worship of the Supreme Brahma is produced 'earnestness' therefore the *Vedanta* insists on the propriety of that worship as a means to the practice of earnestness of mind. But if on the other hand, a person receives instruction on the worship of the Impersonal Brahma, without his having practised earnestness, his devotional exercises will help him to that end and there is no doubt about it.

106. Now the practice of the Impersonal worship is being set forth. To think on the light of Brahma, to study the utterances on the subject, to fix it in the perception by argument and analysis, and constantly to meditate on It are called the practice of the Impersonal worship.

107. "A qualified person possessed of the four means for the acquisition of self-knowledge and actuated with a desire for release, regards each individuated self as the Supreme self, and without any trace of doubt left concerning their oneness and non-duality, devotes himself earnestly to assimilate this solemn truth into knowledge and leaves off speaking, dwelling upon, or thinking on things that are no-t

self: for, speaking entails labor on the tongue, as thinking does on the mind."

108. To the same end, the *Sruti* says [*Gita* Chap. IX., v. 22.] "He who contemplates self to be one with, and non-different from Brahma and always worships me [Krishna] in that way, for him I bring about the accomplishment of the several varieties of *Yoga*, called acquisition of the unattained, and preservation of what has already been attained."

The *Sruti* and *Smriti* are cited by way of illustration:— For the purpose of keeping away antagonistic ideas, in regard to self they insist upon creating an earnestness of the intellect; and that always.

110. The mistaken notions of the body, organs, etc., being identical with self and the reality of phenomena, are called antagonistic ideas. It may be asked why? To account for it, the indications of antagonistic ideas are being cited. To perceive a thing in a way different from its actual condition is called antagonistic idea. As for instance, when nacre is preceived as silver, its original condition of shell is left out of consideration and it is perceived in a different light. In the same way, to perceive self to be one with the physical body and the rest is to leave out of consideration his actual condition and introduce something quite foreign to his nature. Similarly, the belief or perception of a disobedient son, that his father is his enemy, is an antagonistic idea.

111. Now self is distinct from the physical body etc., and phenomena are unreal, yet to believe in an opposite direction and confound him with the body and the rest, and to believe in the permanence of the objective world is nothing else but an antagonistic idea.

112. But it has been said, that an antagonistic idea is removed by earnestness of the mind. This is now being particularly set forth. By constant dwelling on the actual condition of self, and considering his difference from the body and the rest, as also by regarding the impermanence of all

material objects and constantly fixing it in the mind, the intellect is cleared of all antagonistic ideas. Hence it is said, a person desirous of release should never cease to think on the impermanence and unreality of phenomena and the distinction of self from the body, organs of sense, mind, etc.

113. A dissenter stops to enquire whether there are any rules required, like the performance of devotional exercise, for bringing about the perception of distinction of self with the body, etc., and the unreality of material phenomena. Whether like the recanting of sacred texts, or meditating on the image of Vishnu, etc., it is necessary that one should adopt certain rules in bringing about the perception of distinction of self from the body, etc., and the unreality of the universe, or it follows as a matter of course, without the observance of any rules like the ordinary practices in vogue amongst men.

114. The reply is. To dwell upon the actual condition of self and the material universe constantly, requires no other rules, because of its result being visibly perceptible. As for instance, a person desirous of satisfying the cravings of hunger, observes no rules like the performance of a devotional exercise to appease it while sitting at dinner, on the other hand, eats till he is satiated.

115. A hungry person whether at his dinner, or without it, or by any other means, out of his own desire appeases it. That is to say, when his dinner is ready he eats, when it is not, he engages his mind in play or something else, so as to spend the time and divert his attention from the pangs of hunger, or in conversation or sleep; anyhow, he eats his dinner out of his desire. Therefore the visible result of eating is to appease or remove the pangs of hunger, but so far as the *Sruti* and *Smriti* are concerned, the rules laid down there refer to an hereafter (after death) and not for a destruction of the pangs attendant on hunger.

116. The difference between devotional exercise and

hunger is thus being declared :—There are rules to be observed because if left undone, sin or de-merit is produced, and if performed indifferently, *i.e.*, the sacred texts pronounced without attending to the long and short accents, or incorrectly, they fail to produce the desired result; but on the other hand, prove injurious or harmful to the worshipper, as happened to Vretrasur from incorrect pronounciation. Thus then, the propriety of observing rules in the performance of worship or devotion is plainly established.

117. Antagonistic ideas are a source of perceptible grief, like the pangs of hunger, and it is proper, therefore, by some means or other, to conquer them. But for that conquest, there is no consecutive beginning. In other words, the grief brought about by antagonistic ideas is easily experienced, therefore self-evident, and meditation removes it, so that for the destruction of that visible grief—its result is visible too—there is no necessity for any rules, but it is proper that one should begin to meditate without them.

118. Now the means for the prevention of antagonistic ideas—to dwell on Brahma constantly, etc.,—have already been mentioned. There are no such rules as are enjoined in worship to sit with the face towards the east; but as in worshipping the Saligram one dwells mentally on Vishnu, so one may apprehend the rule here is to produce an unswerving earnestness of the mind and to fix it on Brahma. But on that concentrating of the mind on Brahma, like contemplation, there is no rule nor restraint.

119. Casting aside thoughts of other objects, to dwell constantly with the mind on some particular form of Deva, with undivided attention is called Contemplation (*Dhyana*). And there are injunctions for practising it, for it removes the fickleness or unstability of the mind and steadies it.

120. As for instance in the *Gita* (Chapter VI., v. 34.) "Oh Krishna! I confess the mind to be naturally fickle, causing want of steadiness; strong, so as to be unrestrainable; and

firm in being led away by good and bad objects as to be well nigh impracticable to control it, yet like restraining the air, it is with some pain and inconvenience capable of being subjugated."

122. Vashista says in regard to the difficulty with which it is subjected :—"It is more difficult than draining away a sea, or uprooting the Golden Mountain (*Sumeru*), or eating fire, and such other feats of tradition."

122. Like a body restrained from movement by a chain, there is no restraint for speaking and thinking on Brahma; on the contrary, history and biography, recording, as they do, the lives of great men, create mental enjoyment just as the sight of a dance is enlivening.

123. But that study of history and biography, or hearing them read, does not do away with profound contemplation; for self is intelligence only, and is neither the physical body nor the sensory organs, etc., which are like the objective world material and prone to destruction; and as the purport of historical works and biography go the same way, their literal signification, therefore, does not tell against 'profound contemplation.'

124. Agriculture, commerce, service, etc., together with a study of poetical works, fiction, and the *Nyaya Shastra* produce distraction of the intellect, inasmuch as it is impossible for them to bring in a recollection of the Real Brahma.

125—126. But it may be asked, eating is also alike incapable of creating a remembrance of Reality, and it should be therefore abandoned? The reply is, there can be no extreme mental distraction from eating, and as after it is over, a person comes to remember the Real Brahma, it is therefore not to be abandoned. Thus then, since eating creates only for the time being, a break of the mental flow of recollection which can never be disastrous in its effects, and after it is over, the Reality is all at once recollected, it creates no antagonistic ideas which alone are ruinous, hence not necessary to do away with it.

127. Proofs are now adduced in support of what has been said against Poetry, *Nyaya Shastra*, etc., and their inutility to produce a desire of enquiring after self or creating Self-knowledge. A person engaged in studying *Nyaya* has no leisure to recollect the Supreme Self. But this does not hold exclusively true with regard to it alone; for Poetry and Logic, inasmuch as they are opposed to self-knowledge, make those who study them, forget him altogether.

128. For which, it is necessary that they should be abandoned. To this end the *Sruti* says:—"Know that One-Self and leave other discussions [and studies] aside. He is the bridge gulfing over eternity and leading to emancipation." And "Leave off other words, for they are a source of error;" but constantly abide in him.

129. If it be contended, since there is no interdiction for food, though there is a likelihood of its causing a person forget the Supreme Self while in the act of eating, so to do away with the other *Shastras*, Logic, Poetry, and the rest is not needed. The reply is, since no one can live without food, consequently it is impossible to abandon it, though it may be opposed to the remembrance of self, very slightly; but no harm to life occurs to a person if he abandons studying the other *Shastras*, save and beyond the *Vedanta*. Why then show such eagerness for their study? Since without it, the mind is freed from the shackles of contending doctrines and it comes to realise the perception of the secondless Reality.

130. If it be asked, how could Janak maintain his sovereignty, since the administration of state is against self-knowledge. The reply is, the king had such a firm knowledge of self, that it could not be affected by the duties of his exalted position, though naturally they are conflicting and opposed to one another; if your knowledge, be as firm as his, there is

no restriction for your study or following the occupation of an agriculturist, etc., as you may fix your choice upon.

131. Because, after the world has once been known to be unreal and that knowledge has been confirmed, there is no more experience of misery; a desire of consummation of fructescent works alone remains in a theosophist, and from the force of them springs his inclination for present actions.

132. But that does not necessarily imply a theosophist has any inclination for bad or sinful actions. Do not think his dependence or fructescent works leads him to sin, they simply lead him to perform other works; even assuming such harmful works being actually done by the overwhelming force of fructescent works, there is no resisting them.*

133. Thus then so far as the consummation of fructescent works go, an ignorant person as well as a theosophist are

---

* Two opposite doctrines prevail in regard to restraint or immunity of restraint. There are texts in the *Upanishad* which clearly maintain, a theosophist is no longer bound by any consideration, he may act as best he likes without having anything to dread for their consequence. Because gnosis once arisen destroys the seeds of future re-birth and he is freed in life, only waiting for his emancipation to become an accomplished fact after he parts with his body. Our author is against it, and he contends, in that case what is the difference between a theosophist and a dog that lives on impure food? Nrisinha Sarasawati says, in the face of the texts of Revelation and tradition it is impossible to deny the immunity of a theosophist from all restraints, but it is never intended that he should act thus. They are simply eulogistic of knowledge. In this connection it remains to be observed that there are three sorts of actions mentioned in the Systems, *viz.*, Accumulated (*Sanchita*), Fructescent (*Prarabdha*), and Current (*Kriyamana*). The first and last are destroyed by knowledge, leading unaffected the second which can only be exhausted by enjoying happiness or suffering misery according to the merit or de-merit of a prior birth.

equally circumstanced. If this be contended, their difference is now being declared, to remove it. Though equally placed in that respect, yet a theosophist is patient in his suffering, while an ignorant person is impatient and always clamours for the grief he is subjected to suffer, as a retribution for past actions which have already commenced to bear fruit in the present life.

134. For example, two persons travelling on a road miss their way, their destinations are different, but one of them who knows that he cannot be very far from the village he is bound for, with patience continues to walk, and arrives soon, while the other ignorant of how much distance, he has yet to cover sits by the road-side to rest.

135. One who has a tangible perception of self, and done away with the usual mistake of connecting him with this or that, (the physical body, organs of sense, etc.,) has no more desire left in him for enjoyment. He therefore feels no grief for whatever happens to his body.

136. After knowledge has arisen, when the objective world and its contents are reduced to impermanence, and regarded unreal, a theosophist has no desire for anything left, and in the absence of a desired object, his desire is said to cease; consequently for him there can be no grief or misery [from unfulfilled gratifications]. Just as a lamp is extinguished from want of oil, so are his desires extinguished from want of objects of desire, and with their destruction his grief too is extinguished.

137. But it may be asked, how can want of desired objects produce want of desire? Things produced in a magical performance, from illusion, are never desired by any one, on the other hand, they are discarded and thrown, away simply because they are known to be false.*

---

* Juggler's art flourished to perfection in India, centuries hence; they would create a Mango tree in your presence with

138. Similarly a man of discrimination and judgment is never led away by the fascination of sandal, garland and other sensuous enjoyments, though at first they appear to be very pleasant; but on the contrary, shews an aversion, by considering the impermanence of such pleasures, and he desires them not. [In this way, to attribute the usual defects which all pleasures have naturally in them, is a potent cause of creating supreme indifference for them, which is the key to knowledge].

139. These defects are now being pointed out. For the acquisition of wealth a person has to suffer many hardships, he must go abroad, serve somebody, flatter his vanity or caprice, etc., its accumulation is also attended with several disasters, it excites the envy of some, and cupidity of others, it is to be protected from thieves and robbers, then again when it is lost, a person's grief knows no bounds.

140. Where is the beauty in a woman? She is made of flesh and tendons, fickle in nature; and in her wonderful organ, there is nothing very exquisite.

141. What have thus been mentioned in connection with wealth and women, apply with equal force to all objects, and in the *Shastras* these defects have been declared, so that men constantly dwelling on, or considering them, may shew an aversion for material enjoyment and beget indifference.

142. A person may be extremely pressed by hunger, yet that would not make him desirous of eating poison for satisfying his cravings of food; how then can a person of discrimination who has quenched his thirst with sweets, ever shew the least inclination to take a dish of poisoned food, knowing poison to be there? [In other words, a man of discrimination knows all sensuous enjoyments to be poisonous, and his

---

blossom and fruit, and present them to you pressing you to taste, but no one shews any inclination, because he knows the fruit to be no mango at all.

thirst for them having already been satiated with a full knowledge of their impermanence and defects, he has no more desire for them.]

143. From a predominating influence of fructescent works though a theosophist may be actuated with a desire of enjoying material comforts, yet such enjoyments bring him pain, instead of pleasure, just as in the case of a forced and unpaid working man, he finishes his allotted task with difficulty experiencing pain instead of pleasure.

144. And in the midst of that consummation of the fructescent, a theosophist with faith in knowledge of Brahma but a family man too, always repeats mentally that his fructescent has not even exhausted then, and longs for the day when it will be so.

145. Now this grief of a theosophist is no indication for a longing for the good things of life and regret for the sorrows which his fructescent works are bringing forth, on the contrary it is his supreme indifference for the good and unpleasant, and utter disregard of happiness or its reverse; because he is devoid of illusion and hence free from longing.

146. Then again, in the midst of consummation of the fructescent he suffers pain and therefore he is satisfied with a small share of enjoyment for his discrimination of its transitory duration, unlike the ignorant who are never satiated, though they may have it infinitely [without end].

147. To clear away the misapprehension of an ignorant person being satiated with enjoyment and the inutility of discrimination which makes a theosophist satisfied with little, it is said in the *Sruti*, "Desire of enjoyment can never cease from the acquisition of the object desired, but like butter poured in fire, the more a person enjoys, the more he is desirous of fresh objects of enjoyment to acquire."

148. If the desired object be known to be temporary in duration and the happiness it yields will be short-lived, then only will it produce satiety; just as serving a thief, knowing

him to be so, makes him a friend and he is no more a thief to his accomplice.

149. To a person whose mind has been duly subjugated, and senses restrained or kept away from sensuous objects, little enjoyment is enough, for he knows to a certainty the defects attending it, which are a source of misery. Therefore with a fear of avoiding such inconvenience and pain which all enjoyments have in them, he is satisfied with little, as his share of pain will also be thus minimised:

150. Like a king attacked by a combined force of some of his brother chiefs, despoiled of territories and satisfied with the little that remains, which he considers to be ample, but till he was so attacked and despoiled, his kingdom he regarded to be small and insufficient.

151. If it be alleged how can the fructescent works produce in a theosophist a desire of enjoyment, since he knows clearly from discrimination the usual defects inherent in it?

152. There is no inconsistency whatever in it; for actually we find a variety of fructescent works caused by desire, absence of desire, and at the instance of a second person's desire.

153. These are now being particularly declared. As an instance of the first variety, who may mention the desire of a patient or invalid to eat what is unwholesome; of a thief to steal; of a profligate to enjoy the king's daughter. They know the gratification of such desires will bring forth evil consequences, yet from a force of fructescent they are engaged in them: hence they are called fructescent works caused by desire.

154. Even Iswara is incapable of preventing them from taking effect as pointed out by Sree Krishna in his discourse with Arjuna (Vide *Gita*, Chapt., VI. v. 35).

155. Since therefore a theosophist is subject to the fructescent, what more is to be said of others; all beings are equally affected by them. But then it may be asked, if every

one of us be entirely dependent upon our fructescent works, Of what avail is mental restraint and subjugation of the senses by the practice of *Yoga*?

156. If there would have been the slightest chance of influencing the future course of the fructescent, neither Ramachandra, Yudhisthira, nor Nala of *Purana* celebrity, would then have suffered such extreme and unbroken miseries for several years in succession, as they did.

157. And the impotency of Iswara to influence or control them, does not create any discord in his sovereignty or universal control, for it was his wish that fructescent works would continue to bear fruit, and know of no interruption or modification from any extraneous influence.

158. The second variety of fructescent works caused by an absence of desire, is mentioned in Krishna's discourse with Arjuna, in the third chapter of the *Gita*, commencing with verse 36th. Hear what he says:—

159. Asks Arjuna: When a virtuous man is forced to do a sinful act, like a thief compelled to work in prison, who or what compels him?

160. Krishna. Desire produced by the active quality of the individual, is the cause of destroying meritorious actions and bringing forth injury or de-merit. Anger is another modification of desire, the two incite a person to sinful actions:

161. Therefore Arjuna, when you desire not to do a thing, your fructescent will make you entirely subservient to your desire and anger, and induce you to do that; there is no doubt about it.

162. When there is neither desire nor absence of it, to do a thing, but simply for benefiting a third person, one is induced to do it, and thus made to experience either happiness or its reverse, it is called fructescent works created by a desire of [benefiting] another.

163. Thus then, as from force of fructescent works even the wise are not free from desire, it may be contended, how

can it tally with the *Sruti*, where its absence is maintained thus, "What more he is to desire?" But this is conceived in error, for the utterance of the *Sruti* goes to establish not want of desire, but simply its want of potency to create any inclination for further enjoyments, just as parched grains are deprived of fruit-bearing powers or germination.

164. That is to say, as parched grains are incapable of germinating and producing any crop, so a theosophist's desire, though present, is incapable of producing any inclination for frail works,* inasmuch as knowledge has established the impermanence or unreality of all objects, and thus stands in collision of its fructifying.

165. It is impossible to maintain an opposite doctrine, and to say, since a theosophist is never desirous of enjoying any fruits, he has virtually no desire: for as in the case of parched grains, though incapable of producing a crop yet are they capable of being exten and are fit food for men, so does a theosophist's desire produce little enjoyment and bring forth no calamity.

166. His fructescent works are exhausted (from consummation) by enjoying their fruits, therefore they produce no calamity, which follows only, when from ignorance, a person is deluded into the belief of reality of all objects which he is desirous of enjoying, and there is no end of such desire,—virtually he is never satiated.

167. And that calamity assumes pretty often this shape. "Let my enjoyments never come to an end, but let them gradually increase, and there be no impediment to them. I consider myself blessed in having so many things to enjoy."

* Frailty arising from desire or anger includes ten vices coming under calamity, as:—hunting, gambling, day-sleeping, calumny, whoring, dancing, singing, playing, idle-roaming, drinking. Fate comprehends eight:—depravity, violence, injury, envy, malice, abuse and assault.

Mistakes like these, occurring in the ignorant, are a fruitful source of calamity, misfortune and frailty.

168. Its means of destruction are now being declared. To ponder in mind and unceasingly to confirm the belief that fructescent cannot by any power be prevented, and what is to happen, cannot be anyhow avoided, and what is not to be, can never come to pass, causes the destruction of the poison of constant thoughts as to when shall my troubles cease, and better days dawn.

169. From an absence of particular distinction between the wise and ignorant, so far as present enjoyments brought about from the fructescent are concerned, how can calamity be said to befall the ignorant and not affect the wise? What is the cause of this difference? Enjoyments though equal, yet an ignorant person is subject to the illusion of reality of all objects of enjoyment to which the wise is not, therefore calamity affects the former and not the latter, who is devoid of ignorance, and determination, for the acquisition of material well-being—riches, property and the rest.

170. A theosophist knows the unreality and impermanence of all objects of enjoyment, for they are material and liable to destruction, he therefore minimises his desire, and begets no inclination for an extensive sphere of enjoyment, nor is he bent after its pursuit; under such circumstances how can evil befall him?

171. But it may be alleged, how can a false object produce perception of happiness which follows during its enjoyment? Therefore it is said, his desire of enjoyment can never be reduced. To this contention the reply is: How can a theosophist have any regard for the objective world which is material and impermanent, as unreal as objects seen in a dream or in a performance of magic?

172—173. With the experience of dreaming and waking in his own person, and constant study of the unreality of the universe, though it appears as a living reality while awake, he has ceased to be convinced of its reality, and takes it all for a dream, consequently he heeds it not, and pays very little regard.

174. This indescribable universe, made of matter, is but an illusion, like objects seen in a magical performance; from a firm conviction of the unreality of phenomena, in this way, he keeps off all illusions as to their reality, and as a result, whatever enjoyments he may have from his fructescent works, produce no calamity to him.

175. For, the knowledge of unreality of phenomena is a helping cause for Self-knowledge: while fructescent works are only a source of enjoyment or suffering for an individual.

176. Thus from a natural difference in the effects they produce, self-knowledge and fructescent works are not opposed to each other; for, we find a person deriving pleasure and amusement from the sight of a magical performance, though he knows the things produced are all unreal. Thus for a difference of subjects, fructescent works do not stand in the way of Self-knowledge.

177. When an ignorant person enjoys the fruits of actions already commenced to bear fruit, with a firm conviction of the reality of the world in spite of its impermanence, such knowledge is destructive of Self-knowledge. And his conviction of reality cannot make it real when it is naturally unreal.

178. As dream-objects though naturally unreal, are enjoyed, so are unreal objects of the waking condition to be regarded as capable of being enjoyed.

179. If knowledge of Supreme Self could destroy all enjoyable objects it would then cause destruction of fructescent works and be regarded in that light: virtually it does no such thing, it simply establishes their impermanence and unreality, and does not cause their destruction, therefore Self-knowledge is no antagonist or destroyer of the fructescent.

180. As without the destruction of a thing produced in a magic show, its very sight causes mirth to a spectator though he knows it to be unreal; so without the destruction of all objects of enjoyment, self-knowledge offers no impediment to their enjoyment, with a simple knowledge of their unreality from the force of fructescent works.

181. If it be said, repeated mention is made in the *Sruti*, of a man of discrimination reaching that stage when he regards everything non-different from self; in such a state who is then to see, hear, or smell, and what is he to speak?

182. Therefore, when there is no possibility for gnosis to arise without destruction of phenomena, how can a knower of the Secondless Brahma, non-distinct from self, be said to enjoy objectively?

183. Listen to the reply that is being given. The above *Sruti* text has no reference to the period when a person is engaged in the acquirement of knowledge, for it is distinctly mentioned in the *Shariraka Sutras* (Chapt. IV., *Sutra* 16,) as an illustration of profound slumber and emancipation; of them, the dependence of either one, as subject of that condition when he regards everything to be self, is maintained in the *Sruti*.

184. If that is not admitted, Yajnavalkya will cease to be a professor, because when he sees the external world, his knowledge of non-duality is virtually at an end, and when he sees it not, no words can flow. [In other words, if no regard be paid to the explanation just given about profound slumber or emancipation, there would be no professor of self-knowledge, for in the waking condition he is practically related to the external world, his knowledge of its illusion is then at an end; and when he sees it not, from want of adequate words to help the perception of his pupils, his words would cease to instil into their minds knowledge of non-duality, so that the traditional doctrine of the efficacy of knowledge will be nullified.]

185. If you regard that variety of 'profound unconscious meditation' when there is no distinction kept up between knower, knowledge, and the subject to be known, for this want of perception, as visible knowledge* of self, why is not profound slumber to be equally regarded?

186. If you contend, there is want of knowledge of self in profound slumber, and hence it is not admitted as knowledge, that is to say, the external world then ceases to exist relatively to the individual, and for want of a subject to cover or take possession of self, profound slumber cannot be looked upon as knowledge, it virtually amounts to an exclusion of phe-

---

* There are two varieties of knowledge, the invisible and visible. "Brahma is" is an instance of the first, "I am Brahma," of the second kind: the 'invisible' destroys the non-being of Brahma, visibility destroys ignorance with its trammels.

"The non-being of Brahma, due to 'envelopment,' is destroyed by the knowledge of the 'invisible kind,' which clearly defines Its existence by the expression "There is Brahma." For the two are antagonistic to each other, and cannot co-exist; hence the admission of the existence of Brahma, must do away with Its non-existence or non-being; and as such a perception is dim and vague, (nothing definite) it is called invisible. "I am Brahma" is a definite perception, hence it is called 'visible knowledge [or knowledge marked by visibility]'; and it causes the destruction of ignorance with its trammels. For this knowledge is antagonistic of that ignorance which says "I know not Brahma," and of that other kind, which declares "There is no Brahma." "It cannot be cognized"—varieties of concealment or envelopment as have just been remarked;—and to the declaration "I am not a Brahma," but an agent of virtue and vice, and an instrument for enjoying weal or suffering woe, *i.e.*, the same as Jiva, which is a mistake; and these are the trammels or nets of ignorance which cannot exist with the real, definite, and visible perception of Brahma, which is expressed by "I am Brahma."—DHOLE'S *Vicharsagar*, p. 117.

nomena and perception of "I am I" as knowledge. And such is fit to be considered so, for I have a similar purport too.

187. If you say, knowledge of non-duality and total forgetfulness of phenomena, the two combined, constitute Self-knowledge; all insentient objects, a jar, a cloth, etc., would in that case form half subjects of knowledge, for though virtually they cannot claim any knowledge of non-duality, yet it is quite natural to credit them with the forgetfulness of the external world.

188. Thus then, as in the case of jar and other insentient objects, there is total frightfulness of the external world [they have no cognition to take hold of it] so you can never have a similar forgetfulness of phenomena in profound meditation, for there are thousand and one cause for distracting your mind, as for instance, buzzing of musquitoes, etc.

189. If you abandon the position you seek to maintan of knowledge of non-duality and forgetfulness of phenomena, the two together, constituting Self-knowledge and admit knowledge of self to be supreme, may you live long, for that amounts to an admission of what I have been contending for: and as I hold earnestness of the mind necessary to that supreme knowledge of self, may you be successful in it.

190. Since visible perception of phenomena is an illusion, a theosophist's desire of enjoyment is therefore not firm, for he knows it to be impermanent, and it is consequently unlike that of ignorant persons, who are firm in their desire.

191. Two distinct doctrines prevail in the *Shastras*, for instance, "Desire is characteristic of the ignorant,"* and "Passions and desires are found even in a theosophist," but they are not meant to imply any contradiction. For, desire is the play-ground of the internal organ, and as the cavern of a tree

* As from the sight of smoke in a mountain the natural inference is the presence of fire in it, so is the presence of fond attachment a sign or indication of the ignorant.

containing fire* kills it, by destroying its sap, and its greenness is gone; so do the sacred writings interdict passions and desires in the wise, for they are detrimental to emancipation. Hence it is said, when their purport is gathered, and cognition of the Secondless Reality firmly established, a person is no longer affected by his desires, because they are simply the attributes of the internal organ. But then, as a theosophist's desires are not firm, consequently their want is established, hence admission and interdiction of a theosophist's desire in the sacred writings, as they refer to firmness or firm attachment (which he has not) and its want, does not signify any opposite condition, but simply want of fond attachment.

192. As the unreality of phenomena is firmly established in the wise, so is his knowledge of self, being unconditioned

---

* If from some cause or other, there be fire in the cavern of a tree, its sap is destroyed: so is tranquility of mind destroyed by desire produced from ignorance of the Supreme Self and his distinction with the individual spirit or *Atma*, therefore it is said to be his sign. A theosophist's desire is not firm, that is to say, from a relation of its proximate cause, the internal organ, and a similar relation with the material cause, its friendly object, an exclusive want of desire is called 'unfirm desire.' An ignorant person has also his relation with the internal organ but no want of desire; we feel no desire in sound sleep, but there is no relation of the internal organ too; impressions only continue then. In the ignorant, notwithstanding a relation of the internal organ, a desire is absent when trying for the accomplishment of an object, but there is no recollection of objects conformable or friendly and adjacent or near. A similar relation with the internal organ and conformable objects are found to be present along with a theosophist's desire when he is not in the discriminating mood, but that is not constant or exclusively so. In the *Gita* (Chap. II., v. 59.) is mentioned, "Desires cease in an individual after the cognition of Brahma." Hence unfirm desires of a theosophist are faultless.

and unrelated, he has no more desire for any object; therefore it is said: "What more is he to desire and continue attached to the body?" It is not to be supposed, want of objects produce cessation of desire; on the other hand, from an absence of agent or instrument of enjoyment, desire is destroyed: and that does not signify the death or destruction of the agent, but only his instrumentality of enjoyment.

193. "A husband and wife are not desired for their gratification, but for enjoyment of Self." *Sruti.* In other words, affection for wife or son does not proceed from any other motive but self-interest; a person has his own desires to serve, therefore the above passage from the *Sruti*, like similar others, are intended to show desire for wife and children, husband, and other objects proceed not for making them enjoy happiness, but for the happiness of one's own self. But it may be objected, as self is not an instrument or agent, it is futile, to do away with the idea of his enjoyment; though this is a fact, yet prior to gnosis has arisen, he is apt to be taken for an instrument, and individual experience likewise establishes it. This is again corroborated by the above *Sruti* text.

194. Who is the agent? Whether the Uniform Intelligence or its reflected shadow is so, or the two together combined? Now as regards the first, it is clearly untenable, because Uniform Intelligence is unassociated and unrelated:

195. Because enjoyment is a modification of conceit in happiness and its reverse; and as the Uniform Intelligence is subject to no modification (it is unchangeable) therefore if it were to be an instrument of enjoyment, its uniformity will be destroyed and it will then be subject to change, and change cannot abide in uniformity—the two are opposed to one another. To be more explicit:—Enjoyment of happiness and misery assumes this shape "I am happy," "I am miserable," etc., for which it is called a changed condition of conceit, in the form of happiness or its reverse. Now intelligence that is uniform, and knows no change, cannot be con-

nected with that conceit, inasmuch as change does not reside in the same place with uniformity, for they are naturally opposed.

196. Neither can reflex intelligence be regarded as an instrument. Because though dependent on Intellect which is always undergoing change, and for that, it is possible to attribute changeability to it, yet as a reflected shadow, it cannot abide independently of the Uniform Intelligence; but as this one is no instrument, its shadow, the reflex intelligence can neither be so. Then again, as there can be no mistake of snake without a rope being present,—here rope is the abiding substance on which the snake is attributed through illusion—so without Uniform Intelligence being present, there can be no reflex, and this one cannot be mistaken for that other.

197. Thus then, if neither the Uniform Intelligence nor its reflected shadow be an instrument, the two together are practically regarded so, though in point of truth they are not. "This one is unassociated." "The cognitional sheath is a subject of the vital airs, etc." From these texts, self is established as one unconditioned, and Intellect is a manner of witness. Therefore, one may object to the view taken, and apprehend truly also, about the two Intelligences together, as instrument, and not a mere matter of popular belief. The *Sruti* never intended to establish the truth of such instrumentality or agency, therefore to say, the nature of such agent is true, is improper. In the same manner, has the *Sruti* done away with the agency beginning with self and ending in the Uniform Intelligence. [As will appear in the sequel.]

198. King Janak enquired of Yajnavalkya who is sel ? The sage pointed out one after the other, beginning with the 'cognitional sheath'* and ending in the unassociated, for help-

* There are five sheaths each of which is regarded as Self, Yajnavalka refuted them by demonstrating arguments and proofs, one by one, thus helping to instil in the mud of his pupil a correct knowledge of self ultimately, by the passage quoted "This one etc."

ing him to comprehend, finally resting on the text, "This one is unassociated;" and that unassociated Uniform Intelligence is Self. [*Brihadaranyak Upanishad.*]

199. There are other *Sruti* texts in the *Aitareya Upanishad* and elsewhere to the same purpose. "Who is Self that is to be worshipped?" Beginning with the associate of the internal organ, and ending in the Uniform Intelligence, this one has been declared to be self, after thorough analysis, in the *Upanishad* above named. Therefore, if the method used there be followed closely, it would appear, the Uniform Intelligence and its reflected shadow—the two—are not agents: and in point of truth, the former is unassociated, hence neither an instrument nor an agent.

200. If the attribution of an enjoyer to self be false, how and why does an individual experience it to be a fact? From want of discrimination of self, the truth of the Uniform Intelligence is attributed to the two, and from illusion actually regarded as an enjoyer with hardly a desire for abandoning enjoyment, knowing such enjoyment to be real—a mistake.

201. For his self-enjoyment, an enjoyer desires to have a wife and *vice versa*; even in the *Sruti* we find a confirmation of this popular belief.

202. All enjoyable things are dependent on him, therefore to shew any attachment for them is vain; on the other hand, it is advisable, there should be no desire for them but only for self, who is the principal enjoyer, true and free.

203. On this subject the evidence of the *Purana* is as follows:—

"The attachment which ignorant persons have for material objects, which are not eternal, Lord, do out of thine grace I beseech thee, impart me a similar firm attachment for thee, so that I may never forget thee from my heart."

204. In this manner, by discrimination, after all fond desires for non-eternal objects have been abandoned, one is

indelibly to fix his love on the true nature of the real enjoyer and thus know him.

205. As from forgetfulness of self, the ignorant fix their attachment firmly on objects of senses, garland, sandal, wife, clothing, and gold, so is a theosophist to fix and concentrate it on the real nature of the enjoyer (self); and he forgets him not.

206. As one desirous of victory over his rivals, is always engaged in the study of Dramatic works, Logic, etc., so does a person desirous of release study discrimination of Self.

207. As a man of faith is engaged in devotional exercise and sacrificial works, enjoined in the *Shastras*, with a desire of acquiring the blissful abode of heaven, so does the emancipated show his faith in self.

208. As a Yogi with much perseverance and labour acquires the power of concentrating his mind on one object, so does an emancipated person fix his attention on the Real Brahma, with the object of acquiring lightness and heaviness, etc.

209. As repetition of practice leads to skilfulness in those desirous of victory, men of faith, and *Yogis*; so does discrimination of self, by repetition, clear him of all mistakes and purify self-knowledge in the emancipated.

210. Then a person of discrimination by analysing the real nature of the enjoyer inferentially and differentially, knows the witnessing Uniform Intelligence to be unassociated and unconditioned, in waking, dreaming and profound slumbering conditions.

211. For example. Whatever objects are experienced in the three conditions of waking, dreaming and profound slumber (be they gross, subtle or in the form of felicity), for the purpose of enjoyment, that experience is present only in that particular condition where they are seen or felt, though the witness who is to cognise, is present in all conditions.

And against this, there is no dissentient voice for it is the universal experience.

212. Now in reference to inferential and differential analysis for the discrimination of self, the *Vedas* are proofs too. With this purpose the *Sruti* testimony is being cited. "That self when he cognises the enjoyable objects of any of the three conditions is not transferred by them from one state to another; they continue where they are, but he passes over to another state, without taking hold of virtue and sin, and their results, happiness and misery."

213. "Brahma, which is ever-lasting intelligence and bliss, and witness, discovers all objects in the three conditions of time,—waking, dreaming and dreamless slumber; and That am I." "I am neither intellect nor reflection of intelligence nor any thing else besides." He who has come to identify self in this manner, is freed from the usual mistake of confounding him with an agent and instrument.

214. Self is one in all the three conditions, and with discrimination one who has come to realize him as distinct and separate from them, is no more subjected to birth and death.

215. Whatever enjoyable things are to be found in those conditions and whatever enjoyments may proceed from them to their enjoyers,* self is over and above, that is to say, quite distinct from them, he is intelligence and supreme felicity, and That am I.

216. Who then is the enjoyer?

From what has been said in regard to the discrimination of self, it would appear that the literal signification of the word "cognitional" referring as it does to the reflex intelligence, for its being subject to change is the enjoyer.

217. "This reflex intelligence is illusory or material."

---

* Viswa, Taijas and Prajna are the enjoyers. Enjoyments are gross, subtle and felicity.

(*Sruti.*) Experience confirms it too. Because the objective world is material and reflex intelligence (*Jiva*) is included in it. Like things produced in a magical performance both are unreal.

218. In trance and profound slumber, the reflex intelligence is destroyed, and that is experienced by the Witnessing Uniform Intelligence. If it be asked, What benefit can the experience of its destruction bring forth? It is therefore said, a person is led over and over to consider what his self really is. In other words, the remnant of consciousness abiding in profound slumber experienced by a person on rising "I was sleeping soundly and knew nothing then" proves self to be no other than the Uniform Intelligence, unchangeable and indestructible: but this reflected shadow is subject to change and liable to destruction, for it is unreal,—because material.

219. Thus then, having ascertained the unreality of the enjoyer [reflex intelligence] a person no more desires for any enjoyments; just as a person on his death-bed never desires to marry.

220. And as prior to knowledge he was accustomed to say "I am the enjoyer," but like a person with a split nose he is now ashamed and says, "Even now my fructescent works are bearing fruit." Thus he suffers them to have their course with patience.

221. When therefore the reflex intelligence [Jiva] is ashamed to be reckoned as an enjoyer, he attributes it to the witnessing intelligence abiding in him. Therefore it is futile to ask who is the enjoyer?

222. Thus then, it would appear from the preceeding verses that the *Sruti* text "for what desire etc.," has its purpose in interdicting the belief of an enjoyer. Both the Uniform and Reflex Intelligences are truly, no enjoyers; ignorance attributes enjoyment to them, so that when gnosis has arisen, a person has no more desire of enjoyment left in him: hence it is said, subsequent to knowledge, what desires would attach a person

to his body and make him follow the bent of its inclinations? None.

223. That a theosophist is never attached to his body, nor is affected by its pains is now being declared by a passing reference to the three varieties of body and their pains. Every individual has three varieties of bodies, physical, subtle and cause; and each of them has its separate ailments.

224. The diseases of the physical body are apparent enough, they are innumerable, and produced from wind, bile and mucus; among the symptoms are to be found bad smell, disfiguration, burning of the body, huskiness of the voice, and several others, which every one has experience of.

225. Those of the subtle body are desire, anger, covetousness, bewilderment or distraction, pride, and passivity, self-control, abstinence, endurance, intensity of thought and faith; they are called diseases, inasmuch as the presence of the former and want of the latter (passivity and the rest) are equally productive of pain.

226. The diseases of the cause-body are now being cited from the *Chhandogya Upanishad.* When Ignorance, the material cause of the universe is destroyed in profound slumber, a person can no longer know either himself or another, but the seed for future misery which continues to abide even then, is called disease of the subtle body; so Indra said to Brahma.

227. Now these varieties of diseases are naturally connected with the three different bodies, inasmuch as in their absence, the bodies cannot last.

228. Just as with the separation of its yarn, a cloth cannot continue, and with that of earth, a jar is destroyed; so with the separation of diseases, the body is destroyed.

229. Neither the reflex intelligence, which is Jiva, nor the Witnessing Intelligence, which is ISWARA, has got any disease, as will appear immediately.

230. It is impossible for any disease to affect the intelli-

gence of the individual; for no discrepancy can effect its natural illumination. Since therefore, the reflected shadow of intelligence is devoid of disease, its counterpart, the Witness or Uniform is likewise free from it. And whatever disease is experienced by the individual and said to affect him, is an illusion created by ignorance [for that belongs to the body and not to intelligence].

231. The truth of the witnessing intelligence is an illusion created by ignorance. From illusory attribution, the three bodies,—physical, subtle, and cause,—are regarded as semblance of the reflex intelligence, and real.

232. During that illusion, a person affected with diseases of those bodies exclaims "I am unwell," "I am suffering from fever," etc. In point of truth, this experience is unreal: just as illusion attributes bondage to the Intelligence which is free and not subject to birth and death.

233. As in the case of illness affecting a wife, or child, a person is affected with painful thoughts and considers himself to be so affected; so out of ignorance, diseases of the three bodies are attributed to self, experienced in that connection, and expressed in this manner: "I am ill."

234. But subsequent to knowledge, when the nature of self has been ascertained, all divisions are at an end, and he no longer connects the Witnessing Intelligence with those diseases, so that by discriminating the real nature of self, he ceases to express any regret for whatever happens to his body.

235. For example. As in the illusion of snake in a rope, the sight of that false snake makes a person run away from it, and when with the discovery of the rope, that false snake is destroyed, he is ashamed at his cowardice; similarly, subsequent to knowledge of self, his previous conception about his being a subject of disease is destroyed, and he is ashamed at his ignorance.

236. Just as a person asks forgiveness of another, who has been offended by his false calumny, for pacifying him; so in

the mistaken attribution of birth and death to self, a person is to pacify by taking protection of the Witnessing Intelligence.

237. Just as for repeated destruction of sin, penances are performed over and over, so for the destruction of illusory attribution, an individual is always to meditate on Self as the Uniform Witnessing Intelligence.

238. As a woman with cancer of the uterus feels ashamed when in the act of being co-habited, so a theosophist is ashamed at the mistaken notions, which he entertained, prior to gnosis of self.

239. As a Brahman accidentally coming in contact with an unclean person, has recourse to usual penance and never afterwards found associating with him, so a theosophist subsequent to knowledge, ceases to have a conceipt for his three bodies and connects them not with self: As "I am, etc."

240. As a prince regent governing the kingdom of his father, is bent after the happiness of his subjects, with the view of being duly installed; so with the view of being one with Brahma, a theosophist meditates on the Witnessing Intelligence and its resemblance with self.

241. "A knower of Brahma is himself a Brahma." Here is *Sruti* evidence, having for its purport destruction of misery and disregard for what a theosophist used to practice prior to knowledge. In other words, he should concentrate his desire to know Brahma and leave off everything else.

242. As a person with the desire of acquiring the condition of Deva, seeks self-destruction in fire, or by falling from the summit of a mountain, or submerging in the Ganges, or at the confluence of the three sacred rivers at Allahabad; so for the results abiding in the discovery of the Witnessing Intelligence being no other than self, a theosophist seeks the destruction of the reflex intelligence (Jiva)—the more so, as his inclination for knowledge of Brahma may be intensified.

243. But in the above instance, so long as the body lasts he continues to be a man, and with its destruction (when it is

reduced into ashes) he becomes a Deva; so till the consummation of fructescent works, practically a person cannot do away with the reflex intelligence, but continues as Jiva [to be one with Brahma after the separation of the present body].

244. As the sight of snake in a rope, at once strikes a person with fright, which does not go away immediately with the discovery of his mistake, but subsides gradually, and as a repetition of the snake-illusion is apt to recur when he comes across a bit of string in the dark—stretching in his path :

245—246. So with the rising of knowledge, his fructescent do not abruptly come to an end, but are gradually exhausted with consummation of their results, and during a subsequent period of enjoyment he is apt to conceive "I am a man".

247. As in the instance of the "tenth person" the person counting the rest forgetting to count himself, invariably comes to stop at number nine, and the party thinking their 'tenth' to have met with a watery grave, while in the act of crossing the river, give vent to their grief and strike their forehead, till pointed out by another, when discovering their mistake, their grief is replaced by happiness; but that pain in the forehead takes a little time to subside, and not at once :

248. So a theosophist even after attaining to the condition of one delivered in life, has yet to exhaust his fructescent and enjoy or suffer according to their merit or de-merit; and they cannot abruptly come to a close; and his emancipation destroys the miseries of the fructescent.

249. Now this condition of delivered in life is not an observance of religious ceremony or any particular practice,* but a mere resting on the Impartite Brahma, so that, if from a preponderance of the fructescent, there follows any illusion, to cause mental distraction, it should be guided by repeated discrimination of self, just as one having taken mercury, or

* Like the fasting observed in the 11th phase of moon.

sulphuret of arsenic cannot stand the pangs of hunger for a single day, but eats over and over.

250. As in the aforesaid instance of the missing 'tenth,' when in the height of their grief, the rest of the company beat their foreheads forcibly to cause pain, but perceive it not, till their mistake is pointed out and the missing tenth is visibly produced, when in the midst of happiness, they feel pain which subsides after the application of medicines; so a theosophist exhausts his fructescent by enjoying their results and subsequently attains to that Brahma, whose sole essence is joy, *i.e.*, experiences the supreme felicity of emancipation.

251. Whatever mention has been made in the present treatise from the first verse, for the destruction of misery and 'desire of release,' that constitutes the 6th condition of an individual, a reflected shadow of the Uniform or Witnessing Intelligence; the seventh is that supreme felicity in the form of satiety called *Nirvan*, which is now being determined.

252. Satiety proceeding from the enjoyment of material prosperity, riches, position, rank, wife and children, etc., is called excessive, but this seventh form is supreme; because with the attainment of the attainable [Brahma], one considers himself successful in achieving his end, and is supremely satiated.

253. Prior to his knowledge, whatever avocation a person follows for the acquisition of felicity, or sacrificial offerings undertaken for the acquirement of the blissful abode of heaven, which is non-eternal, or whether practising the usual means* for the acquisition of knowledge to help his emancipation, all these, were a part of his duty, it was proper for

* The four 'means' for attaining self-knowledge are :—

(1). Discrimination of things eternal and transient.

(2). Disregard of reaping any benefits here or hereafter.

(3). Passivity, self-control, abstinence, endurance, etc.

(4). Desire of deliverance [from future re-births].

him, that they should be done; but subsequent to knowledge, in the absence of a desire for enjoying any results relating to earth-life, and for an experience of the felicity of Brahma, all that he had done cease to produce any more fruits to a theosophist: they are dead and abortive so to speak, and as he has nothing proper for him to do, he is therefore said to be successful in having done what was proper. [Just as a candidate for examination is said to be successful when he has answered the questions set and satisfied his examiners, so that nothing remains for him to do, so far as the examination is concerned; so a theosophist is said to be successful when he has a visible cognition of Brahma and he has nothing proper for him to do, or be engaged in.—Because the usual means,—devotional exercises, etc.,—have brought forth their results in paving the way to knowledge, which has produced emancipation in turn, and that is the goal.]

254. In this manner, having done what was proper for him to do, and finding nothing left that was proper to be done, he recollects it and is supremely satisfied (with his success).

255. Miserable persons steeped in ignorance of Self-knowledge are absorbed in their desire for a wife, children and material prosperity: let them continue so. [But as] "I am full of supreme bliss" what desire can I possibly have to continue attached to earth-life?

256. Let them who desire the blissful abode of heaven practise sacrificial offerings, but "I am a knower of self" what occasion have I for practising any more action?

257. Let those who are qualified for studying the *Shastras* read them, or let them study the *Vedas*: my knowledge of self is ripe, hence "I am actionless" and not qualified for any thing else.

258. Really I do not sleep, nor go out for begging, neither do I bathe, nor conform to any previous habits; and if any one were to attribute them to me, that cannot cause any harm to my self.

259. As a heap of *Abrus precatorius* appears from distance to be fire, and in spite of that appearance it has no burning property, so the attribution of others about my being a worldly man, will not make my-self so.

260. Let an enquirer of self-knowledge who has not succeeded in the cognition of his oneness with the Impartite Brahma, continue to be engaged in the usual means for its acquisition; "I am a knower of the Supreme Brahma," therefore have no more a necessity for them. Let them that are affected with doubts practise 'consideration,' "I am free from doubt;" and have therefore no occasion for it.

261. Let him who has antagonistic ideas concerning the Supreme Brahma, have recourse to 'contemplation,' but "I am free from conflicting ideas." Why then am I to undertake its practices?

262. Even in spite of conflicting ideas from a force of confirmed habit and as a result of fructescent works, a theosophist is apt to exlaim "I am a man." [That is, not Brahma.]

263. But with the exhaustion of the fructescent, by enjoying their results, the above practice ceases: otherwise a thousand contemplations over and over, are quite powerless to destroy it so long as the fructescent continue.

264. If the practical use of the above expression "I am a man" appears conflicting to knowledge and for seeking its destruction you think it desirable to be engaged in contemplation, that may be necessary for you; but seeing that practice to be opposed to knowledge why "am I" to contemplate?

265. For I am free from mental distraction, and therefore there is no occasion for me to have recourse to profound meditation. Both distraction and profound meditation are the attributes of an unrestrained and changeable [fickle] mind.

266. I am not an agent, neither a beggar, nor a student of the sacred scriptures; I am no doer of sacrifice, or devotional exercise, from the force of the fructescent; no practice,

either popular or religious, or anything else, can cause me injury.

267. Or, if after having done all that was proper to be done, for the sake of securing popular favor I follow the practice enjoined in the *Shastras*, even that does not cause me any harm.

268. Whether my body is engaged in devotion and worship, bathing, and cleanliness, or begging for food, and my words, in recanting the mystic '*Om*,' or hearing the *Upanishads*;

269. Whether my intellect be engaged in contemplating Vishnu, or absorbed in the felicity of Brahma, "I am the eternal, pure, Witnessing Intelligence," and have neither any inclination for works, nor create it in any.

270. For this difference between a theosophist and doer of works, there is hardly any ground of contention or dispute between them, just as two seas situated apart cannot mix their waters or form a junction.

271. Because a doer of works and worship has for his pursuit body, speech and intellect, which a theosophist has not, (his is the Witnessing Intelligence). Thus for a difference of subjects, there is no common ground of contention. [In other words, not-self, and self are situated quite apart from one another, not-self is the subject of a doer of works, and self that of a theosophist, hence for a difference of pursuit, of not-self by the former and self by the latter, there is no apprehension of any quarrel between them.]

272. In spite of this difference, if they would quarrel, from an ignorance of each other, that can only create mirth to a person of intellect, just as to deaf persons quarrelling from an incapacity of hearing what one says to the other, excites laughter.

273. A doer of works and worship has no cognition of the Witnessing Intelligence, but a theosophist knows it to be

Brahma, and how can that knowledge of the latter be injurious to the former?

274. A theosophist has discovered self, and he mistakes him not with the physical body and the rest, which are non-eternal, therefore they engage not his attention; but for a doer of works to be engaged quite in the contrary direction, cannot be harmful to the former.

275. If it be contended, for a theosophist to be engaged in works and worship is not proper, but where is the propriety of their cessation? And if cessation of works, be the extraordinary cause of knowledge, in that case, there can be no inclination for the acquisition of Self-knowledge.

276. If it be said, subsequent to knowledge, there is no necessity for inclination to cause it, the inference naturally will be: What is the necessity for cessation of works to bring forth knowledge, inasmuch as they cannot cause any obstruction to, or destroy it?

277. Neither ignorance, nor conceit, (egoism) can cause any obstruction to it, for they have been destroyed in the first stage of knowledge, by discrimination of self.

278. Therefore ignorance, already destroyed, can create no obstruction to, or cause destruction of knowledge. When a live rat flies at the sight or approach of a cat, how can a dead rat injure him.

279. When a person stands uninjured after receiving the thrust of *Pashupat* weapon, how will a lighter one without steel points cause his destruction?

280. When from performance of works and worship in an infinite variety of ways, a person has come out victorious in his fight with the fructescent works, and landed in full knowledge of self, he can never be affected in a manner so as to have it destroyed.

281. Though destruction of ignorance and its product, caused by knowledge, allow that ignorance to continue like a

dead body, yet such appearance is not injurious to him, on the other hand, it proclaims his glory.

282. He who does not alienate himself from this all-powerful knowledge in any way, has nothing to fear either from inclination or its reverse—they cause him no injury.

283. It is always proper for the ignorant to be engaged in works and worship, for they help the attainment of heaven : or by rendering the internal organ faultless, pave the way to the acquisition of knowledge, whereby to be emancipated.

284. When a theosophist lives in the company of such an ignorant person, no harm can befall him, if he be engaged in similar works at his intercession.

285. But in the company of the wise, he should discard all works, increase his stock of knowledge by attributing defects to them.

286. And for a theosophist to be engaged in works, in the company of the ignorant, in the manner aforesaid, implies no fault.

287. Just as a father when thrown to the ground by his child, or scolded and made bad use of, feels neither pain nor is angry with him, but caresses all the same ;

288. So a theosophist either caluminated, or praised by the ignorant, returns it not, but tries to create knowledge in them. And thus he uses them.

289. Now the result of this practice of a theosophist among the ignorant is being declared. That which helps the cognition of self in the ignorant, a theosophist should do ; he has nothing else proper for him.

290. And satisfied with the accomplishment of what was proper for him to do, he mentally reflects in the following manner.

291. I have a tangible perception of the eternal Self, therefore I am blessed. The supreme felicity of Brahma is plainly manifested to me, therefore I am blessed.

292. The miseries of earth-life touch me not, therefore I am blessed. The darkness of ignorance has left me, therefore I am blessed.

293. I have nothing proper left to be done, therefore I am blessed. My desires have all been now accomplished, hence I am blessed.

94. Verily I am blessed, I am blessed, my satisfaction is unrivalled; I am blessed, and blessed and blessed, and twice more blessed.

295. My merit is producing fruit "I am supreme good," my merit is extremely wonderful, and for that, "I am wonderful too."

296. How very wonderful are the *Sacred Writings*, Guru and knowledge; and how incomparably exquisite is the felicity which I am now master of.

297. Now the result of studying this treatise is set forth:— He who studies it always, is immersed in the felicity of Brahma and experiences supreme felicity always.

SECTION VIII.

On the Discovery of the Uniform Intelligence.

WITHOUT clearing the signification of 'That' and Thou' of the transcendental phrase "That art Thou," there can be no knowledge of oneness of individual self and the Parabrahma as a means of emancipation, therefore in the present treatise the literal and indicated signification of 'Thou' is to be first ascertained. Just as the ordinary light of sun discovers a wall and other objects, but by concentrating that light on a glass and reflecting it on them, they are emblazoned and strikingly illuminated, so is the Uniform Intelligence vivifying or illuminating our bodies, intensely manifested by the individual Intelligence centred in the Intellect or Spiritual Soul (*Boodhi*) and gains doubly in brilliancy.

2. As in the sun's light reflected through a lens on a wall, here and there a stray ray of light retains its ordinary luminosity and absence of that junction of the lens with sun-light makes no difference in it:

3. So the function of intellect, endowed with the reflected shadow of Intelligence, helping the cognition of external objects by forming a junction with them [in waking], or its want [in profound slumber], is discovered by the Uuiform Intelligence. Know it to be distinct from the reflex intelligence with the function of intellect.

4. That reflection of intelligence seated in intellect, assumes the shape of an external object which it seeks to cognise, and discovers it so: "This is a jar." But knowledge of its properties, etc., is brought about by the Uniform Intelligence as "I know a jar."

5. Prior to the modification of intellect in the shape of a jar, "I knew not a jar" arises from the Brahmaic Intelligence

[uniform] ; and subsequent to its perception in the modified intellect, a person discovers it and says, "I know a jar." This is the difference between the intelligences, Individual and Brahmaic, [uniform].

6. As in a steel knife, its sharp edge is confined to one side, so the modification or function of intellect resides in one part or province of reflex intelligence and ignorance—the two pervading a jar, are said to make it known or otherwise.

7. Like an unknown jar discovered by the Uniform (Brahmaic) Intelligence, known jar is also discovered by it. Why? Because reflex intelligence simply creates a knowledge of jar,* and that known jar is discovered by Brahmaic Intelligence.

8. Intellect, without the reflex intelligence, can produce no cognition of an object, consequently, in the cognition of jar as a lump of clay, there can be no difference apprehended between the reflex intelligence and modification of intellect of clay.

9. As without knowing it, on one can say, that he knows a jar, so without reflex intelligence, simple pervasion of a jar by intellect cannot be admitted to cause it to be known.

10. From what has been said, it would appear mental

---

* Says The *Vedantasara* :—

In the cognition of "This is a jar" the mental function assumes the shape of, or pervades the unknown jar and dispels the ignorance which rests there. By its reflected intelligence, it then discovers or renders it visible. As is mentioned in the *Shastras*, "the mental perception and its indwelling Intelligence both occupy the jar, the first dispels the ignorance about it, the second brings it out to view, (*i. e.*, renders it visible." As the light of a lamp taking possession of such articles as 'a jar,' 'a cloth,' etc., which occupy a dark corner, dispels the surrounding darkness and bring them out to view by its own brilliance, so the mental function after dispelling the ignorance which occupies an unknown jar, brings it out or renders it cognizable to the senses by its indwelling reflex intelligence.—*Vide* DHOLE'S *Vedantasara*, pp. 43-44.

function (Intellect) with reflex intelligence assuming the modification of an object which they prevade are the source of its cognition; and that knowledge is not to be expected as capable of being brought about by the Uniform Intelligence, since it was existing prior to its being known [or discovered by the intellect with reflex intelligence].

11. This view is not opposed to what SURESWAR ACHARYA (*Bartikara*) holds, as maintained by the supporters of the discriminating view of intelligence known by the name of *Avacheda vadi*, Cognition of external objects, a jar etc., is caused by intelligence, therefore the cause of that knowledge is intelligence, for which, the result is the subject to be known or demonstrated:—and this intelligence is the subject that is to be known from Vedantic utterances, which are its proofs.

12. Therefore SURESWAR wants to establish the reflex intelligence, which resembles the Uniform or Brahma, to be a result of proof, and not the latter; for in the *Upadesha Sahashri* of SANKARACHARYA (his preceptor) occurs the distinction between the two intelligences.

13. Since then, the distinction between the Uniform and Reflex Intelligences is an admitted fact, mental function, arising in the shape of Reflex Intelligence pervading a jar is the cause of its cognition, and the resulting knowledge, like ignorance, is fit for being discovered by the Uniform Intelligence. In other words, cognition or knowledge is discovered by Brahma [Uniform Intelligence] like an unknown jar, inasmuch as the modification of intellect, reflection of intelligence and external objects, jar etc., all are discovered by Brahma, while for its being a single subject, a jar is discovered by the reflex.

14. Thus then, mental function issuing through the sensory organs, reflex intelligence, and jar, all three, are manifested by the Brahmaic or Uniform Intelligence, and for the reflex being seated in the jar only in the form of result, which it pervades for cognizing it, that jar is discovered by the reflex intelligence.

15. Therefore, the knowledge of a known jar is discovered by both the Reflex and Uniform Intelligences, and this is called by a Naiyayika (*Anubyabsaya*) knowledge of knowledge.

16. From the reflex intelligence proceeds particular knowledge, as "This is a jar;" while the Uniform creates an ordinary acquaintance with it, as a "known jar."

17. Just as in the cognition of external objects, both the Reflex and Uniform Intelligences are ascertained, so are they to be considered in reference to the physical body.

18. But it may be alleged in reference to external objects, the mental function pervades them, and as inside the body there is no subject to be pervaded by the modification of intellect, consequently there is no necessity for admitting reflex intelligence. Therefore it is said, Egoism is present and the pervasion of reflex intelligence is required to discover it. Just as in a ball of red hot iron, fire pervades it, and is present, intimately combined with the iron, so does reflex intelligence pervade Egoism, passions and desires, by mixing with them.

19. And as that ball of iron manifests itself and is incapable of discovering any other object, so do the modifications of Egoism, passions, etc., with the reflex intelligence discover themselves.

20. These aforesaid modifications, separated by the intervals of waking and dreaming, are apt to arise, as they disappear during profound slumber, trance, fainting and profound meditation.

21. That unchangeable Intelligence which discovers the junction or union of those modifications and their want, is the Uniform Brahmaic Intelligence.

22. As in the cognition of an external object, a jar, the reflex discovers only, "This is a jar," and the knowledge of that jar is discovered by Brahmaic Intelligence, we have therefore both the intelligences; so in regard to the internal modifications, Egoism, etc., we have a similar play of both intelligences. And that double display of intelligence in junction

with those modifications make them more strongly manifested than external objects.

23. Unlike external objects which are capable of being ascertained either known or unknown, internal objects of mental perception are not; because that perception cannot take hold of or cover itself, and ignorance is destroyed by it.

24. If it be asked, so far as intelligence goes, both the reflex and uniform are identical, why then is the former called changeable and the latter, uniform or unchangeable? Because that double intelligence is liable to birth and death, therefore it is Jiva, while the uniform distinct from it is unchangeable and eternal,—the Supreme Brahma.

25. Older professors have, in various places of their writings, mentioned the Uniform Intelligence as the witness of mental perception and its modifications.

26. As in the reflection of face in a mirror, all the three (face, its reflection and mirror) are visibly perceptible, so by the help of the sacred writings and their arguments are to be known, Self (Uniform Intelligence) his reflection (reflected shadow of Intelligence) and its site or receptacle (the internal organ). In the *Upadesha Sahashri*, Uniform Intelligence is described as distinct from the reflex in the following wise. "It is the witness of the mind and intellect." And in the *Sruti* "Like the associate of the internal organ the reflex is only a reflected shadow" [of Intelligence *i.e.*, self].

27. If it be alleged, since the Uniform Intelligence is everywhere equally present, let that Intelligence seated in the intellect, be the subject of transmigration (like the ether in a jar) and there will be no necessity for imagining the reflex intelligence to be Jiva?

28. The reply is;—That limiting of the Uniform Intelligence would not necessarily convert it into a Jiva, just as the uniform present in a jar and wall and limited by them, or discriminated in that way, are no longer a Jiva.

29. If it be said, from want of luminosity, the Uniform Intelligence present in a jar or wall, and bounded by them, cannot convert them into Jiva, but for the luminosity of intellect, the uniform intelligence seated in and bounded by it, is Jiva: the answer is, there is no occasion for introducing luminosity or its reverse, when you seek to discriminate the Uniform Intelligence by setting a limit to it:

30. Just as the use of a measure made either of brass or a lighter substance, can bring no profit to the seller in dealing out a specified quantity of grains to a purchaser.

31. If you reply, the metallic measure has a particular action, inasmuch as it is capable of reflecting an image, though as a measure it has no difference with one made of wood, then, What prevents a similar reflection of intelligence in Intellect ?

32. And though the manifestibility or luminosity of that reflection of intelligence [in intellect] is very slight, and distinct from the Uniform Intelligence which is luminous, light-like, yet it is endowed with powers of discovery. And the same cause that deprives a shadow of the signs of the light whose shadow it is, and makes it manifested, produces the reflection of that light.*

---

* In the work *Vibarana*, Jiva is defined as a reflection and Iswara light [subject of reflection]. According to the doctrine of VIDYARANYA SWAMI, Iswara is the reflection of Intelligence in *Maya* abounding in pure goodness, and Jiva, a reflection of intelligence in *Avidya* abounding in pure goodness, which is a proximate cause of the internal organ. Though in the *Panchadasi*, VIDYARANYA SWAMI mentions Jiva to be a reflection in the internal organ, and as that internal organ is not present in the profound slumbering condition, consequently then, there should be no Jiva also ; but as *Prajna*, almost ignorant—a form of Jiva—continues in dreamless profound slumber, therefore what the SWAMI purports to mean is, the particle of ignorance modified or changed into the form of internal organ, and intelligence re-

33. [To be more explicit]. Inasmuch as the Reflex is associated and changeable, while the light of Uniform intelligence is unassociated and unchangeable, therefore the former

---

flected therein is called Jiva, and that ignorance is never wanting in profound slumber, consequently *Prajna* also is not wanting then. Moreover, reflection of intelligence alone does not constitute either a Jiva or Iswara, but intelligence abiding in Maya, and the reflex intelligence with Maya, constitute Iswara; and intelligence abiding in ignorance, and the reflex intelligence with the particle of ignorance, constitute Jiva. In the associate of Iswara, there is pure goodness, for which he is omnipotent, omniscient, etc.; while the associate of Jiva is composed of impure goodness, hence he is parviscient, parvipotent and the rest. This is said by the supporters of the Reflex Theory.

The associates of Jiva and Iswara are identical according to the view of the author of *Vibarana*, who connects them with Ignorance. In such a consideration, both Iswara and Jiva must be parviscient. But it is not so; because it is the nature of a thing in which there is a reflection, to impart its defects to the reflection, and not to the image: as for instance, when a face is reflected in a mirror (its associate) the defects belonging to the mirror will prevent a faithful reproduction of the face itself. Hence the defects, though present in the mirror, are not cognized or rendered visible till the face is reflected in a mirror, for which it is said, reflection determines defects. Similarly in the reflection of the Jiva, in the mirror of ignorance, are produced the defects caused by it, such as parviscience, etc., while Iswara (in the form of image of pure Intelligence) who is the visage, has none of them, for which He is omniscient. This is the cause of His omnipotence, omniscience etc., and the parvipotence and parviscience of a 'being.' Now between the respective doctrines set up by these supporters of reflection and reflected image, the difference is this—A reflection is false, but a reflected image is true, and not false. For, the expounders of reflected image conclude as a natural inference that the reflected image of the face in a mirror, is not a shadow of that face, inasmuch as a shadow is situated in the same site, where its original is placed; but in the case of a face reflected in a mirror, it is said to be wanting in the indications of the latter, and hence distinct; but its luminosity is manifested like that of the Uniform.

34. As an earthen jar is non-different in its composition from earth, so is reflex intelligence non-different from (*Boodhi*) Intellect, for an identity of their condition. But it may be

---

is always placed in front, or exactly opposite to the original, hence a reflected image is not a shadow in a looking-glass. But for making a subject of the mirror, the function of the internal organ, projected by the organ of sight, makes that mirror its subject, at the same time, it ceases or retreats from that mirror, and makes the face, situated on the neck, its subject. As quick playing (*Bunite*) makes the wheel of a fire-brand perceived, while actually it has no wheel, so the velocity of mental function for making a subject of the mirror and face, produces the perception of that face in the glass as situated in it; while actually it is placed on the region of the neck, and not in the glass, and is not a shadow: and, by the velocity of the mental function, the knowledge of a face in a glass, is reflection. In this manner, from the connection of the associated mirror, the face placed on the region of the neck appears both as a visage and its reflection. Moreover, on due reflection, it is to be found, there is no reflection. Similarly by the close connection of the associate formed by Ignorance, the site of visage in the unassociated Intelligence is known Iswara, and its reflection, *Jiva*. And there are no separate conditions of *Iswara* and *Jiva*.

The perception of a *Jiva* in Intelligence, from Ignorance is called its reflection in Ignorance; so that, both the considerations of visage and its reflection are unreal, while actually they are true; for the site of their actuality is the face and its reflection in a mirror; and in the subject of the illustration—Intelligence—that face and intelligence are true. According to this view, as a reflection proceeds from the original, it is consequently true; and a reflected shadow, for its being the shadow, is untrue. This then is the difference between the expressions 'reflection' and 'refletcted shadow.'—DHOLE's Edition of *Vicharsagar*, pp. 328-330.

apprehended: in that case, distinction of intellect from the physical body, will be done away with; therefore to settle the question, it is said, what is maintained by a theosophist is very little to the purpose, because it is easy to admit intellect as not an additional entity distinct from the body.

35. If it be alleged, subsequent to death, when the physical body is absent, existence of intellect is established from the testimony of the *Sruti*; then as in the *Prabesha Sruti*, 'reflex' is described to be distinct from Intellect, it is but proper to regard it in that way.

36. If you say, it is possible for the associate of Intellect to enter a body: the reply is, self distinct from Intellect is said to enter according to the authority of the *Ailerya Upanishad*:—" Self distinct from Intellect with a desire of entering, enters the body."

37. " This body with its insentient sensory organs cannot exist without the intelligence of Self," having considered in this manner, he enters the body through the cavity of Brahma situated on the crown of the head, corresponding to the anterior fontanele, and experiences waking, dreaming and profound slumber.

38. If it be contended, How can the unassociated Supreme Self enter a body? It may as well be said in reply, in that case it is impossible to attribute to him the instrumentality of creation. Thus then, both his entrance and instrumentaiity or causation equally are due to *Maya*, and with the destruction of that Illusion, they too are equally destroyed, therefore the cause of their destruction is alike.

39. YAJNAVALKYA in his discourse on Self-knowledge with his wife Maitreyi, cites passages from the *Sruti* to explain the destruction of associate as follows:—" The Supreme Intelligence Self, taking his birth with the physical body, organs sensory and active, etc., dies with the destruction of the body, and subsequent to its demise no knowledge abides in it." In other words, though distinct from the body and the

rest, which are material, self for keeping company with them. appears to be destroyed when the associates succumb to death.

40. " The Supreme Self is eternal, and unassociated, his associates are destroyed only," [and not he]. In this manner, *Sruti* explains the Uniform Intelligence (Self) devoid of associate, to be distinct from the associated reflex intelligence. " He is indestructible." And "unconnected with the body and the rest."

41. " When leaving the physical body, Jíva does not die; because he is without birth and death, the body alone dies." In this passage, the *Sruti* does not seek to expound that with death, he is emancipated and freed, but subjected to metempsychosis.

42. If then the associated Jiva is subjected to destruction, how can he have any identity of relation with, "I who am the Supreme Brahma and indestructible?" Therefore it is said, this knowledge is not of identity; it is community of reference and that is capable of existing even in the presence of obstacle or antagonism.*

---

* Though the spiritual soul or intelligence (Boodhi) with the reflex is the seat of the perception ' I am Brahma,' and not the Uniform, yet such reflex knows that the Uniform Intelligence and its principle of individuality are the *Atma*, indicated by the first personal pronoun ' I,' which also is the same as '*Aham*.' Now '*Aham*' establishes the Uniform intelligence as always non-different from Brahma, as the space covered by jar is always one with the infinite space from which it cannot be in any way demarcated. Hence the Vedantin describes this mutual relationship of the Uniform with Brahma as '*Mukshya Samanadhikarana*' a main predicament or inference in which several things are included.

When a thing is always non-different from another thing, their association is called a *Mukshya Samanadhikarana.* As for instancee the space engrossed by a jar is always non-different

43. As from mistake or illusion when the stump of a tree is taken for a man, not to know it as a stump does not affect the other knowledge that it is a man; so when the perception of egoism "I am an agent, and instrument" is destroyed by the knowledge "I am the Supreme Brahma," the objective world is destroyed.

44. SURESWAR ACHARYA has in this manner pointed out in his work *Niskarmya Siddhi** the antagonism of community of

---

from the infinite space which is ever present along with it, therefore the jar-space is the infinite space—and as such, the first has in relation to the last, the condition of a predicament in which it is included with it. In the same manner, the Uniform Intelligence has in connection with Brahma a similar 'main inclusive predicament,' because they are always non-different from one another.

Or, as in a person mistaking the stump of a tree for man, after the tree is known, the form of man disappears and the tree is rendered apparent. Here the person has a community of reference to the tree, of the second kind; similarly by the disappearance of the reflected Intelligence, it becomes one with Universal Intelligence, which is one with *Brahma,* hence its reference to 'I' is the same with *Brahma,* and not distinct from it. Such a 'community of reference' the reflex intelligence has with *Brahma* by merging or disappearing into it.

* SURESWARA, the reputed disciple of SANKARACHARYA, is the author of *Niskarmya Siddhi.* He is opposed to the doctrine of a theosophist's acting with impunity. For him there is nothing proper to do; to this end says the *Vicharsagar* :—"If after hearing the utterances of *Vedanta,* any one has an inclination still left in him as to what is proper, he has not learnt the first principle, or primitive truth. For this reason, the constant removal of the useless, and which answers no purpose, and acquirement of felicity, that is constantly got as a result of hearing the *Vedanta,* is mentioned by the Deva Guru in *Niskarmya Siddhi.*—*Vicharsagar,* DHOLE's Edition, pp. 120-121.

reference : for this reason, community of reference is destroyed in the expression "I am Brahma."

45. As in "All this is indeed Brahma" the Supreme Brahma has a community of reference with "all this"—the objective world—so in "I am Brahma" there is possible for the same reference with Jiva.

46. But objection may be taken to it, for in his work *Vivarana*, PRAKASHATMACHARAN SWAMI, speaks of the opposition of community of reference (*Vadh Samanadhikarana*). To explain this, it is said :—With a desire of declaring self to be identical with Uniform Intelligence, the author of *Vivarana* ascertains the incompatibility of community of reference and seeks to do away with it.*

47. Both in the *Vivarana* and other works, professors have sought to establish the indication of 'Thou' in the Uniform Intelligence—the Supreme Brahma, and having ascertained the incompatible community of reference (*Vadh Samanadhikarana*) have spoken of the main inclusive predicament referring to the same subject.†

48. Intelligence abiding in, and mistaken for, Jiva—who is the reflected shadow of Intelligence combined in the gross and subtle body, is in the *Vedanta* declared to be the Uniform.

49. And Brahma is the substrate of Intelligence pervading everywhere, and completely in phenomena fabricated out of illusion.

---

* *Vadha Samanadhikarana* means that condition of mutual relationship, when a thing establishes its non-difference with its companion by lapsing into it. Here the thing is a *Vadha samanadhikarana* to its companion. As for instance, the reflection of a face merges into the face (when the mirror is withdrawn) hence they are non-distinct; the reflection is the face itself and not something different, and this mutual relationship of the reflection with the face is called (*Vadha samanadhikarana*) 'community of reference by merging.'—*Vicharsagar*, DHOLE's Edition p. 121.

† *Vide* note pp. 212—213.

50. Since therefore illusion attributes the unreal world, and mistakes it for the indestructible and unchangeable Intelligence, the substrate of all, it is not at all surprising that Jiva, who is the reflected shadow of Intelligence should be similarly attributed, as there, Jiva is a part of the material world.

51. For a difference in associate, the material world and Jiva included in it, 'That' and 'Thou' appear to be distinct; virtually they refer to one intelligence.

52. That reflex Intelligence (Jiva) assumes the attributes of the spiritual soul, intellect or *Boodhi*, *viz.*, as an agent or instrument and demonstrator, and the illumination of self; for which, it is said to be an illusion [just as in nacre no silver is present, but illusion attributes or super-imposes on it. Here we have two conditions "This nacre" is the seat or abiding place of silver, and the other, attribution or superimposition of illusion: so in the superimposition of reflex on the Uniform Intelligence there ought to be the two conditions of abiding and superimposition; and in the absence of discerning their attributes how can illusion be established in them? This is what a dissenter objects to. Therefore, it is said, the reflex is only an illusion; for agency and instrumentality are properties of the Intellect, and illumination belongs to Self, who is the Uniform Intelligence. Barring them, what remains of Jiva? Nothing.

53. And the cause of that mistake or illusion is ignorance. What is Intellect? What is this reflex intelligence or Jiva? What is Self? And what is this material world? From want of discriminating them, is engendered error, which error or illusion is fit to be destroyed, for it is nothing less than the world we live in.

54. But it may be asked how is illusion to be destroyed? By proper discrimination when a person has come to know the nature of the several entities, intellect, reflex and Uniform Intelligences, etc., he is a real knower of Self and freed. So says the *Vedanta*.

55. Thus then, we find discrimination and its want are the cause of emancipation and consecutive re-births, and the Naiyayika's jeering taunts to his adversary about bondage and emancipation being uncertain, according to a non-dualist's standpoint, is easily refuted by the arguments employed in *Khandan*, by its author SRIHARSA.

56. Having ascertained the nature of Uniform Intelligence from *Sruti* texts and arguments based on analogy and reason, the testimony of the *Puranas* is now being declared. "That Uniform Intelligence is witness of the modification of intellect, and of its prior condition, when it has not arisen; of desire of enquiring and its prior condition of ignorance, when a person says "I am Ignorant;" and for its being so, it is said to be full of felicity.

57. For its being the resting place [substrate] of the unreal objective world, it is truth; for its being the discoverer of all insentient objects, it is Intelligence, as the site of affection always, blissfulness; and as the illuminator of all objects having connection with them, it is perfect.*

* Various are the objections raised against what has been said of the felicity, intelligence, etc., of the Uniform Intelligence or self. Thus felicity is disputed:—a difference in the modification of intellect creates a difference in it, because it is the witness of modification, and where no such difference affects it, it is no more a witness of those modifications. Then again, it is contended how can the site of an unreal substance be real? As they are naturally opposed to each other. In the snake-illusion, the site of that snake is a real rope: there can be no snake-illusion without seeing a rope, a bit of straw, etc., in the dark, on which is super-imposed the form of snake through ignorance: we have therefore a trite instance which sets at rest the second contention. Similarly as it is said to be a discoverer of insentient objects only, it can lay no claim to intelligence, and if it is no intelligence, it can be no discoverer, but is virtually insentient like a jar. But without intelligence, there can follow no discovery; in short like rabbit's horns

58. In this manner, Uniform Intelligence is described in the *Siva Purana*, to be neither a Jiva nor Iswara, but self-illuminated Intelligence, full of blissfulness.

59. How? Because both Jiva and Iswara are declared in the *Sruti* to be "formed of *Maya* and reflex intelligence." It may be apprehended, if they are thus material, there will be no distinction between them, and the insentient physical body, etc. To clear this, it is said, just as there is distinction between a glass and earthen jar, though equally material, for the one is transparent, which the other is not, so are Jiva and Iswara distinct from the physical body and the rest.

60. Just as body and mind (modified products of food) are different from one another, inasmuch as the former is insentient which the latter is not; so Iswara and Jiva though material, are far more sentient than other objects of the universe.

61. Though Jiva and Iswara are thus material, yet for manifesting intelligence, it is possible to regard them as intelligence itself, and this is plausible enough, since there is nothing impossible for Maya to fabricate.

62. Since even in our slumber, consciousness present in dreams creates Jiva and Iswara: what objection can there be for the Primordial Cosmic Matter to contrive intelligence in Jiva and Iswara?

63. Though equally material with Jiva, yet Iswara is not parviscient like him, for the same Maya shows him to be om-

---

which exist not, the phenomenal would have been similarly conditioned, and remained undiscovered. Without a connection of intelligence, insentient objects can never be known; to say, they are discovered of themselves, and intelligence plays no part is clearly absurd. What is subject of another's affection cannot be blissfulness itself. And for its being universally related, it can be no more an universal illuminator, neither the one nor the other.

niscient. Since it is capable of fabricating Iswara, what possible objection can there be for fabricating his omniscience?

64. It is improper to regard the Uniform Intelligence in the same light with Jiva and Iswara, and to say, it is unreal, and an illusion: for testimony to that effect is wanting.

65. On the other hand, its Reality is explained in all *Vedantic* treatises, and it has no similarity either with the elements or any other substance, for which it can be said to be material.

66. Hitherto for ascertaining the nature of Iswara and Uniform Intelligence—their unreality and reality—testimony of the *Sruti* has been made use of only, and if in the absence of the usual arguments to help that, any one be inclined to raise objections, it is therefore declared: our purpose is only to disclose the real meaning of *Sruti* texts and not to invite discussion so that a Naiyayika, fond of dispute, should have any cause of misapprehension.

67. Following the method adopted here, one should abstain from ill-matched arguments and disputes and depend entirely on what the *Sruti* says. And there we find it stated "Maya creates Jiva and Iswara."

68. Beginning with creation till his entry in all objects is the work of Iswara, and that of Jiva ranges between the conditions of waking and emancipation.

69. From the *Sruti* we gather:—"The Uniform Intelligence is without decline and growth, always uniform." And it is proper to discriminate it, in that manner.

70. Who is without birth and death, and not subjected to re-birth, can have no concern for practising the means of emancipation from metempsychosis; who is neither desirous of such release, nor free is the Real, Indestructible, Uniform Intelligence.

71. As it is unspeakable and unthinkable, therefore the *Sruti*, for explaining and ascertaining its nature, has described

it by reference to Jiva and Iswara and the objective world, whose substrate it is.

72. There can be no objection in what manner soever a person begets an inclination to know self, and for a theosophist it is always proper so to do.

73. Because from failing to comprehend the drift of *Sruti* utterences, dull and ignorant persons are entranced, and made to wander in illusion ; while a person of discrimination with his knowledge of self is immersed in his supreme felicity :

74. And he knows it for certain, that the cloud of illusion is constantly raining in the form of this material expanse, and the Uniform Intelligence is like ether, quite unconnected with it, and can suffer no injury from that mistake, or derive any profit, [for he is unassociated and blissful].

75. He who studies the present treatise and ascertains its drift, gets an insight of knowledge of Self and experiences supreme felicity by his unbroken presence in the luminosity of that Uniform Intelligence. Such is its result.

SECTION IX.

On the Light of Meditation.

IN beginning the present treatise, the emancipation which proceeds from the worship of Brahma (like that accruing from knowledge of Supreme Brahma) is being pointed out. An illusion is to know a thing different from what it is, and to mistake it for something else. It is of two sorts (*a*) Agreeable and (*b*) Disagreeable. They are defined as follows :—

(*a*). When a mistake of different substance helps the acquirement of the desired object by going to it, it is called agreeable or conformable mistake.

(*b*). When it does not help the accomplishment of the desired result it is called unconformable or disagreeable. Like the acquisition of desired results from a conformable mistake, worship of the Supreme Brahma is also productive of emancipation; for which, various are the forms of worship mentioned in the *Uttara Tapniya.*

2. If the ray of a gem be mistaken by one man for a gem, and the ray of a lamp mistaken for a gem by another man, though both of them are equally subject to mistake, yet there is difference; for if they are tempted to run after the objects of their illusion, the first person, inspite of his mistake, becomes the master of the gem, while the second for his mistaking a lamp for it, can never have the gem: hence the first is an instance of agreeable or conformable mistake, and the second, its reverse, *viz.*, uncomformable or disagreeable.

3. If the light of a lamp inside a house issuing from a door falls outside; and elsewhere, the ray of a brilliant jewel is similarly projected :

4. Two persons viewing the two rays of light at a distance, run after them, knowing them to be jewels; both of them are similarly influenced by mistake caused by the ray.

5. But that one, who had mistaken the ray of lamp-light for a gem and had accordingly run in that direction to seize the prize, is disappointed, while the other, who for his knowledge of a jewel had mistaken it in its ray, is elated with the success attending his search.

6. Illustrations of the above two varieties of mistake are now again particularly set forth. Though the two mistakes are equal, yet for an absence of result in the second, namely lamp-light mistaken for a gem, it is called disagreeing or unconformable, and the mistake of gem in its light, is called agreeable or conformable—for it leads to the possession of the desired gem.

7. If the sight of vapory exhalations rising from a spot, induce a person to infer fire, and he goes in quest of it, mistaking vapor for smoke, and accidently gets it, it can be called an instance of conformable mistake.

8. And if a person believing the waters of the Godavery to be Ganges water, bathes in it with a desire of being benefited, and that bath does produce good results, then it is a conformable mistake.

9. If a person suffering from typhoid fever, pronounces the name of Narayana mistaking it to be the name of a friend, or his son, whom he wants to summon; and subsequent to death, inherits the blissful abode of heaven [for that act], it is a conformable mistake.

10. The above are a few of the many instances of conformable mistake, either visible or inferred, mentioned in the *Shastras*.

11. If a conformable mistake be not regarded to be productive of result in the manner aforesaid, how then can images made of clay, wood, stone, etc., which are all material and subject to destruction, be regarded as *Devas*? And in Knowledge of the five mystic fires, how can woman be worshipped as fire?

12. Moreover it is visibly seen, that a different knowledge

accidentally produces a different result, as in the story of the fruit of palm falling from the flight of a crow; hence it is reasonable to expect conformable mistakes producing results.

13. As conformable mistake, though an error, is productive of results; so is the worship of Brahma, like the knowledgè of Impersonal Brahma, is a cause of person's attaining emancipation.

14. With the help of the four means (passivity, self-control, and the rest) and the arguments used in the *Vedanta*, one is to ascertain the ordinarily invisible Parabrahma, establish his oneness with It and worship thus: "I am that Parabrahma."

15. On the subject of the worship of Parabrahma, the nature of invisible knowledge is thus set forth. Instead of internally contemplating on the Supreme Brahma as impartite bliss, like the worship of the invisible form of Vishnu, ordinarily to know "Brahma is," from the proofs mentioned in the sacred writings, is here meant for 'invisible knowledge.'

16. Though Vishnu is pointed out in the *Shastras* to have four hands, etc., yet during worship, instead of taking cognisance of that form by the eyes, the wise simply pronounce his name in the act of worshipping, and that is acknowledged as invisible knowledge.

17. Now this knowledgė of theirs cannot be called untrue, inasmuch as from the testimony of the *Shastras*, knowledge of his true form shines there intensely.

18. Inspite of knowing self as eternal intelligence, and bliss, according to the *Shastras*, if intelligence be not duly contemplated on as the Impartite, such knowledge does not constitute visible knowledge of Parabrahma.

19. Knowledge of self as eternal, intelligence and bliss from the testimony of the sacred writings, though invisible, is reckoned as knowledge of reality, for it is not erroneous.

20. Moreover, it is worth remarking, though invisible knowledge of Brahma is comparatively slight, since for Its

visible perception the transcendental phrase "That art Thou" has been explained in the *Shastras*, to help the cognition of each self as Brahma, yet as that knowledge can never accrue to the ignorant without due discrimination, therefore the 'invisible' is but another means of knowledge and properly regarded so.

21. Why is visible knowledge of Brahma so difficult of being obtained from want of discrimination in the ignorant? To men of ordinary calibre, self is mistaken for the body, senses, etc., and as that erroneous conception is ever present, they are prevented from grasping self as Brahma,—hence invisible.

22. In men having faith in the *Shastras*, and understanding them, invisible knowledge of Brahma is easily produced; for the visible perception of phenomena—a duality—is no bar to that non-duality;

23. As in the visible perception of stone, no antagonism is created of the invisible knowledge of a Deva, whose image that stone is, and in the well-known image of Vishnu there is never any dispute.

24. And regarding that invisible or visible knowledge, the examples of persons wanting in faith is not worth being taken into consideration, inasmuch as in the *Vedas*, only persons having faith are said to be qualified to undertake works.

25. After having once received instruction from a professor free from error, invisible knowledge is sure to follow, and no argument is necessary for it, as the instruction in regard to the form of Vishnu stands in no need of *Mimansa*.

26. Thus then, though there is no necessity for arguments or discussion to have an invisible knowledge of the Supreme Self in the manner aforesaid, yet the arguments used in the *Shastras* for discussion of works and devotional exercise are only for determining the inutility of practising works and

worship to that end :* otherwise it is impossible for any one to deal with them as they are divided interminably.

---

* In other words, for knowledge of self, neither works nor worship is needed. Why? Because they are naturally antagonistic : knowledge produces emancipation which is eternal, works and worship enable a person to attain a better sphere hereafter, therefore their effects are non-eternal ; knowledge destroys ignorance which is the material cause of re-birth, for which a theosophist is no more subjected to re-births ; and that ignorance consists in regarding Self to be identical either with the physical body, sensory organs, mind, Intellect, etc. The wise are free from illusion, they have no belief in the agency or instrumentality of Self, he is neither a doer of works, nor an enjoyer of their results, consequently they abstain from works save the fructescent, which must be exhausted by actual consummation of their results. Caste, state of life and condition belong to the body, whose properties they are, and not of Self, who is distinct from it, and no other than Brahma. For this visible knowledge of Self, and the mistaken attribution of caste, and the rest, to Self, having been totally destroyed, they, the wise are not engaged in any action.

The same rule applies to worship ; a difference between a Deva and one's Self is an error originating from the intellect ; the wise are free from such error. They regard all phenomena to be unreal, just as objects created in a dream : the only Reality is Intelligence pervading everywhere and that intelligence is called severally Self, Brahma, Atma, and Paramatma. They are all one. If we pause to enquire into the nature of results produced by devotional exercise, we shall find it to be invisible. For, according to the *Shastras*, a worshipper expects to derive benefit by an abode in heaven, of which he has an invisible knowledge produced from the same source. But knowledge of Brahma produces visible results, inasmuch as the person who has acquired it, experiences felicity in life, and his miseries are all removed. Hence for this difference of products from worship and Self-knowledge, they are opposed to each other—that is to say, knowledge produces visible and worship invisible results : they are naturally opposed, hence

27. In the *Kalpa Sutra*, works and worship have been mentioned in a connected form, but when a person has no faith, it is impossible for him to practise without proper discrimination, as to what is proper to be done.

---

a knower of Brahma has no need of worship. He has no faith in the common belief which sets up bondage in self; that has been destroyed by knowledge. Works and worship are not needed for it, just as in the destruction of snake-illusion, knowledge of the rope is enough and nothing more is needed. It would thus be evident, there is a difference in results between those of knowledge and works, etc., hence they are respectively called visible and invisible. The 'visible result' is exemplified in the illustrations of cloth produced by the weaving loom and brush, or thirst and hunger appeased by drink and food. Inasmuch as all illusions or mistakes are removed by knowledge of the abiding seat on which they are superimposed, therefore that destruction of mistake or error is a visible result of knowledge: similarly knowledge of self removes the mistaken notion of his bondage, and emancipation proceeds as a matter of course. But it may be contended why is self not subject to re-birth? Because, he is eternal, and naturally unrelated, *i.e.*, free. What is eternal can never be subject to birth and death; and what is free can never be an agent or instrument. If bondage were true, works and devotion would be required to cause its destruction, but as it is not, therefore that ignorance which creates it on self, is removed with his thorough knowledge; in the same way, as the snake created by ignorance in a bit of string, is destroyed when a light is brought to bear on it, thus helping its knowledge. Just as in the snake-illusion, no work can remove it, but knowledge of the rope [in all its parts] is enough to dispel it, so a thorough knowledge of the oneness of self with Brahma, destroys the illusion of bondage and the other mistakes as to his identity with the body and the rest. Emancipation has been spoken of as a 'visible result,' for the *Vedas* mention it in that way. If it were otherwise, it will be in opposition to them, for emancipation is either eternal release, or a temporary abode in heaven. Now of them, the

28. Worship has been described in several works written by *Rishis* in a practical form, but those who understand them not, nor are capable of discussing the comparative merits of a particular form, when they hear them read, repair to a professor for the necessary instruction and pay all reverence to him.

---

latter is non-eternal, and therefore cannot be same with eternal release; actions and worship procure heaven; knowledge, emancipation; actions are non-eternal, their results, equally so; knowledge is eternal, and its product is eternal release. Enough has already been said to shew knowledge alone, and not works and devotion, or the three together, to be the source of emancipation, and to say that like watering the roots of a plant yielding fruit, is the fruit emancipation produced by works and devotion is improper. Because, watering a tree does not invariably make it bear fruits. It may be requisite for its growth and vitality, so far well; but in the matter of seed-bearing, other causes are at work: for instance, the usual laws of male and female flowers, and carriage of the fertilizing pollen through the pistil into the ovary; some trees have only male flowers, the pollen is conveyed either by the wind or the wings of the bee and butterfly unknowingly acting as a medium; for as they come and sit in the flower cup to suck the honey, a little of the powder which has adhered to the wings or feet adhere into the pistil, thence to come in contact with the ovisac, and impregnation is complete: when so much is involved in the process, how can watering a plant would make it yield fruit? On the other hand, this may be said of it, when a tree is deprived of its supply of water, it withers and dries. Plants suck the moisture by their roots and the food is conveyed in a soluble form, to be mixed up with the sap, afterwards elaborated into chlorophyle, carbon, and so forth; hence it is said, just as stopping the water leads to premature decay and death, and it dries; so if works and worship are done away with, knowledge already produced is destroyed, and the result emancipation follows not. But it is a mistake. Because, the example does not apply; for, so far as the withering of a tree goes, it is to a certain extent true, especially

29. Then again, with a view of determining the signification of *Vedic* words, men analyse and solve them, but in the precepts of a trustworthy performer of practice, there is a chance of practices being enforced.

30. As without proper discussion, but simply from instruction, a person may be trained in devotional exercise, so from simple instruction no one can have visible knowledge of Brahma.

31. As want of faith is the one impediment for invisible

---

in countries where the heat is intense and the usual rainfall very scanty, but to say, abandonding works and worship will bring the mind back into its original condition of unsteadiness and make it faulty, is far from correct; so that, like the withered tree of the dry land, knowledge will be destroyed, is an assertion not authenticated by proofs either personal or authoritative. In the first place, let it be ascertained what shape does the knowledge assume, to see if it be ever removed or replaced by anything else? Everywhere, in the *Vedanta*, the doctrine of non-duality has been established, and it is maintained: when a person has realized that oneness of self and Brahma, he exclaims, "I am Brahma." To say, that by ceasing to have recourse to actions and devotion a theosophist loses this knowledge, is clearly contraindicated: for, on appealing to experience, we find the reverse is true. A theosophist is never engaged in works and worship, but his perception of Brahma is clear enough. His natural love for all creatures is the best proof. For Self is the source of affection, and he pervades everywhere, hence, "All this is full of Self," consequently he loves them equally with Self. Then again, such knowledge is eternal, and, therefore, not liable to destruction; it stands in no need of protecting care, like that of water as in the case of tree; their discontinuance affects it not, one way or the other; for when the mind has once assumed the modification of the Impartite Brahma, all ignorance ceases, and after its destruction, that knowledge of oneness with Brahma requires no protection from anything injurious. Ignorance is the enemy to knowledge, and when it is destroyed, what can injure knowledge? Clearly nothing.

knowledge, so want of proper discussion and exercise of judgment is the obstacle to visible knowledge; therefore it is necessary to have recourse to arguments and analysis for visible knowledge of BRAHMA.

32. If after particular and attentive discussion, no visible knowledge follows, yet such is to be repeated over and over for that knowledge to set in.

33. And if discussion, and analysis continued till death, brings no cognition of self visibly, even that would not be in vain, for in the next re-incarnation it will be accomplished.

34. Because VYAS, the author of *Vedanta Sutras*, has ascertained it to be a fact, and persons of dull intellect hearing it, fail to comprehend its import, though it is certain for knowledge to yield fruits even in another re-incarnation.

35. As for instance, in the case of BAMDEVA: while in his mother's womb he had known BRAHMA, as a result of knowledge of a prior existence.

36. As in the case of study, where the meaning is not comprehended, for a part not committed to memory after repeated trials and if the subject be not taken up the next day or shortly after, yet from repeatedly remembering, it is confirmed.

37. As repeated tilling a piece of land makes it fertile and it yields abundant crops, so by gradual practice, even Self-knowledge will unmistakably bear fruits.

38. Owing to the presence of three obstacles, some are unable to know the Supreme Self, from repeated analysis and discussion: this has been fully mentioned by *Bartikara*.

39. How can those obstacles be removed? By searching after the cause of their destruction, the social bonds are torn, and they are destroyed of themselves. The obstacles are past, future, and present.

40. Even study of the *Vedanta* proves ineffectual owing to the above obstacles. This has been illustrated in the *Sruti* by the example of HIRANYANIDHI.

41. Of them, the past obstacle is as follows:—Owing to an attachment for a milch-buffalow, from the force of habit acquired previous to their retirement from society, some recluse fail to have a firm knowledge of self; this is known too well:

42. But when after receiving instruction from a *Guru*, by kind and sympathising words, the obstacles are destroyed then their Self-knowledge becomes firm,—it is confirmed.

43. Present obstacle is of this nature:—Firm attachment to property, riches and the rest, is called present obstacle. It spoils knowledge, creates illusion, raises ill assorted objections, and begets an inclination to dispute and wrangle.

44. But passivity, self-control, etc., and hearing, consideration, etc., requisite for the time being, destroy it with the rest, and pave the way for the fruits of knowledge to accrue easily.

45. Future obstacle is in this wise:—On the subject of the rising of knowledge in BAMDEVA, it has been said, the presence of fructescent works, for the next or another incarnation, is called future obstacle. It was exhausted in him by enjoying during his sojourn in one incarnation, but BHARAT had to enjoy them in three successive re-incarnations, before they were exhausted.

46. A person who has failed in Yoga, or been deprived of it, exhausts his obstacle by the practices of several incarnations, inasmuch as there can never be an undoing of the results of discussion and analysis. To this end KRISHNA says to ARJUNA (*Gita*, Chapt. 6., V. 41.) as follows:—

47. "From the meritorious actions of prior life, after having inherited the blissful abode of heaven, etc., he is born from the force of Self-knowledge, in a noble family, with wealth and rank, as best he wishes.

48. "Or, from the strength of that virtue, and discussion of BRAHMA, he is born in the family of an intellectual Yogi free from any desire, but this is extremely rare:

49. "Because, in that life, after having been re-possessed of his previous knowledge and connected with intellect, he again follows the path that leads to knowledge of BRAHMA.

50. "Attracted by the impression of former practices which have well nigh from disuse become deadened, his attachment to them grows strong; in this manner, after having passed through several re-incarnations and realised the fruits of knowledge, ultimately merges into the Absolute, and is freed."

51. Even with a desire of acquiring the abode of *Brahmá* being present, when a person restrains it, and enquires into the Supreme Self with due discrimination, he does not get a direct knowledge of the SUPREME BRAHMA, visibly, it is true:

52. But after having ascertained it, in the manner laid down in the *Vedanta*, he goes to the abode of *Brahmá*, to enjoy felicity for a time, ultimately in the end of *Kalpa** to be freed with *Brahmá*.

53. In some, knowledge of a previous life, acquired by the help of the arguments used in the *Vedanta*, is concluded by falling into the practice of works, inasmuch as some are unable even to hear the reality of Supreme Self being talked of or read; and some fail to comprehend its import even after having heard it.

54. But either from dullness of intellect or want of purity of mind, when a person is incapacitated from ascertaining self by the help of supporting arguments, it is proper for him to be constantly engaged in the worship of the SUPREME BRAHMA in the invisible manner. As "BRAHMA is."

55. To worship the Impersonal BRAHMA in the above manner [invisible form] is not inconsistent; as in the personal method, the flow of the mental function is directed towards him, so here also, there is a likelihood of his faith in the

---

* A day and night of *Brahmá*—a period of 4,320,000,000 solar sidereal years.

existence of BRAHMA being confirmed and thus invisible knowledge resulting [ultimately].

56. If it be asked since the form of BRAHMA is beyond the reach of word and mind, how then it is possible to worship Him invisibly? In that case, let there be no visible krowledge produced.

57. If you know Him to be beyond the reach of word and mind, why not admit his invisible worship in that manner?

58. If you say:—To acknowledge BRAHMA as an object of worship will reduce him to a Personal [God], possessing attributes? But then how can you do away with it in his visible knowledge? Therefore worship him invisibly by Indicative Indications.

59. In the *Sruti* occurs the passage "What is beyond the reach of word and mind, know that to be BRAHMA." And "Whom people worship is not BRAHMA.

60. If you admit the above, then as "BRAHMA is distinct from the known and unknown" (*Sruti*): this passage would necessarily make us refuse his visible knowledge;—for, as his worship is interdictible so is his knowableness equally.

61. If you regard BRAHMA to be unknowable, what prevents you from acknowledging BRAHMA to be not worshippable? inasmuch as knowledge and worship are equally functions of the internal organ and pervaded by it.

62. If you ask, why am I so fond of worship as to maintain its practice and explain it? I may stop to enquire, why are you so averse to it? to say proofs are wanting for impersonal worship is quite inconsistent.

63. For proofs to that effect abound in the *Uttar Tapniya*, *Prashna*, *Katho* and *Mandukya Upanishads*.

64. The method of its practice has been mentioned in connection with quintuplication, if you admit it to be a means for the acquisition of knowledge, I have no objection.

65. If you say, no one has ever practised the invisible

worship of the SUPREME BRAHMA: the reply is that does not indicate any defect in the worship, but it is the fault of the person who does not practise it.

66. For, no matter whether an ignorant person be engaged in the recantation of the formulæ for making a person submissive, considering it to be easier than worship, or the stupid considering cultivation to be easier still, be engaged in it accordingly, that does not imply any fault in worship.

67. So far as the inclination of the dull and ignorant are concerned, though there may be other points of discussion, it is proper to judge becomingly as to the superiority of the Impersonal worship; owing to the unity of all the ordained knowledges in the *Vedanta,* the well-known attributes, over and over declared in all Branches of the *Vedas*, are in the end centred in the Invisibly to be worshipped PARABRAHMA.

68. Bliss, etc., are all centred in PARABRAHMA, in the end, by VYAS in the 11 *Sutra* of the 3rd Sect. Chapt., III., of the *Shariraka.*

69. In the 33rd *Sutra* of the same work, VYAS describes BRAHMA in the end as neither gross nor diminutive—qualities which are fit for being excluded.

70. If therefore any one were to contend:—to attribute qualities to the Impersonal BRAHMA is unreasonable and inconsistent, that remark applies to VYAS who wrote so, and not to us.

71. If you say, since there is no mention of *Hiranyakesha, Hiranyashashru,* Sun or other forms by way of illustration, I admit the above worship to be Impersonal. The reply is, be you content with that.

72. Then again, if to enquire into the attributes, you say to be purposeless though admitting the desirability of knowing BRAHMA by Indication, be you engaged in that form of Its worship.

73. That self who is indicated by blissfulness, or who is not gross (*i. e.,* subtle), is one Impartite with the Supreme

Self. And "That am I:" this is the way by which you should worship him.

74. If it be asked what is the distinction between knowledge and worship? The reply is:—There is particular distinction between them, knowledge is dependent on the substance that is to be known, while worship is dependent on individual desire.

75. From discrimination or exercise of judgment is produced knowledge; when that has once been confirmed, in spite of disinclination on the part of the person, it cannot be prevented. With knowledge, illusion of the reality of phenomena is at once destroyed.

76. Thus a theosophist is successful in accomplishing what he was about, and attains perfect contentment. He is "delivered in life" waiting only for the consummation of his fructescent works.

77. A person of faith believing on the Reality of instruction received from a preceptor, should always with due disrimination and judgment enquire after, and become one with it, by concentrating his mind with earnest attention.

78. So long as he knows not self to be non-distinct from Parabrahma, he should constantly give himself up to meditation; and when that non-duality has been firmly established, there is no more necessity for thinking: he will then be freed from death.

79. A *Brahmachari* worshipper of non-distinction from self with Brahma, keeps that non-duality constantly in mind and is engaged in begging for his daily bread.

80. To worship in this way, or not to worship, or to do it in any other manner, proceeds from a person's desire which is its extraordinary cause, so that to remove that want of desire will make the current of the internal organ constantly assume the modification of Brahma.

81. As a person studying the *Vedas*, from the habit of constant study bereft of all doubts and mistakes, in dream

also is engaged in that study; or like one engaged in repeating the sacred texts from desire, a worshipper, from the force of practice is engaged in meditation while in dream.

82. When contending knowledge is cured, and a person is always engaged in thinking of self, in dream also he acquires the habit of meditation.

83. Even during the consummation of fructescent works, from a good deal of faith, one is able to meditate constantly, and no doubts remain on that subject:

84. Like a woman fond of associating with her lover, though engaged in the performance of her household duties, is ever thinking of tasting the sweets of that illicit intercourse.

85. And though her household works are not managed *quite* irregularly yet they are only done in a perfunctory manner.

86. Like a house-wife busy with her household work, that other woman desirous of courting her lover's embrace can never show a similar attention or order and regularity in performing her duties, for she is wanting in earnestness:

87. So is a person engaged in meditation able to keep up a trace of the ordinary popular practices, and a theosophist is quite able to keep up with them, as they cannot destroy or affect his knowledge in any way.

88. The world is illusory and self is intelligence: in this knowledge there is no antagonism to popular practice.

89. A theosophist knowing the unreality of the world, still uses it, and knowing self to be intelligence is yet engaged in the usual means of that knowledge as in use among men:

90. Because the means to that end, mind, word, body and external objects he cannot do away with, consequently it is very natural that he should be using them.

91. One who by thinking, has his mind freed from its ever changing function is not a theosophist, he is called a 'meditator'; for in determining the nature of external objects

which are in daily use, as a jar, etc., there is no necessity for making the mind so firm.

92. With the manifestation of the mental function once, a jar is known, why is not *Atma* who is self-illuminated to be discovered without the destruction of the mind?

93. If it be said, though BRAHMA is self-illuminated, yet the flow of the mental function directed to It, is called knowledge of self, but that modification of the mental function is liable to destruction every moment, consequently it is necessary to rest it on BRAHMA over and over. The reply is:—It holds equally true in the cognition of a jar, etc.

94. If you reply, after the intellect has discovered a jar to a certainty, even with its destruction, it is quite easy to cognise it again; analogy will draw a similar conclusion with regard to Self.

95. After the intellect has been once fixed in self, whatever may a theosophist desire, he is enabled to consider or meditate; and to say, what another has in mind.

96. And if like a worshipper, a theosophist engaged in meditation forgets the usual practices, it is then said to be produced from meditation, because knowledge never creates such forgetfulness of popular practices.

97. To a theosophist meditation is optional,—dependent on his desire, because emancipation results from knowledge, as mentioned in the *Shastras* over and over. "Knowledge produces non-duality."

98. If a theosophist does not betake to meditation, but is engaged in the external practices of men, let him go on with them; for there is no impediment to his being so engaged in the daily routine of practice.

99. If for a theosophist to be engaged with worldly practices, you say, imply excess of attachment, the question is what do you call excess of attachment? If you refer to the sanction and prohibition of *Shastras* that does not apply to him.

100. One who has a conceit for his caste, station in life, condition, etc., to him only does that sanction and prohibition laid down in the sacred writings apply; but to a theosophist free from conceit, it is inapplicable.

101. Caste, station and the rest are from illusion attributed to the physical body, but to self, who is eternal and intelligence they belong not; and this is the firm knowledge of a theosophist.

102. No matter whether they practise profound meditation, works, etc., or not, from want of faith in the reality of the universe in their internal organ, they are called pure Theosophists and "delivered in life."

103. Works or no works can produce no injury to them, and meditation or no meditation, or recanting of sacred formulæ or its reverse, can produce neither benefit nor injury; for their minds are free from desire.

104. Self is unassociated, eternal intelligence; saving him, everything else is due to *Maya* or illusion, as unreal as things produced in a magical performance: when such an impression has been confirmed, there is no room for any desire to remain in the mind.

105. If therefore, for a theosophist there is nothing proper and improper, in short the sanctioned and forbidden rites can bring him neither merit nor demerit where then is his excess of attachment? That can only hold good in a person who has attachment, but to speak of excess in connection with him who has no attachment whatever, is illogical.

106. As in the absence of sanction or law, that excess does not hold good with regard to boys, so there being neither any rule nor prohibition, so far as theosophists are concerned, it is impossible to apprehend any excess of attachment in them.

107. If it be alleged, boys have no knowledge of what is lawful and unlawful, consequently the rule of sanction and prohibition does not apply to them; it may as well be said in

regard to a theosophist, that as he knows the unreality of this material expanse and reality of self and his non-distinction from BRAHMA, he has nothing lawful and unlawful; for that sanction and prohibition has been mentioned in the *Shastras*, only for the guidance of the less knowing, and no rules have been laid down either for theosophists or the ignorant.

108. Any one possessing the power of cursing and blessing another [so as to make them actually come to pass] should not be regarded as a theosophist; for the ability to curse and bless effectually is a result of devout and rigid austerities (*Tapasya*).

109. Nor shall knowledge be credited with powers like those which the supremely wise VYAS and others had, for they are the result of devout austerities. And that (*Tapasya*) devotion, which causes knowledge, has no such result: knowledge is its [only] product.

110. One who has achieved success both in devout austerities and devotion (the cause of knowledge) gets both the ability of cursing, etc., as well as knowledge; otherwise there does not follow one set of results from one sort of practice, when he betakes to the other for acquiring Self-knowledge. One engaged in practising the means of knowledge gets only knowledge as a result.

111. If you say, men conforming to no sanctioned practice and without any ability are spoken ill of by ascetics (*Yati*). That is not so very grave a charge, inasmuch as men devoted to sensual pleasures speak disparagingly of ascetics, thus each in turn is equally a subject of reproach from the other.

112. And those sensualists revile in this wise :—If ascetics betake to begging for the sake of enjoyment, wear the usual clothing, etc., for the sake of happiness, how astonishingly exquisite is their asceticism? Indeed under weight of asceticism has their indifference to worldly enjoyments succumbed!

113. If you say, to be thus reviled by ignorant persons can bring forth no injury to them, it may as well be said of a

theosophist, that the treatment which he meets with, at the hands of persons who consider self to be their physical body, etc., is of little import.

114. In this way, without removing external objects, as a means of knowledge, a theosophist is yet able to carry on the ordinary duties of a king and administrator or the usual popular practices without suffering any detrimental effect.

115. If it be alleged, after having discovered all material objects to be unreal, a wise person can have no more desire for them; the reply is, certainly it is so far true, but fructescent actions engage him either in meditation, or practice [common amongst men, as eating, sleeping and the rest] as he likes.

116. A devout worshipper should always betake to meditation, for like attaining the abode of *Vishnu*, through meditation he has become BRAHMA [by his knowledge of non-duality].

117. What is caused by meditation, should naturally be undone by its want? Hence a worshipper should always meditate; but after a person has known self to be no other than BRAHMA, if he were to abandon the means of knowledge, that would not destroy it.

118. Knowledge is only for the attainment of BRAHMA (not its cause), and it assures a person that he is so; therefore, in the absence of knowledge, and non-existence of knower, firm persuasion of the identity of self with BRAHMA is never destroyed.

119. And if you regard a worshipper to have accomplished his identity with the eternal PARABRAHMA what prevents you from looking dull and ignorant persons as well the lower animals from an equal accomplishment of their identity with It?

120. For, in the absence of Self-knowledge both are equally placed, so far as emancipation goes. As to beg for bread is better than starvation, so it is better to have recourse to meditation instead of doing nothing.

121. Instead of following the course of practice in vogue among the ignorant, to have recourse to the usual actions [sanctioned in the sacred writings] is preferable, better than that is the form of Personal worship, and Impersonal worship is the best of all.

122. So long as a person reaches not the portal of knowledge, his progression gets gradually advanced; but Impersonal worship is afterwards developed into Self-knowledge and counted as such.

123. As during the time of reaping results, a conformable mistake can be looked upon as correct proof, so is matured Impersonal worship equal to Self-knowledge, during emancipation.

124. If you say, a person inclined to a conformable mistake accomplishes the desired result by other proofs, what harm is there for worship becoming a cause of Self-knowledge by any other proof, during emancipation?

125. If any sort of Personal worship or recanting sacred formulæ, etc., by clearing the mind of all blemishes leads indirectly, *i.e.*, secondhand, to visible knowledge, and they are therefore regarded as its cause, yet as a direct cause of knowledge, Impersonal worship has many points of particularity.

126. That Impersonal worship when matured, ultimately leads to profound meditation, hence by profound unconscious meditation it is easily attainable.

127. After that profound unconscious meditation,* has been thoroughly practised and one has become proficient in it, there remains only the unassociated Intelligence in the inter-

* When the mind comes to centre all its thoughts on the Impartite (Universal) Consciousness, after having surmounted the four obstacles, like the unflickering light of a lamp, by devout and profound meditation, it is called the (*Nirvikalpa Samadhi*) Unconscious meditation.

nal organ, and when by repeated practice that has been removed, he discovers his oneness with the SUPREME BRAHMA as expounded in the signification of "That art Thou?"

128. And the unchangeable unassociated, eternal self-illuminated Intelligence of PARABRAHMA is easily fixed in the intellect.

129. This has been fully declared in the *Amritabindu Upanishad*. Thus then, for the sake of acquiring Self-knowledge by means of profound unconscious meditation, Impersonal worship is the best and superior to personal, etc.

130. Those who undertake the Personal form of worship, heeding not what has just been said about the superiority of the Impersonal leading to Self-knowledge by its direct means of profound unconscious meditation, are best compared with the popular illustration of refusing to take what is in the hand and getting satisfied with licking it by the tongue.

131. The above illustration applies equally to those who are engaged in Impersonal worship leaving off discrimination of self. For this reason, worship has been laid down authoritatively necessary to those, with whom exercise of judgment or analysis for discrimination of self is impossible.

132. A person whose mind is distracted with several things, say accumulation of riches, aggrandisement of others, etc., has no possibility of acquiring Self-knowledge by due discrimination; consequently worship is essentially necessary to him, for clearing the internal organ of all blemishes and making it faultless.

133. But those, who are desirous of release, have been cured of unsteadiness or fickleness of mind [hence worship is not needed for them]. Their internal organ is simply enveloped in fascination, and discrimination of self is very desirable, as it is superior to all other means—for it easily leads to emancipation.

134. In evidence of Self-knowledge, as a means of the particular forms of emancipation mentioned in *Yoga* and *Sankhya*,

the *Gita* says :—"Whatever result is obtainable from *Sankhya*, is equally produced by *Yoga* ; therefore, he who knows them to be non-distinct, is a real knower of the purport of the *Shastra*." (Chap. V., v., 5)

135. Nor is the *Gita* the only authority, for we find proofs to that effect in the *Sruti* :—"Knowledge of self is expounded in *Yoga* and *Sankhya Philosophy* as a source of emancipation. Here both the *Sruti* and the two above-mentioned Systems agree, but in matters where they disagree from the *Sruti* they should not be considered as proofs.

136. A person unsuccessful in maturing worship in his present life, attains the abode of *Brahmd* after death, and in a subsequent, emancipation, *from Self-knowledge.

---

* "*Om* is BRAHMA, and you should look upon its alphabets, representing the SUPREME BRAHMA, to be non-different from yourself, and have your mental function so moulded after it, that it may remain fixed or impressed there. No other meditation can equal this: and in his work on *Quintuplication*, SURESWAR has particularly dealt on it. Though many of the *Upanishads* treat on *Pranab*, yet the *Munduka* has particular reference to it : and from the annotations of the Commentator as well as those of ANANDAGIRI, the subject has been clearly explained. *Vartikara* [SURESWAR ACHARYA] has also adopted the same method in his work on *Quintuplication*.

Meditating on the mystic '*Om*' can be done in two ways according to the *Upanishads* ; one is to identify it with the SUPREME BRAHMA, aud thus to reflect and meditate profoundly on that abstract condition of impersonality which is devoid of qualities. The other is to meditate on BRAHMA with qualities (personal). Now the Impersonal BRAHMA is called the SUPREME BRAHMA, while that other is called the (Personal) BRAHMA with qualities ; and one engaged in the first sort of devotion obtains 'release ;' while to the follower of the second method can accrue the abode of *Brahmd*. Thus then, we find meditation of '*Om*,' from a difference in the method and subject of worship, is divided into two sorts, of which the Impersonal alone will be considered here.

137. Whatever ideas take hold of a dying person's mind, after death he assumes that condition accordingly; for concentration of mind invariably produces the result of similarity of condition.

138. The future life of the individual is determined by his good or bad thoughts during his last moments; if that be certain, it is natural to infer that like a worshipper centering his east thoughts on this Personal worship, having his mind moulded after Him, the follower of Impersonal worship has his knowledge moulded after the Impersonal BRAHMA.

139. Emancipation and attainment of BRAHMA are only a difference in name; otherwise both have for their signification deliverance, and like conformable mistake, are equally productive of result.

140. Though Impersonal worship is a variety of mental action, and not a direct cause of emancipation, yet it leads to knowledge by which ignorance is removed; as meditation of Benares (which itself is not free) produces knowledge of BRAHMA.

141. In the *Tapaniya Upanishad* is thus mentioned emancipation produced as a result of Impersonal worship:—"With desire, without desire, without body, without senses, without

---

For, the worshippers of the personal creator are actuated with a desire of enjoying the fruit of their devotion, and this they get by inheriting the blissful abode of BRAHMA; and as that very desire stands an obstacle in the way of impersonal devotion, they are prevented from acquiring the necessary knowledge, and, therefore, subjected to bondage, and never freed. Now while enjoining the blissful abode of *Brahmâ*, and sharing all enjoyments equally with *Hiranyagarbha*, if the individual acquires knowledge, he may yet be freed. But those who have no desire of inherting the *Brahmaloka*, acquire knowledge here and are freed. Thus then, the results of the Personal worship are included in the Impersonal.—*Vicharsagar*, pp. 199-200.

any fear are the indications of emancipation in Impersonal worship.

142. According to the strength of worship is produced knowledge, the cause of emancipation. "Therefore, without knowledge there are no other means of emancipation," as mentioned in the *Shastras*, implies no antagonism to worship.

143. For this purpose it is said "Worship without any desire of reaping its result produces emancipation" (*Tapaniya*). "And worship with desire leads to the abode of truth" (*Prashnopanishad*).

144. One who worships *Om* with a desire of being benefited, attains the abode of *Brahmá*, where after acquiring Self-knowledge he is released with its king, at the end of *Kalpa*.*

145. The *Shariraka Sutras* (Chapt. IV., p. III., *Sutra* XV.,) mention the attainment of the abode of *Brahmá* as a result of Personal worship, according to the desire of the individual:

146. "From the force of Impersonal Worship after reaching there, he acquires Self-knowledge to be released with *Brahmá* when his time comes at the expiry of the *Kalpá*."

147. Worship of *Om* has everywhere been described as almost Impersonal. In some places, it is said to be Personal, and their results have thus been ascertained :—

148. *Om* is the proof on which rests both Personal and Impersonal forms of worship. This was the instruction given to MAHAKAM by PIPLADA in reply to his question.

149. Thus knowing *Om* to be the prop, whatever worship a person undertakes either of the Personal or Impersonal BRAHMA, he gets results according to his desire ; so said *Yama* to NACHIKETA (*Kathopanishad*).

---

* "A day and night of *Brahmá*, a period of 4,320,000,000 Solarsydereal-years of mortals, measuring the duration of the world, and as many, the interval of its annihilation."—WILSON.

150. To the worshipper of the Impersonal is produced visible knowledge of PARABRAHMA either in his present life or the next, or in the abode of *Brahma*; and the result of that worship can never remain unfructified:

151. Therefore one who is unable to weigh and make proper use of the arguments used, should constantly worship self, as clearly set forth in the *Atma Gita*.

152. For example:—"He who is unable to know me manifestly, should depend on me without any fear and misapprehension, and when subsequently that has been confirmed, in due time, I shall appear unto him as the giver of result."

153. "As when a deep mine has been discovered, there is no other means save that of digging, for getting at the gem; so without reflection of self, there is no other means by which I can be manifestly known."

154. How reflection of self produces visible knowledge of PARABRAHMA is thus being declared:—By removing the bit of stone in the shape of the physical body from the ground, and repeatedly turning the sod by the spade of intellect, mind is cleared of all-blemishes, and a person desirous of release is successful in discovering me—like the gem in a mine. And there is no doubt about it.

155. Advisableness of meditation for one not qualified to Self-knowledge is thus illustrated:—One who is not qualified in discovering PARABRAHMA should think and reflect "I am PARABRAHMA." Since unreal objects can be had from meditation, Why is the Real BRAHMA, who is eternal and free, should not be had in that way?

156. From meditation, is gradually destroyed the usual knowledge of not-Self in self; and one who knows this and yet keeps himself off from meditation is a brute.

157. By abandoning conceit for the body, and cognising BRAHMA in self, *Jiva* becomes immortal, and enjoys the supreme felicity of BRAHMA in his present life.

158. Now for the result:—Having thoroughly understood the present treatise, who keeps it constantly present in his mind, is freed from all doubts and is delivered from metempsychosis, for his constant meditation and reflection of self.

SECTION X.

Illustration by comparision to a Theatrical Performance.

ILLUSORY attribution and its withdrawal, are now being introduced in opening the present treatise, with the view of helping the comprehension of self and enabling a pupil easily to acquire that knowledge. Prior to the evolution of the world there existed the one and secondless Supreme Self, full of bliss. Out of his desire, created He the world with *Maya*, and entered each individual in the form of *Jiva*.

2. Created He the superior bodies of *Devas*, and entering them, himself became *Deva*; in the same way, did he create the mean and worthless bodies of images and entering them, became their worshipper out of ignorance.

3. After having been engaged in several prior births till death, in worship, a person begets an inclination for Self-knowledge; subsequently by discrimination and exercise of judgment, when spiritual ignorance about the reality of phenomena and attachment to mundane enjoyments is destroyed, and associates removed, he knows self to be pure and eternal, and thus abides his time.

4. The Supreme Self is secondless and blissful, but to consider otherwise and to regard him as subject to grief and misery is called bondage; and to rest on his real nature is called emancipation.

5. Want of discrimination causing the bondage in self is removed by discrimination. Therefore it is imperatively necessary always to reflect on the points of resemblance and difference between *Jiva* and *Paramatma*.

6. Apart from the body and organs of sense and action, *Jiva* for his conceit of egoism is the literal signification of "I am I," the agent or instrument; and mind is his instrument of action. Actions produced by the internal or external functions are all his.

7. The internal function modified into "I am I" expresses the agent or instrument. And the external modification of 'this' discovers all phenomena.

8. Subjects of external knowledge are characterised with distinct properties: for instance, smell, form, taste, sound, and touch; and for perceiving each of them, we have five organs of external sense, which are called instruments of action accordingly.

9. Now the witnessing Intelligence or Supreme Self is the discoverer of *Jiva* as an agent, mental action, and of the five properties of objects abovementioned at one time.

10. As the light of a theatre discovers equally the proprietor, dancing girls, actors and spectators who have assembled to witness a performance; and when none of them are there, the light burns and illuminates itself:

11. So, sight, hearing, smell, taste and touch; and egoism, function of intellect, and phenomena are illuminated coetaneously by the light of Witnessing Intelligence;

12. And in their absence, it burns intensely and is as conspicuous as before.

13. From the incessant resplendency of the light of Uniform Intelligence, the individual intellect draws its powers of discovery, and assumes several modifications, just as dancing girls throw their figures in several attitudes to make it more attractive.

14. And the particular distinction is this:—Egoism is the householder; objects resemble the audience; intellect, *danseuse*; senses, musicians; witnessing intelligence, light. Such a theatre is fit for the intellect to dance in.

15. As the light in the theatre though confined in one spot illuminates the whole place equally, so the Witnessing Intelligence though resting quietly, discovers internally and externally at the same time.

16. ('Internal' and 'external' have reference to the

relation of the body: the first stands for egoism, etc.; and the second, objects situated external to the body).

17. Though Intellect is situated inside the body, yet in connection with the sensory organs it repeatedly pervades external objects which it seeks to cognise; and its fickle and unsteady nature discovered or illuminated by the Witnessing Intelligence is from illusion attributed to the Witness in vain,—for it is steady and tranquil and has no wavering fickleness.

18. As by moving the hand to and fro, in a few rays of fixed light entering a room through a crevice, makes that light appear to be moving, while virtually it is fixed:

19. Similarly the Witnessing Intelligence though situated in its own site, and neither gets in or out, is apt to be taken for the unsteadiness of intellect,—as going out and coming in—which virtually it never does.

20. That Intelligence has neither any locality external nor internal, which belongs to the Intellect. And when the interminable associates of intellect are destroyed, it rests in the resplendent effulgence of its own light.

21. Though after destruction of all associates, in the absence of a province, it is impossible for its manifestibility to continue everywhere, yet in the presence of a practical province its pervasion is admissible from that relation.

22. Like Its pervasion, PARABRAHMA is everywhere a witness. As Intellect is capable of going either internally or externally everywhere, whatever may be the time, and however distant a subject may be which it wishes to take cognition of, so does PARABRAHMA, for It is the witness that discovers all phenomena, and the intellect is a mere reflected shadow of Its intelligence.

23. Whatever objects with form, etc., are cognised by the intellect, they are all discovered by PARABRAHMA, as their witness; though virtually, He is beyond the reach of word and intellect.

24. It may be contended, since Self is beyond the reach of word and thought how is he then to be grasped? Cease doing it then. Discrimination of the Reality of Self and unreality of the material universe, removes the perception of its being something tangible; and when it has ceased to exist to all intents and purposes, then as the residue of its destruction, Self is manifested in the form of truth, and thus continues to subsist.

25. No proofs are necessary to make Self visible, for he is self-illuminated. And if proofs be needed to help the intellect, repair to a professor and receive instruction from him in the *Sruti*.

26. Having in the aforesaid manner taught the means of discriminating Self to a superiorly qualified person, another method is now being pointed out for the benefit of others who are incapable of practising it.—Those unable to cast away material perceptions, should take protection of their intellect. Because as through that intellect all objects, both external and internal, are known, and e Supreme Self as their witness is dependent on it, therefore is he to be inferred as such witness.

SECTION XI.

*Brahmananda.**

(*a*) *Yogananda.*

[WITH the view of producing an inclination in the pupil to study the work, its importance is thus set forth]:—I shall now speak of BRAHMAIC felicity, which being known, a person abandons all works, as they are based on ignorance, and experiences happiness by becoming BRAHMA.

2. To demonstrate the truth of the assertion "knowledge of BRAHMA destroys ignorance together with its product the objective world, and procures emancipation," the author quotes two texts from the *Taiteriya Upanishad* "A knower of BRAHMA attains the Supreme BRAHMA." "A knower of Self surmounts all grief." And explains them in the following wise:—One who knows BRAHMA acquires the supreme blissfulness of BRAHMA; and one, who knows Self to be infinite, surmounts all grief, inasmuch as any ill befalling one connected to him fails to affect him. If it be contended, the word 'Supreme BRAHMA' in the first passage cannot have for its signification felicity, but that it expresses secondlessness: therefore to remove such a misapprehension it is said, BRAHMA as Self is the essence, and a theosophist knowing his oneness with It experiences happiness, and save this knowledge there are no other means capable of producing it.

3. When a theosophist rests on the Supreme Self knowing him to be non-distinct from his individual Self, his fears

---

* The five following treatises are all explanatory of BRAHMAIC felicity, for which they have been laid down as so many chapters of one book "Brahmananda." Now the felicity which arises from concentration of the mind *(Yoga)* is also included in it, and this is the subject of the present work. It is proper here to observe that instead of following the author's classification we would go on with the serial number of the Sections, otherwise the *Panchadasi* (composed of fifteen works would be incomplete.

cease; and one who does not, but believes them to be distinct, is subject to fear.

4. "Notwithstanding the practice of religious observances and meritorious works in a prior state of existence, this knowledge of distinction (duality) has been the cause of fear; and for that fear of *Brahma*, Air, Sun, Fire and Death are engaged in their several spheres.

5. "After the cognition of the felicity of BRAHMA, a person is no more affected with any fears concerning the present or future. For a theosophist is never distressed with thoughts of good actions left undone and bad deeds done, like the common run of humanity; [inasmuch as he knows Self to be actionless, and no doer or enjoyer.]

6. "Abandoning works good and bad, such a theosophist, remembering his non-difference with BRAHMA is always engaged in meditating on Self, and actions (good and bad) done and looked upon as Self.*

7. "Visible knowledge of the Supreme† Self destroys all maladies of the internal organ, clears away doubts, and extinguishes good and bad works.

8. "And for surmounting death, there is no other means save the knowledge that each individual Self is BRAHMA; it weakens the fetters—passions and desires—removes misery and prevents metempsychosis.

---

* How are actions regarded as self? When virtue and vice, or merit and demerit have equally been discarded, they can no more cause any pain; moreover, works are the result of the physical body, with its organs of action and sense, and a theosophist sees self everywhere. For "whatever is, is self," so that for want of distinction between him and works, they are regarded one with him.

† The word "Supreme" need not unnecessarily create an anthropomorphic deity, what it is very apt to signify. what is sought to be conveyed is the infinite superiority of self over *Hiranyagarbha*, etc.

9. "That knowledge enable men of tranquil mind to be above pleasure and pain even in the present life; and neither bad nor good works done or left undone bring forth any pain."

10. Are these the only proofs? No. Knowledge of Self as a source of destroying ignorance and removing worthless and harmful works is amply testified in the *Sruti*, *Puran*, and *Smriti*. As for instance, "When a person knows full well the physical body, he knows the truth, and when he mistakes it for Self, suffers pain." "A knower of BRAHMA is never subject to death; stupid and ignorant persons are re-incarnated to suffer in a subsequent sphere of objective existence." "Those among the *Devas*, who know BRAHMA, become one with the Supreme Self." "Those, who know their individual Self to be one with BRAHMA, enjoy all manner of temporal happiness" (*Sruti*). "Self is present everywhere in all material objects, as they are in him; and a person engaged in considering his oneness with BRAHMA, attains emancipation." "BRAHMA, the Universal Witness, when seen as Self, destroys ignorance together with its product, the source of all harm." So say the *Puran* and *Smriti*. [Therefore] knowledge of BRAHMA destroys all injurious and harmful works and produces felicity."

11. There are three distinct varieties of felicity, *viz.*, BRAHMANANDA, VIDYANANDA, and VISHAYANANDA. Of them, the first is now being considered.

12. BHRIGU, the son of VARUNA, hearing the indications of BRAHMA from his father, ceased regarding the foodful, vital, mental and cognitional sheaths as BRAHMA, and identified blissfulness with It. [The subject of the discourse between the father and son, who was being instructed in knowledge of BRAHMA, ran as follows; "From whom all living things have sprung into existence, continue to exist, and unto whom after death return, know that to be BRAHMA." This indication of BRAHMA does not apply to the several sheaths, foodful and the

rest, consequently after abandoning them, blissfulness was ascertained to be BRAHMA.

13. If it be asked, how did BHRIGU connect blissfulness with the indication of BRAHMA? The reply is, inasmuch as all creatures owe their existence to the gratification of sexual appetite, and after being born, continue to live by means of temporal enjoyments in the shape of food, etc., and in death enter into a condition of blissfulness resembling that of profound slumber, therefore blissfulness is BRAHMA.

14. [This is further corroborated by a passing reference to the conversation of SANATKUMAR and NARAD (*Vide Chhandogya Upanishad*, Chap. VIII)]. "Prior to the evolution of the elements, and their products,—viviparous, oviparous, etc., and the threefold entities,—knower, knowledge and the object to be known, there existed the Supreme Self, unlimited by time and place, *i.e.*, infinite." And in *Pralaya*, they—knower (internal organ) knowledge (modification of the mind) and the object of cognition (jar, etc.,)—are absent.

15. The cognitional sheath is the knower; the mental, knowledge; and sound, form, etc., are subjects of cognition. They did not exist prior to the evolution of the universe. [That is to say, *Jiva* with his associate of intellect, forming the cognitional sheath, derived from the Supreme Self, is the knower; the mental sheath is knowledge; and sound, form, taste, smell and touch are the well-known properties by which objects are known—all these being products could not exist prior to the cause from which they are derived, and from that cause—the Supreme Self—they are not distinct.

16. Thus, in the absence of the three entities (knower, etc.,) the secondless Supreme Self is perfect, [*i.e.*, unlimited by time and place,] and this is easy to understand. When is He experienced? In profound unconscious meditation, dreamless slumber, and in fainting swoon that Self is experienced as secondless. [To a theosophist accustomed to practise unconscious meditation, and to the generality of men

profound slumber and fainting fits are trite examples. For, after recovering consciousness, the common experience is absence of recollection of what passed in the interim ; and that recollection of the total disappearance of phenomena proceeds from the abiding Intelligence or consciousness which is no other but BRAHMA, the Supreme Self. In the same way, in the twilight of creation—prior to the evolution of the elements and their products—as there was nothing to limit, It is therefore said to be perfect.]

17. [If it be contended, BRAHMA may be perfect and infinite, but that does not imply supreme felicity; to clear such a misapprehension it is said:—What is perfect is full of bliss and no happiness is to be found in what is finite and limited by the three distinctions of knower, knowledge and the object to be known; therefore, as BRAHMA is secondless, It is full of bliss. So spoke SANATKUMAR to NARAD when he came to enquire of Self-knowledge to remove his extreme unhappiness.

18. Though NARAD was well read in the *Puranas*, *Vedas* and the other *Shastras*, yet was he devoid of Self-knowledge, consequently felt very miserable. (*Chhandogya Upanishad*, Chapter VII.)

19. Previous to his studying the *Vedas*, he was worried with the three varieties of misery,—personal, accidental and elementary,—but subsequently in addition to them, the pain attending study, and the mortification of forgetfulness, besides censure from one superior in learning, and the feeling of pride towards his inferior—all these—come for his share.

20. Then he repaired to the sage SANATKUMAR and said. "*Bhagavan*! I am extremely miserable, do impart me the necessary instruction that I may surmount all grief." And the sage replied, "Happiness is the only remedy."

21. Inasmuch as worldly enjoyments are covered with thousand miseries, it is proper to regard them as such; there-

fore what has already been said about finite substances containing no happiness holds true.

22. If it be contended, material objects as they are finite may be devoid of happiness, but the secondless Reality is also similarly conditioned; if it were otherwise, one should have experienced that felicity, and since such experience is wanting, it cannot be present. Then again, the admission of its experience involves duality, for there must be a knower to experience felicity, and the subject of knowledge. Thus will duality be established, antagonistic to the secondless, non-dual BRAHMA and injurious to It.

23. [To this the *Siddhanti* replies.] The secondless is not the seat of, but happiness itself. The same cause which makes the secondless happiness, prevents it also from being its seat or receptacle. If proofs be wanted, they are not necessary, because BRAHMA is self-illuminated.

24. And regarding the selfmanifestibility of BRAHMA I admit your words as proof, inasmuch as you confess the secondlessness, but contend only for an absence of felicity.

25. If you say, you never intended to admit the secondless BRAHMA, but simply referred to our words, to advance objections against them; then say what existed prior to the evolution of this vast material expanse?

26. Whether in that prior condition, there existed the secondless BRAHMA, or the objective world, or something different from both? Now something different from duality and non-duality is inadmissible, for it exists nowhere. Duality could not exist prior to the secondless BRAHMA, as that had not yet been ushered into existence, consequently you are forced to fall back upon the secondless.

27. If you say, this only establishes the secondless BRAHMA analogically, and not by inference. May I then enquire of you whether you call that to be an argument based on reason and analogy which is with or without illustration? There does not exist a third form.

28. An argument without inference and example is worthless. Therefore in connection with the first variety (*i. e.*, with example) adduce an illustration that will be conformable to the sacred writings.

29. If you say, like the imperception of phenomena in profound slumber, cyclic periods of destruction are secondless, owing to similar imperception; then the question for you to answer is, whether in regard to profound slumber being secondless, you refer to your own slumber or that of another person for an example. If your own slumber be the example of secondlessness, what is the illustration of that slumber? Do reply.

30. If the profound slumber of another person be regarded as such example, how grand is your device? A person who knows not his profound slumber can have very little knowledge of it in another.

31. Just as in my own case, I do nothing while sleeping, so in the case of another, when he is actionless, that is his profound slumber; if you draw your inference in this way, that necessarily amounts to an inferential admission of the self-manifestibility of your own profound slumber.

32. And that self-manifestibility is such a condition where no sensory organ can go, and of which there is no example, yet it cannot but be admitted.

33. If you say, let profound slumber be secondless and self-manifested, but how can there be any felicity in it? The answer is, since there is no misery, you are constrained to admit the existence of felicity in profound slumber.

34. Where is the proof of absence of misery in profound slumber? Universal experience and the *Sruti* alike establish it. "A blind person forgets his blindness, one pierced in the ears forgets that he is so, and a sickman imagines in sleep that he is in health." And this is ratified by experience.

35. If it be contended, absence of misery does not amount to happiness, for in stones, etc., misery is absent yet

there is no happiness. Such a contention is untenable and extremely opposed to profound slumber—the subject of dispute.

36. Presence of happiness and absence of misery can be inferred from the appearance of a person. The usual marks by which one or the other, or both, are made out, are too well-known, so that the face may properly be regarded as the index of what a man has for his share; but so far as stones are concerned, from an absence of the usual signs by which happiness or its reverse can be traced, it is impossible to conclude that misery only is wanting in them.

37. Individual happiness and misery are a matter of personal experience, and they cannot be inferentially known; but like their presence known from experience, their absence is known too.

38. Thus then, like the perception of happiness, want of misery in profound slumber is likewise established from the same source (experience); and for such absence of misery, it must be admitted as a condition of uninterrupted felicity.

39. If that condition of profound slumber were not one of felicity, what necessity would there be to undergo trouble and expense for making the bed soft, neat and tidy to induce sleep?

40. If the bedding be looked upon as a means for the removal of pain, it is natural to believe its capability of producing happiness in a bed-ridden patient by removing his pain. And in health—in the absence of pain attending illness, the necessity for its removal is likewise wanting—that bedding and the rest are the means of procuring happiness.

41. But since such happiness of profound slumber is accomplished by the usual means—bedding, cot, and the rest, it must be material. To such a contention, the reply is, whether happiness preceding the advent of sleep, or during it, is considered material? The *Vedantin* inclines to the first view, and says happiness felt prior to the advent of sleep may

be declared material, *i.e.*, derived from material resources—bedding and posture.

42. Now for the second query. Happiness attending profound slumber is not due to any cause. Then, knowledge of the usual means, bedding, etc., is wanting, consequently the happiness felt cannot be ascribed to them as its source. But it may be argued, if the happiness of profound slumber be not material, *i.e.*, uncreate and eternal, why is it not experienced like material enjoyment? Because the sleeper who experiences that happiness in sleep, being immersed in happiness, it is not perceived like happiness proceeding from material enjoyment. Hence it is said, prior to sleep, the intellect of the sleeper approaches the felicity produced from bedding, etc., and subsequently during slumber, is immersed in exquisite felicity.

43. To be more explicit.—*Jiva*, engaged in work during the hours of wakefulness, gets tired, and repairs to his bed for sleep; the fatigue, produced from work, is removed, and with the return of mental quiet, brought about by rest, he feels the happiness caused by the bedding, etc.

44. What is the nature of material happiness? Pain following an ungratified desire in the shape of material acquisition (say wealth, etc.,) is experienced by the individual during the course of his daily labor, for destroying which he repairs to his bed; his intellect is now directed inwards where it meets with the reflection of natural felicity [of Self]; and this reflection of felicity is material happiness. Here too, after experiencing that material happiness, the individual who experiences it, as well as his experience and the subject of that experience, subject him to work and fatigue.

45. And for the removal of that labour and fatigue, *Jiva* runs at once into the blissfulness of BRAHMA to be one with It. As in the *Sruti* "Pupil! then (in profound slumber) *Jiva* merges into BRAHMA to be one with It."

46. Five examples are adduced in the *Sruti* to illustrate

the blissfulness of profound slumber, *viz.*, of the eagle, hawk, infant, emperor, and *Mahabrahmana* (an eminent *Brahman* learned in the *Shastras*). These are :—

47. Just as an eagle, with its leg tied to a string round its keeper's wrist, tempted to fly hither and thither at the sight of prey, but unable to find any comfortable resting spot alights upon the hand where the other end of the string is attached :

48. So is the mind of the individual (his associate), for the sake of experiencing the fruit of actions, good and bad, *viz.*, happiness and misery, engaged between the hours of dreaming slumber and wakefulness, and after the consummation of fructescent works, merges into Ignorance, his formal cause. Then with the dissolution of the mind, *Jiva,* a form of its associate, becomes the Supreme Self.

49. Like the hawk tired with flying in the air in quest of food, vehemently bending its way towards its nest for the sake of rest ; *Jiva* (reflection of intelligence with the associate of mind) desirous of the blissfulness of Self at once repairs to the region of the heart for profound slumber.

50. Just as an infant, suckling its mother's breast to the fill, lying in a soft bed, and having neither any discrimination of 'I' and 'mine,' nor any desire and passion, is the very picture of happiness ;

51. Or like an emperor, satiated with all sorts of human enjoyments, feeling himself supremely blessed ;

52. Or like an eminent *Brahman*, learned in self-knowledge, experiencing happiness after reaching the confines of blissfulness derived from knowledge of his oneness with BRAHMA ; do all individuals attain the felicity of BRAHMA in profound slumber.

53. But it may be asked, why other examples are excluded, and allusion made only to the infant, emperor and an eminent *Brahman?* Because, the happiness of an infant, emperor and a *Brahman* devoted to BRAHMA is proverbial, while the

condition of other persons is only miserable. Persons wanting in discrimination are apt to conclude the condition of an infant to be happy, while those with an ordinary amount of discrimination consider a king to be happy; but the really discriminating person knows for certain that happiness belongs to him who has cognised Self to be no other than BRAHMA; and the rest are miserable, for they are affected with passions and desires which give them no rest. They are, therefore, not proper illustrations to explain the felicity of profound slumber.

54. Let infant and the rest be happy, but what connection is there between them and a person in profound slumber? "Like the happiness of an infant, emperor and a Brahman devoted to BRAHMA, a person in profound slumber attains the blissfulness of BRAHMA." And "like a fond husband embracing his dearly beloved wife, knowing neither out nor in, but experiencing happiness; a person in sleep, having merged into BRAHMA, knows neither out nor in, but is transformed into blissfulness."

55. As the word 'out' in the illustration includes all places from cross-ways to the narrowest lane, and 'in' has reference to houshold work and and inside the house; so are subjects of the waking condition and dreams respectively called 'out' and 'in.' Because dream is the impression of objects seen during wakefulness, and manifested inside the vessels of the body.

56. In profound slumber "a father is no more a father." This and similar other *Sruti* texts, shew that the individual loses his ordinary condition, and the usual relation of father and son, brother and husband is no more perceived then; so that, there remains the condition of BRAHMA.

57. The conceit that "I am a father," etc., is the source of happiness and misery according as it fares well or ill with his relations, but when it is destroyed [and the illusory attri-

bution of Self to not-Self beginning with son to nothing is removed] a person surmounts all grief.

58. "Dnring profound slumber when this material expanse has disappeared temporarily into its formal cause, Ignorance abounding in darkness, the individual for this envelopment of ignorance (*Prakriti*) enjoys felicity." So says the *Kaivalya Sruti* (*Atharva Veda*).

59. And this is alike corroborated by universal experience. For a person on rising from sleep exclaims,—"I was happy in sleep and knew nothing then." In this manner, the happiness felt during sleep and want of knowledge or ignorance of what happened then, is remembered by him.

60. Since there can be no recollection of substances which one has no experience of, it is natural to infer the presence of experience in connection with the recollection of happiness in profound slumber; hence it is said, experience of happiness and of ignorance are both present then. If it be contended, the mind is in a state of abeyance in sleep, consequently in the absence of its instrument, how can experience be possibly present? To such a contention it may be asked, whether the instrument of experiencing happiness, or the instrument of ignorance is meant to be absent? Both of them are untenable. Because, happiness is self-manifested intelligence and stands in no need of any instrument. And Self who is intelligence is manifested in the form of bliss; and from that self-manifested bliss is discovered ignorance which envelops it.

61. Nor can it be contended, that the admission of the self-manifested happiness of profound slumber does not necessarily amount to Self being the blissful BRAHMA: for in the *Bajsaneya Upanishad* we read "Intelligence is the blissful BRAHMA." Therefore that self-manifested happiness is no other but BRAHMA.

62. Since experience and recollection have invariably the same seat, it may be argued that the usual experience of a person on rising from sleep "I was sleeping happily and

knew nothing then" being remembered by the sleeper (the predicate of the word cognitional) he is their experiencer. To avoid such a misapprehension, it is said, inasmuch as the internal organ (a product of his associated ignorance) merges into or disappears in ignorance, *Jiva* with the associate of the internal organ is not the experiencer of happiness or ignorance. In other words "I knew nothing then" is an inferential proof of the presence of ignorance in profound slumber experienced by the sleeper and recollected immediately on his waking; and in the absence of ignorance it is impossible for him to say so; then again, as both the demonstrator or witness of that ignorance (the cognitional sheath) and its proof (the mental sheath) are so transformed that they abandon their respective forms and rest in the shape of the cause-ignorance; therefore, intelligence, associated with the internal organ, can never be the instrument which experiences it. Why? Because sleep is said to be the condition of destruction of both the cognitional and mental sheaths, and that sleep is ignorance.

63. If it be asked, since the cognitional sheath is literally wanting in profound slumber during the time when felicity and ignorance are both experienced, how can it be credited with the power of remembering them with the return of wakefulness? Just as butter liquifying with heat is restored to its original consistence by the action of cold; so from the exhaustion of fructescent works in the hours of wakefulness, the internal organ disappears in sleep to be again modified into the shape of the internal organ from the force of the fructescent during the next waking condition, and thus appears in the gross condition; for which self, the associate of the internal organ, is also converted into the consistence of the cognitional sheath; and that Self in the first condition of profound slumber when his associate has been destroyed is called by the name of 'blissful sheath.'

64. That is to say, immediately prior to profound slumber that modification of intellect which combined with the re-

flection of happiness, subsequently disappears in sleep in connection with the (reflection of happiness) and is called the 'blissful.'

65. The blissful sheath, a product of the modification of intellect with the reflection of happiness directed internally, (an associate of ignorance together with its impression) experiences the felicity of BRAHMA in profound slumber by means of a subtle modification of ignorance combined with the reflection of intelligence.

66. If it be asked, like the expression "I feel happy," used by individuals in waking condition, why is not a similar conceit present in connection with the profound slumber? Because, modification of ignorance is subtle, and of intellect, apparent: as declared by persons well-read in the *Vedanta*.

67. For authority to prove what has already been said about the blissful sheath as the experiencer of the blissfulness of BRAHMA by a subtle modification of ignorance, the *Mandukya* and *Tapniya Upanishads* are cited:—"The blissful [sheath] is the agent and instrument, and respecting the felicity of BRAHMA it is the enjoyer." Self who has assumed one form, or blended with, ordinary intelligence in profound slumber is full of bliss; for he enjoys felicity by the modification of reflected intelligence.

69. To be more explicit.—In the waking condition Self who is regarded as BRAHMA, ("That art thou,") and one with the cognitional, vital and mental sheaths; who has eyes, ears, etc.; who is earthy, watery, aerial, fiery and etherial, and not; full of desire and free from it; full of anger and without it, as cited in the *Sruti*, is separated from the associates of mind and intellect in profound slumber and assumes one form; like flour ground out of a handful of rice where the separate form of each grain is lost.

70. In the waking condition, the mental function assumes the modification of a jar to cognise it; but in sleep the jar is no more cognisable: it is then said to be non-existent as an

object of cognition, and the mental function or intellect blends into intelligence to be one with it: just as drops of rain falling from the clouds are solidified into hail-stones.

71. And this intelligence (in which the mental function has blended) is in common parlance said to be the witness and free from misery by the *Vaisheshikas* and others who are ignorant of the drift of the Sacred Scriptures for an absence of the usual modifications of misery in profound slumber.

72. For tasting the blissfulness of BRAHMA] in profound slumber, intelligence reflected in the modification of ignorance is the principal means. But it may be asked, if *Jiva* enjoys such felicity in sleep why does he abandon it and get up from sleep to be a subject of misery produced from his connection with home, family and the rest? Because, bound as he is by the chain of actions—good and bad, he is constrained to abandon that BRAHMAIC felicity after having tasted it as a result of good *Karma*, to wake up for tasting the misery incidental to every human being* [as a result of past misdeeds].

73. To this effect the *Kaibalya Sruti* says, "From the effect of works of prior births a person reverts from profound slumber to dreams and wakefulness."

74. Even after waking, a person experiences for a short

* Just as a child leaving its mother's lap is seen to go out in company with its playmates, and when tired with play returns to the mother to experience felicity; so is profound slumber the house; ignorance (cause-body) mother; its projection, lap; and the internal organ with reflection of intelligence projected, or evolved out of ignorance, the child, which is engaged in the province of wakefulness in play, in company with playmates in the form of fructescent works; and when these works are exhausted during waking hours and dreams, feeling tired retires to its mother's lap to experience felicity in profound slumber and thus forgets fatigue and toil; till roused by the call of its companions again to play and stir out of doors in wakefulness and dreams.

time the impression of BRAHMAIC felicity he had been enjoying while asleep. How is it known? Because, without conceiving of any subject, the mind remains unoccupied; and for this state of (mental) indifference,* he feels happy.

75. Controlled by their actions—good and bad, all creatures are subsequently (while awake) subjected to a variety of grief; and thus forget the blissfulness they had enjoyed for a short time while sleeping profoundly.

76. Therefore, their need be no more contention about the presence of felicity in sleep. Each day, both in the beginning and termination of sleep, every individual has a partiality for it: under such circumstances where is the man of good intellect who will say nay? In other words, every man has a partiality for sleep, both prior to it and at its end; and as in the beginning the usual bed is laid, and after sleep is over, he is yet unwilling to part with the felicity he was enjoying, for which he remains silent, hence there can be no question about it.

77. If what has just been said about the experience of BRAHMAIC felicity after the close of sleep when the individual rests in silence and contentment be a fact, where then is the necessity for the Sacred Scriptures or instruction from a *Guru*? As even without them, idle persons will be successful in attaining that felicity.

78. And the *Siddhanti* replies:—If a person would know the felicity of profound slumber to be Self, and no other than

---

* A person on rising from sleep experiences neither pleasure nor pain; in short, both happiness and its reverse are then absent, for which, it is called the state of indifference. Similarly in wakefulness when both happiness and grief are absent, it is called 'indifference.' In happiness there arises passion or desire, and in grief envy or spite; therefore, absence of desire and envy caused by their respective instruments—happiness and grief is 'indifference' or resting in contentment.

BRAHMA, his emancipation is certain, inasmuch as that ignorance which would fix limits and enjoin him to practise sanctioned works will be destroyed; thus far you are correct. But it is impossible to know BRAHMA without the help of the Sacred Writings and instruction from a Professor.

79. Now I know BRAHMA from what has fallen from your lips; how then can my emancipation be prevented? Just as an ignorant person after having heard something from another considers himself to be learned [as in the following example]:—

80. A rich person once observed in reference to a Pandit, who had studied the four *Vedas*, that he was fit to be rewarded with wealth amply; an ignorant person, present then, hearing that the *Vedas* were four in number, stepped forward and exclaimed, "I know the *Vedas* are four from what you have just said, so please give me money too." And you resemble him.

81. If it be said, that the ignorant person knew nothing of the *Vedas* except their number, then inasmuch as your knowledge of BRAHMA is imperfect [your emancipation is not certain and resemblance with him is complete].

82. If you say, since the *Vedas* have their individual distinction apart from number, and none whatever between Self and BRAHMA, who is impartite bliss; and there is not a particle of ignorance left in you about this knowledge; the illustration which I have adduced is not an apt one; nor can your knowledge be imperfect inasmuch as in respect to the impartite blissfulness of BRAHMA (which is devoid of illusion and its product) neither imperfection nor its reverse is possible:

83. May I then enquire of you, whether you understand the signification of the words impartite, etc., or simply read them? If you read them without comprehending their meaning, your knowledge is necessarily imperfect.

84. Even if you understand what they signify from the

help of grammar, etc., there yet remains the visible knowledge of BRAHMA to be acquired; thus your imperfection is a fact, and it cannot be gainsaid. Till you know that you have nothing proper to do, nor any desired object to acquire, your knowledge of BRAHMA is imperfect.

85. Know then, whenever any happines is felt apart from any subject, it is the impression BRAHMAIC felicity.

86. And when after the acquisition of an object, desire ior it having ceased, the mental function directed internally receives the reflection of felicity from self, it is called (VISHAYANANDA) Material felicity.

87. [Excepting the three varieties of felicity, *viz.*, of BRAHMA, impression and reflection, there is not a fourth variety present in the world. The felicity discovered in profound slumber, and which is self-manifested is called BRAHMAIC felicity; whatever happiness is experienced in the condition of indifference immediately after rising from sleep, is independent of any subject of cognition, for which it receives the name of impressional felicity (VASANANANDA);—because, the mind has not been thoroughly roused into its normal activity so as to pervade any subject. And that happiness which proceeds from the acquisition of a desired object, from the reflection of the

* With the acquisition of a desired object, active quality of the mental function, which had produced desire, ceases; and from its good quality following the knowledge of acquisition is manifested the felicity inherent in intelligence associated with the (desired) object. Now this modification of the mental function has been produced from the object desired, consequently it is called VISHAYANANDA. Or knowledge of the desired object removes the modifications of desire; and with its removal, other modifications directed internally arise, by which felicity associated with the internal organ is discovered; and this internally directed modification, or the reflection of felicity in it, is known severally as 'material happines,' 'reflected happiness,' and 'little happiness,'

felicity of Self on the mind directed internally is called reflected happiness, or as it is otherwise known, temporal or material (*Vishayananda*). These are the three forms of happiness universally felt; beyond them no other variety is recognised. But here it may be contended, that in a previous portion of the present treatise (vide VII. ante) the second finds no mention and *Vidyananda*—felicity produced from Self-knowledge—substituted for it, so that we have an antagonism. Moreover, further on will occur passages like these: "from the force of practice as a person forgets its individuality or sense of Self (egoism), a proportionate keenness of perception will be developed to enable him to infer his own happiness." "Similarly during the state of indifference he avoids all impressions of happiness;" so that we have two more varieties added to the tripartite classification given here. Then again *Atmananda*, *Yogananda*, and *Adwaitananda* are also mentioned, and the first and the last have each a section devoted to them. Thus we have here three distinct forms of happiness and to say, that beyond the three with which the text opens there is not a fourth variety is clearly inconsistent; therefore the subject requires a passing consideration. It would appear subsequently (Sect. XIV. v. 2), that like reflex happiness or better still, enjoyment of felicity produced in connection with material objects, happiness proceeding from self-knowledge is only a modification of the intellect, and the two are not distinct from each other. In the same way, for an absence of distinction between 'own happiness,' 'principal happiness,' 'self-happiness,' 'happiness following mental restraint,' 'secondless blissfulness,' and BRAHMAIC felicity, the apparent antagonism is cleared away. That is to say, the threefold classification mentioned here embraces all other varieties of happiness elsewhere cited. This is more clearly established in the following wise:—"As forgetfulness of egoism or individuality" follows as a result of the practice of *Yoga*, the Yogi experiences the felicity peculiar to such mental restraint and which is no other but his 'own happiness.' "Where no phenomena are manifested, where there is no sleep even, the happiness present in that condition of mental restraint (*Yoga*) is the BRAHMAIC felicity" as KRISHNA spoke to ARJUNA. Now this BRAHMAIC felicity is not distinct from 'own happiness;' so is 'principal happiness' one with felicity of BRAHMA; because as the source of 'reflex' and 'impressional happiness,' BRAHMAIC felicity remains self-manifested. Similarly the blissfulness of Self, and the 'secondless blissfulness' are all forms of BRAHMAIC felicity].

88. Of the aforesaid three forms, that which is self-manifested, and gives rise to material and impressional happiness is fit to be known as the blissfulness of BRAHMA.

89. Having established the blissfulness of profound slumber to be the self-illuminated intelligence of BRAHMA, by the help of *Sruti* texts, logical conclusion and experience, listen to the means of recognising that felicity of BRAHMA in that other condition—of wakefulness. [In the *Sruti* occurs the passage "During sleep when this vast material expanse disappears into its formal cause ignorance, the individual experiences bliss by the envelopment of ignorance." "I was then sleeping happily" is an illustration of recollection of happiness which the sleeper exclaims immediately on getting up; had there been no happiness he could not have said so, thus leading to the only logical conclusion of the presence of happiness; and as the mental function is in abeyance then, consequently it could not take cognition of that happiness, for which it is said to be self-manifested].

90. The same felicity which receives the name of, BRAHMANANDA in profound slumber, is called the 'cognitional sheath' in connection with the dreaming and waking states. A difference in seat produces a difference in name.

91. Wakefulness has its seat in the eyes; dreams, throat; and profound slumber, the lotus of the heart. But 'eyes' here

indicate the whole body; for during wakefulness the whole body from head to foot is prevaded by intelligence.

92. And like an ignited ball of iron [in which the fire and iron though distinct appear one] that intelligence is from illusion, recognised one with the physical body, and used so. As "I am a man."

93. "I am indifferent to pleasure and pain;" "I am happy;" "I am miserable;" these are the three conditions experienced by humanity. Of them happiness and misery are a result of good and bad works; while indifference proceeds naturally; [inasmuch as Self is neither an agent nor doer of works, so that they cannot affect him].

94. Happiness and misery are of two different sorts as they are produced either from external objects of senses or internal (mental) enjoyment; and the intervals between happiness and misery—when the mind rests in contentment—represent the state of indifference.

95. When a person exclaims "Now I have no anxiety and care, but am happy," he expresses the natural blissfulness of Self during the state of indifference; so that even in wakefulness there is manifestation of 'own happiness'; and it is proper that one should know this.

96. But for the presence of a subtle form of egoism in the happiness discovered in the condition of indifference, it is not the principal felicity of Self, but only its impression.

97. Now for an example as to the difference between 'principal happiness' and its impression. As the sensation of cold communicated to the hand by the contact of a jar filled with water is not water, but its quality, from which the presence of water is inferred:

98. So, from repeated practice as egoism is forgotten, wise persons with keen preception infer own happiness.

99. After the mental function has ceased to take cognition of things which are not-Self, and become moulded in the shape

of BRAHMA, so that Self appears one with It; then from repeated (skilful) practice of profound meditation, the individual forgets egotism and tastes the supreme bliss. But this does not signify that sleep is such a subtle condition of egoism. Because though the senses cease to carry on their respective functions there is no want of mind in sleep; and because profound sleep is said to be the resting of the intellect in its cause, ignorance. The presence of mind in sleep is proved by the body not falling to the ground. That is to say, when in profound slumber egoism disappears, the body of the sleeper is seen to fall to the ground, but here it does not; consequently there is no dissolution of egoism, but it rests in the form of the internal organ.

100. "Whatever happiness is felt during profound unconscious meditation, when there is neither knower, knowledge nor the object to be known,—and which is not sleep too,—it is the BRAHMAIC felicity," So spoke KRISHNA to ARJUNA. (*Gita*, Chap. VI).

101. [The *Gita* text is now being set forth :—]

"The person of tranquil intellect, gradually restrains the mind by resting it on Self* and abandoning other thoughts."

102. Mind is naturally unsteady and fickle, and liable to be acted upon by the usual objects of cognition through their individual senses; and when it has discovered their unreality, it is finally led by those objects themselves to show an utter disregard for, or indifference to them; thus impeded or restrained it becomes subservient to Self, tries adequate means to fix all thoughts exclusively on him, leaving everything else. In this manner, a Yogi through the force of practice comes to rest his mind tranquilly on Self.

103. A Yogi free from sin and fascination, and with the

* Resting on Self is to fix the mind on the grand truth "All this is indeed Self, and beyond him there is nothing."

mind tranquilized, knows to a certainty "Indeed all this is BRAHMA;" and experiences undecaying and pure bliss.

104. When from constant practice of Yoga, the mind has been restrained so as not to be led away by sensuous objects; and from profound meditation the internal organ has been rendered pure, the Yogi sees Self as intelligence and feels contentment in him—not in external objects.

105. While resting on Self, he experiences infinite happiness—happiness capable of being grasped by the intellect, though supersensuous [*i. e.*, independent of any subject of cognition by the senses]; so that the internal organ never leaves Self to pervade any thing else.

106. Thus having acquired visible knowledge of Self, he disregards all other acquisitions as inferior; and with the internal organ firmly seated on Self even the pangs of death are unable either to disaffect or move his mind so as to leave Self.

107. Know it to be a form of pain-destroying Yoga. [In short, whatever mention has been made of the particular conditions of Self (beginning with v. 101). come under the category of Yoga; know it by the indication of painlessness, or properties antagonistic to pain]. And that Yoga it is proper to practise with a mind free from pain.

108. A Yogi freed from the obstacles which attend the practice of Yoga, always seeks for Self, and knowing his oneness with BRAHMA experiences ineffable and supreme bliss.

109. Just as sea water removed drop by drop by means of a straw* may ultimately lead to its being dried [in an im-

---

* A bird of the species *Parra jacana* deposited her eggs on the sea coast, but they were washed away by the waves, causing much annoyance to her. She resolved to run it dry, and took hold of a bit of straw by which she commenced operating, removing each time a few drops; other birds saw the hopeless task she

mense distance of time]; so does the practice of Yoga unattended with pain produce mental restraint in a subsequent period of time.

110. Nor is the *Gita* alone in mentioning it, for in the *Maitrayniya sakha* of the *Yayur Veda*, the sage SHAKAYANYA in his discourse with BRIHADRATH speaks of BRAHMAIC felicity in connection with profound meditation.

111. Just as fire deprived of fuel subsides into its cause heat [and its characteristic glowing ceases]; so from the exhaustion of its modifications, the internal organ subsides into its cause. [That is to say, when from the practice of profound meditation the internal organ has been thoroughly restrained, and eased of its natural fickleness—modifications of its active quality— it rests in its cause the good quality, which alone remains].

112. To one desirous of finding out Self, and who for that purpose has reduced his mind to its cause, and subjugated the senses, so as not to allow them being turned away by sensuous objects, happiness produced as a result of his good *karma* appears unreal—for it is material.

113. Virtually mind itself is this material world, and every endeavour should be made use of to render it faultless [by the several means discrimination, indifference and the rest]. For

---

was bent in carrying out, tried to dissuade her, but in vain. At length they too were moved to join her; this novel spectacle affected NARADA, who sent *Garuda* to their help. This produced the desired result; the sea was made to restore the missing eggs. What is meant here to be conveyed is that like the bird engaged in its self-imposed task entailing immense labor and time, steadily bent after it, feeling neither pain nor getting disheartened till relieved by the assistance of *Garuda*; a person bent in restraining his mind receives the kind assistance of ISWARA, and his ultimate success is certain.

It is a golden truth, that results follow according to the nat eu of the mind—(subject thought of).*

114. Earnestness of the mind destroys both good and bad works as mentioned in the *Sruti* and *Smriti.* "As fire destroys in a blaze the filaments of cotton which crown the tops of certain reeds, so does knowledge, all de-merit." "All sins are removed by meditating on BRAHMA in the fourth quarter of night." A person with contentment of mind sees BRAHMA in Self and exclaims, "That am I;" and experiences ineffable bliss.

115. Just as in ordinary persons wanting in self-knowledge, the mind is apt to be drawn away by sensuous objects; if a like attachment to BRAHMA would take place, where is the individual that would not be freed from consecutive re-births?

116. Mind is either pure or impure; these are its two varieties. Impurity results from passions and desires, and purity, in their exclusion.

117. Mind is the cause of metempsychosis and emancipation. Attachment to material objects (temporal enjoyments) is the source of bondage, as its reverse,—emancipation.

118. That happiness which results from the practice of profound meditation, when the mind cured of its blemishes and throughly restrained, firmly rests in Self is so uncommon that it is impossible to be described, but capable of being realized by the mind.

119. Though profound meditation cannot last infinitely yet during its stay for short periods (of which there is no impossibility) the felicity of Self is ascertained.

---

* Just as pure water appears colored blue from the color present in its associate; so is the mind—a product of the good quality of the five elements—converted into the shape of the object thought of; therefore when a person is constantly thinking that he is *Jiva*, his mind is modified, accordingly; similarly, "I am ISWARA" results from the thought of non-difference between Self and BRAHMA. And the results are different too.

120. The reason why a person of faith, bent after the practice of profound meditation, always experiences that felicity of BRAHMA, is because after having once ascertained it [while in his meditation] he is led to believe in its continued presence at other times too—when he rises from his meditation.

121. So does he, during the condition of indifference discarding all impressions of felicity, contemplate on the primary or chief blissfulness of Self.

122. Just as a profligate woman, even in the midst of her household work, mentally dwells on the pleasure experienced in company with her lover :

123. Does a man of faith, with tranquil mind, believing in the Reality of Self, internally taste the supreme felicity of BRAHMA, even in the midst of the usual practices [eating, etc.,].

124. 'Tranquil mind,' is thus explained :—

To turn the senses away from their several subjects and to restrain them with a predominating desire of finding out the natural felicity of Self.

125. Like a person carrying a heavy load on his head, finding rest by easing himself of [and depositing it on the ground], one, who has discarded the world and cut off all connections with it and its goods, exclaims "Now I am at rest." Such a modification of the intellect is expressed by the aforesaid word 'faith.'

126. Just as a person who has found out rest in the manner above explained is bent after the enjoyment of that one and primary blissfnlness of Self during the condition of indifference ; so does he diligently attend to it, even in the midst of happiness and misery which follows as a result of his fructescent works.

127. Just as one bent after immediate self-destruction in fire, considers dress and ornaments which cause delay in carrying it out as his enemy ; so does a person of discrimina-

tion in quest of self-knowledge consider temporal enjoyments inimical to him, and find them all faulty.

128. But in respect to those other enjoyments not inimical to Self, and the exquisite felicity naturally belonging to him, he is found to take hold of them by his intellect one after another; just as the crow uses its eyes.

129. That is to say, as the sight of a crow is influenced by one eye at a time, so that when the left eye sees, the right does not, and *vice versa*; similarly does the intellect of a man of discrimination take hold of one set of enjoyments; for which it is said to come and go between them, one after anothei.

130. A knower of Self enjoying such happiness proceeding from material objects not inimical to him, and the felicity of BRAHMA ascertainable by means of the utterances of the *Upanishads*, knows both of them, as much, as are they known by persons acquainted with the popular and *Vedic* languages.

131. The same cause which enables a man of discrimination to experience or know both material and BRAHMAIC felicities, prevents him from being affected with any misery that may fall to his share as a result of fructescent works subsequent to knowledge, as he used to be, ere gnosis had arisen. In short, even in the midst of misery his perception of the blissfulness of Self remains unimpeded, just as by immersing half the body in water one feels both cold and hot at the same time.

132. As in wakefulness, he experiences that BRAHMAIC felicity constantly. so in dreams too it is ever present: for dreams are a product of impression of objects seen while awake.

133. Impression of ignorance is also a source of dream; hence in common with the ignorant, a theosophist experiences both happiness and misery in dream—a product of the impression of ignorance.

To sum up then :—

The present treatise *Yogananda* forms the first chapter of BRAHMANANDA ; it deals on the discovery of the blissfulness of Self as experienced by a *Yogi*, for which it is called the blissfulness of 'mental restraint.'

—:o:—

SECTION XII.

(b). *Atmananda, or The Blissfulness of Self.*

HAVING in the previous section described the experience of felicity by a person of discrimination following mental restraint; this one will deal with the blissfulness of Self as cognised by an enquirer of self-knowledge with dull intellect, through the consideration of the word 'Thou.' With this purpose the author now begins with an explanation of the query set by his pupil:—Let those who practise *Yoga*, experience the blissfulness of Self as something over and above the impressional and BRAHMAIC felicities, but how would it fare with persons of dull intellect?

2. And the *Guru* replies:—

Persons of dull intellect are not qualified for self-knowledge. From the force of good and bad works they inherit bodies according to their deserts, to die and be born over and over. Hence there is no necessity for ascertaining what becomes of them.

3. If it be said, kindness of a professor to all creatures is proverbial, and that actuates him to impart the necessary instruction to those seeking for knowledge, hence there is already a necessity. [The professor now enquires:] Say then, whether that person of dull intellect is an enquier of self-knowledge or averse to it?

4. If he is averse to enquire after self-knowledge, he should practise adequate works and worship; [one desirous of obtaining the abode of *Brahmá* should have recourse to worship; and works are necessary for him who desires the abode of heaven]. If he is an enquirer, with intellect dull, he should be instructed by the door of self-blissfulness—in short, by the consideration that his individual blissfulness is no other but BRAHMA:

5. As set forth by YAJNAVALKYA in his discourse with his wife MAITREYI.—"Know my dear, that husband is not dear for the sake of husband's enjoyment;" but because he contributes to the happiness of the wife.

6. Husband, wife, wealth, horse and cattle, *Brahmana*, *Kshetriya*; the several abodes—heaven, etc.; *Deva*, *Vedas*, and the elements—earth and the rest; in short all objects of enjoyment are dear because they are beneficial to Self.

7. When a wife is desirous of her husband, she loves him; and when he is hungry, or otherwise employed, or confined in bed with sickness, he desires her not.

8. Therefore it is evident, that the love which a wife bears to her husband is not for his sake, but for her self-gratification; in the same way does the husband express his fondness for her only for the gratification of his desire and not for her sake.

9. But it may be contended, let their individual desire be the incentive for one liking the other, how is it possible for both of them being actuated by the same desire at one time? Surely if self-gratification were concerned in it, that would render such desire being present in one and absent in the other. To this the reply is,—both are actuated by the gratification of their individual desires.

10. For example, a child kissed by the father cries with pain caused by the beard pressing against its cheek; yet instead of desisting he continues his kisses not for gratifying the child but for his own sake.

11. Gems and wealth have no desire of their own, yet a person protects them with care and affection, not for their sake, but for his own benefit.

12. Bullocks and other beasts of burden are never desirous of carrying any burden, yet they are so used by traders. Here the subject of affection for carrying weight is the tradesman's and not the beast's.

13. "I am a *Brahmana*, and qualified to worship." Whatever contentment follows from worship done with a motive of reward, can only be felt by a *Brahmana* who has the above conceit for his caste; but caste (which is insentient) can never have any such experience of contentment.

14. "I am a *Kshetriya* and that is why I am a ruler." Here the happiness is felt by the king and it properly belongs to him; but the insentient (warrior) caste is no more a king; nor does it feel any pleasure naturally connected with that high position. The same holds true with *Vaishya* and other castes.

15. Desire of obtaining the blissful abode of heaven, *Brahmá*, etc., does not cause any benefit to the several abodes themselves; but to the individual who has recourse to adequate works and worship for inheriting them.

16. SIVA, VISHNU and the other *Devas* are worshipped for the destruction of sin; that worship procure them no benefit, for they are sinless; but to the worshipper, it is beneficial.

17. Neglect of studying the *Vedas* on the part of a *Brahmana* is very injurious as it reduces him to the level of the "fallen;" but does not affect the *Vedas*, and it does not matter whether they are read or not; only those qualified to study will incur de-merit, and be reduced to the condition of one who has lost caste from neglect of the initiatory observances.

18. Moreover, all persons are desirous of obtaining a place of rest, of quenching thirst, preparing food, drying clothes, etc., thus shewing a necessity for the elements—earth, water, fire, etc., wherewith to gratify their desires; but they (elements) have no such desire.

19. Master and servant, have each his desire of benefiting self; just as the servant serves his master for the sake of gold which goes to benefit him, so is the master benefited by the services of the servant.

20. So many illustrations have been adduced with the purpose of enquiring into the applicability of the rule that everywhere, in all our practices (eating, etc.), for this love of Self, every thing is dear to us; and the mind should be properly impressed with it.

21—22. If it be contended, affection for all substances as they are conducive to the benefit of Self does not necessarily constitute affection for him; because there are four varieties of it, and this one is distinct from them. Therefore a dissenter asks of what sort is that affection for Self spoken of in the *Sruti*? Whether it is in the form of passion, faith, devotion or desire? Of them 'passion' would only be applicable to wife, etc.; 'faith' for sacrificial works; 'devotion' would have *Guru*, *Deva*, etc., for its subject; and 'desire'—for a thing which one has not got already. Thus then, affection cannot possibly include all conformable things and make them its subject. To this the *Siddhanti* replies:—Let the modification of the good quality of the internal organ which follows happiness only, be called affection then.

23. That [does not necessarily convert affection into desire; for desire at first pervades the subject of happiness which we have not got, whereas affection has for its subject both the got and ungot varieties of happiness, inasmuch as in happiness already present, and when it has been destroyed, there is never wanting affection for Self. This then is the difference between affection and desire. Just as food and drink are dear, for they are associated with and are means of happiness; so for Self being dear, will like them, be a means of happiness?

24. [If then] like food and drink for being dear, Self be regarded as an adequate means of happiness who would be the enjoyer? Regarding food and drink, the substances of enjoyment are the associate for which they are said to produce happiness; but in respect to Self there is no associate in the shape of enjoyable substances, consequently no means

of happiness too. With this purpose the *Siddhanti* asks his opponent, if for Self being dear, he be the means of happiness, who will be the subject of that affection—in short the enjoyer? No one; because apart from Self there is no enjoyer. If it be said, for his being dear, Self is fit to be a subject of affection; then the reply is, to regard the same subject both as action and actor simultaneously implies the presence of properties opposed to each other, hence it is absurd to hold Self as both the subject of benefit as well as the benefiter at the same time.

25. There can only be affection for happiness derived from temporal enjoyments such as wealth, wife, children and the rest, and not its excess. Self is exceedingly dear, hence love of Self is infinitely superior to it. Then again, material happiness is apt to change its site, sometimes pervading one set of objects, which no sooner got possession of, than hungering for others, it does not remain fixed as a rule, which affection for Self never does; therefore love of Self is said to be superior to all.

26. Abandoning one variety of temporal (material) happiness, men are always found bent after the enjoyment of another; but Self is neither capable of being abandoned nor be acceptable, hence Self-love cannot be said to change.

27. Nor can it be said, Self is fit to be disregarded like a bit of straw; inasmuch as he is not a subject of either being abandoned or accepted. Because he* who is to disregard Self is one with him.

28. If it be contended, that the assertion "Self is not a subject of being abandoned" does not hold true; for in illness and anger men are found to express a desire of death, so that

* *Jiva* is reflection of intelligence; his individual self is indestructible intelligence, which is naturally one with him, for which he cannot disregard Self as something distinct and separate like a bit of straw.

from hatred, Self is abandoned. The reply is, that desire caused by hatred has for its subject the gross physical body,—different from self—and the wish to die can only affect it, but not Self who is indestructible.

29. The physical body—which is parted company with at death—is not Self; but its relinquisher—different from it—[*Jiva*] is; and as there can be no hatred regarding the relinquisher, there is therefore no abandonment of self-love in the desire of death.

30. Thus having established the truth of the *Sruti* texts regarding YAJNAVALKA's address to his wife MAITREYI commencing with, "the husband is not dear to the wife for his desire" and ending in "for the gratification of self-desire all are dear to him," the subject is further illustrated by argument.—Husband, wife and the rest, in short all the materials of happiness, inasmuch as they contribute to the welfare of Self are held dear. As the son is dearer to the father than the son's friend; so for their relation with him, all subjects of affection are extremely dear to self.*

* To a theosophist, self is very dear for his being eternal bliss; but with the common herd, the rule is otherwise; ignorant of his natural blissfulness, they are deluded to hunt after temporal enjoyment, which receiving reflection of happiness from him, tempts them to the belief that it is supreme felicity; and to regard with affection the internal organ, which receives that reflection of happiness, the senses situated close to it, and the vital airs, as they are directly related to Self. Now the physical body is incapable of receiving the reflex happiness, so that it has no direct relation with Self: on the contrary, there is a second-hand, indirect or mediate relation between him and the physical body, through the subtle body which is immediately connected with him on the one hand and the physical body on the other. Similarly son, wife, etc., are connected by means of the physical body, as their friends are by them; so that the comparative scale of affection proceeds at a progressive ratio of increment in the proportion of the connection of a thing with Self: that is to say, Self is the

31. On appealing to universal experience it is found that the wish to be always, is the predominating idea uppermost in humanity, and its reverse—not to be—is nowhere prevalent. For instance, "may I live always in happiness, etc." So that here also extreme self-love is manifested.

32. In spite of the authority of the *Sruti*, argument and experience, there are many who from ignorance, or incapability of comprehending *Sruti* texts regard Self as subordinate and inferior to son, wife, etc.:

33. And cite as their authority the text of the *Aiterya Upanishad* where it occurs "Self is born as son." So that here son is spoken of as the principal Self:—

---

center, things closely connected are more loved than those situated at a distance and connected through the second-hand instrument of another; this is why a son is more loved and held dearer than his friend, whose connection is only second-hand through the connection of the son. But it may be asked since Self is all-pervading and naturally blissful, consequently we should expect an equal amount of affection everywhere, and neither excess nor its reverse, as is here pointed out. The reply is very simple; it has already been said, that the internal organ receives the reflection of his felicity, because it is transparent; or what amounts to the same thing, from a preponderance of the pure good quality. A jar is insentient, it abounds in darkness, consequently it cannot receive that reflex happiness, hence it is not dearly loved. Upon the capability of receiving this reflex happiness from Self depends the direct relation of a substance with him; and that relative who is beneficial or conformable to the internal organ with its reflection of intelligence is said to have an affection for substances; and on the difference of its associate in the proportion of its conformableness or its reverse, depends the proportion of excess or diminution of affection. All this refers to the ignorant; but to a theosophist who is devoid of the distinctions created by knower, knowledge and the object to be known, in short who regards him as unassociated, perfect bliss, there is neither diminution nor excess; he sees Self as the center of affection and full of felicity, equally present everywhere.

34. Which means that the Self in the shape of son acts as the substitute of the father, for performing meritorious works, and subsequently in dotage, that other Self (the father's) considering himself benefited by the good deeds done by the son, dies to reap their results; and believes himself to have achieved success in all that was necessary to be done.

35. Of that inferiority of self to son, wife, etc., passages abound in the *Purans* too. For example. "One without a son has no abode hereafter." Since son is the primary self a son-less father (though) having his own Self) has no future abode to inherit after death. Then again the *Sruti* says:— "Learned men speak of a son instructed in the *Vedas* as beneficial to his father's hereafter."

36. Human happiness is capable of being reaped by son only and not by any other means. To a father without son, the usual means, wealth, etc., are a source of creating indifference. A son educated in the *Vedas* is said to be the means of procuring a future abode for his father. "Thou art BRAHMA" and similiar other sacred texts are pronounced by a dying father to instruct his son.

37. Now this inferiority of self to son, etc., does not rest entirely on the *Sruti* and other proofs but likewise on popular practice where this superiority is equally admitted.

38. [For on referring to it we find], a father facing death, and undergoing privations to acquire wealth, that his wife and son may live, (after his death) in happiness, and be free from misery. Thus son and wife are superior; otherwise he would not be so mindful of their happiness at the cost of so much hardship and labour to self.

39. The *Siddhanti* admits the truth of the *Sruti* assertion about the superiority of son to Self and confirmed by popular practice too. He says: Yes what you say about this superiority is true. If it be apprehended, this admission will create discord with those other passages where the superiority of Self (as witness) has been maintained, then the reply is, that

does not necessarily reduce Self into a subordinate position inferior to son and the rest. On the other hand, to establish the superiority or primary importance of a subject practically used as self three varieties of *Atma* are spoken of, *viz.*,—secondary—with the modification of quality;—unreal; and primary.

40. As for instance "DEVADATTA SINHA." Here the first word is the name of a person, and the last stands for lion—a beast of prey; but for the presence of the attributes of the latter in the person called DEVADATTA, they are attributed to him, and the two are non-distinct; similarly Self and son are naturally distinct (like DEVADATTA and lion) but for the attribution of Self to son they are regarded one and non-distinct; for a like modification of quality as in the instance under illustration, the identity of self with son is called *Gouna** or secondary.

41. Just as the stump of a tree taken for a thief, cannot possibly be a thief for the distinction between a tree and a thief, and it is unreal; so for the distinction between the five sheaths and the witnessing intelligence, (Self), the attribution of Self to them is unreal.

---

* Words are capable of being understood either by the primary force inherent in them which is the principal modification, or from the force of 'indication,' from the perquisites of quality. Now this qualitative signification is called *Gcuni Britti*, for instance "DEVADATTA SINHA." Here for the presence of bravery etc., which are characteristic of the lion, to call the person DEVADATTA 'lion' signifies that he is brave. Similarly in regard to Self, whose literal signification is witness, that witness is the principal Self; but in the attribution of unreal qualities to Self, for instance that he is the doer of works for present or future benefit—depends his connection with son, etc., which cannot literally signify Self—hence the signification of son, and the rest as Self (for this modification of quality) is called the secondary Self or Self with quality. *(Gaunatma).*

42. No distinction is seen between the witness (Self), and other things, as manifested in respect to the secondary Self (son, etc.,); nor is there any difference like the unreal Self (the physical body); because there does not exist any thing different from him. And as he is internal to them all, he is necessarily the primary or real self.

43. For this threefold difference, each individual takes that to be his primary self which he has learnt from practice. That is to say, ordinary persons devoid of self-knowledge follow the usual practice, connecting wife, son, body, etc., with Self and believe them to be real; but a theosophist regards every thing else to be unreal, save BRAHMA, the witness. Thus for a difference in practice, whether it be popular, *Vedic* or that of a theosophist, either son, wife, etc., or the physical body, or the witness is regarded as the principal self.

44. [Accordingly we find] in the case of a person in death-bed, his son, wife, etc., appear as the proper parties to look after the house and property and they are his secondary self; because they are desirous of surviving him: but neither the witness (real Self) nor the physical body (unreal Self) are fit for such work, inasmuch as the former is unchangeable, and have no desire, while the latter in confronting death is reduced to helplessness; consequently son and the rest appear as the principal self.

45. For example:—"This reader is fire." Here if the literal acceptation of fire be taken, the sentence loses its meaning; because fire is neither capable of reading nor of pronouncing, and one who can read is the fit person, therefore it would signify, "Boys reading." And this is meant.

46. Similarly, in the ordinary phrase "I have been reduced in flesh and it is necessary that I shall be stout in body," the connection of self with the physical body (their identity) is proper; but for the purpose of regaining flesh it is not necessary that the son should be fed with good food, etc.; hence body is the principal self.

47. "I will practise religious observances to obtain the blissful abode of heaven;" here the agent is the cognitional sheath and it is fit to be regarded as self, but not the physical body. For all desire of material enjoyments are abandoned [which are gratifying to the physical body] and recourse had to the practice of rigid austerities enjoined by religion for benifiting the cognitional sheath in the shape of the desired abode in heaven.

48. "I am bound and will try to be freed." [When a person possessed of the four means of knowledge is desirous of release, then by the help of the preceptor and the sacred writings as to the signification of the transcendental phrase "That art Thou," he obtains visible knowledge of his oneness with BRAHMA, discards the idea of his being an agent and instrument, and exclaims "I am BRAHMÁ."] Here it is proper to connect the witness with pure Intelligence and not the cognitional and other sheaths. In the *Sruti*, Self is spoken of as BRAHMA thus: "BRAHMA is knowledge and bliss." "Self is infinite, internal, perfect, and full of knowledge."

49. Just as *Brahmanas* are qualified to perform the sacrificial ceremony known by the name of *Vrihaspati*, which no *Kshetriya* nor *Vaishya* can; a king, the installation ceremony (*Rajsuya*); and *Vaishya*, the sacrifice called *Vaishyastom*, which no other casteman can; so in respect to the secondary, unreal and primary selves, each has adequate superiority in his own sphere when used properly.

50. [To be more explicit]:—

In uses adequate to and proper for Self there is excessive love; in substances which are not-self but beneficial to him there is only affection; and those other things which are neither Self nor beneficial to him have neither love nor its excess (both are wanting) in them.*

* Things which are subjects of desire are called conformable. Happiness, and want of misery, and their means are objects

51. And those things are divisible into two varieties according as they are either objects of disregard or of hate. For instance, straw and rubbish deposited on the roadside come under the first variety; while tiger and other ferocious animals inasmuch as they cause injury are objects fit to be hated. These are the four sorts of things, to wit:—

52. Self (the dearest), things beneficial (dear), worthless and hateful. But there is no such rule in them that one particular object is the dearest, another dear, a third worthless and fourth hateful; on the other hand, that depends upon action, according as they are beneficial or otherwise.

53. For example:—When a tiger confronts a person with a view of devouring him, it is hateful; but when it returns baffled it is worthless; when wheedled into sport to excite pleasure then it is loved. Thus the same animal from a dif-

---

desired; of which acquisition of happiness and cessation of misery, or its want and their means—these four—are adequate objects of desire and called conformable. But there is this difference between them: Self who is supremely blissful, and wanting in misery is extremely conformable, and for his being the subject of exclusive affection he is said to be very dear; happiness procured from works of the present or past life as it is non-eternal and costs us much trouble and misery is called more conformable, hence for its being the subject of a higher degree of affection than its means which are painful, is said to be dearer; and the means for happiness, and cessation of misery, which are naturally not wanting in either of them, but are helpful to their production, (hence conformable) are merely dear for being the subject of only a slight degree of affection. Beyond these four no other object is ever desired, for which there is no other conformable substance; but differing from it and the unconformable are the inimical, that is to say, inimical substances are never desired, for which they are no subjects of affection and consequently are dear neither. But as they are the subjects of disregard and hate, consequently they are either worthless or hateful.

ference in its action is respectively the subject of hate, disregard, and affection.

54. If it be contended, to admit the presence of the three aforesaid qualities in the same substance will do away with established usage. The reply is, usage is regulated not by the individual quality but by the force of indication. And the indications are friendliness, hostility and their absence. [That is to say, friendliness or conformability to happiness is the indication of affection; what is hostile to happiness and brings on pain is the indication of hate: and what is neither friendly nor hostile indicates worthlessness].

55. To sum up then: each individuated Self is the dearest, and those related to him are dear, and substances different from them are either hateful or worthless;—for they are productive of pain, or incapable of causing either happiness or misery. These are the four separate forms of things regulated by popular usage according to their different uses, and beyond them there is not another. So says YAJNAVALKYA too.

56. It is not to be imagined that the above doctrine 'Self is most beloved' finds mention only in the *Brihadaranyakopanishad*; other passages to that effect occur in the *Punisvidha Brahmana*. For instance:—" Who is dearer than son, house, land, cattle and riches, who is more internal and dearer than the senses, more internal than son and the rest—that Self most intrinsically situated to them all—is the dearest or most beloved."

57. If the purport of the *Sruti* be duly considered, it will be found, that the witnessing Intelligence alone is Self, And that 'due consideration' consists in discriminating the five sheaths foodful and the rest and things subordinate to or included in them, and ascertaining their difference from Self; what is internal to them is Self. In this manner to know him by inference is meant by the verb 'to consider.'

58. How can a substance internally situated be seen? In this wise:—That self-illuminated intelligence which discovers

waking, dreaming, and profound slumber—their appearance and disappearance—is Self.

59. All substances of enjoyment from the Vital air* (*Prana*) to riches are more or less close to Self, for which they are more or less dear to men.

60. A son is dearer than riches, and the physical body is dearer than son. In the same way, the senses are dearer than the body, mind dearer than the senses, and Self dearest in comparison to mind.

61. Though excessive dearness of Self is established in the *Sruti* and other proofs, yet it is a matter of dispute between the wise and ignorant, and for the purpose of settling it, the *Sruti* cites it as an example. If it be asked what does that dispute prove? It proves Self to be the dearest.

62. A theosophist says "of all visible objects Self is the dearest." But ignorant persons say, son, wife, etc., are the dearest, and the witness (Self) for the sake of enjoying them is dear.

63. A pupil qualified for self-knowledge and a dissentient person both regard something other than Self to be dear. A theosophist replies to them in such a manner as to enable the former to have a correct knowledge of Self but to the latter it is a curse.

64. He says:—"That dear of yours will make you cry." [In short, if both of you look upon son, wife, etc., as objects of affection and hold them dear, their death will make you weep.]

---

* Here mind is meant by Vital air or *Prana*. Because it is the receiver of reflected happiness of Self, and is the controller of the senses, for which it is the Lord. When mental distraction is caused by disease of the eye, etc., a person says "if the diseased organ could go I would be happy;" therefore, the mind is to be taken for *Prana*. Then again, as the mind can neither remain in or depart from the body living *Prana*, that is another reason why mind is to be accepted as the meaning of Vital air.

How can the same reply apply both to the pupil and his opponent? Because discrimination enables the former to see the defects present in his own view of the dearness of son. [As set forth in the three following verses.]

65. Till a son is born to them, the parents are very miserable; even after conception, the mother is liable to suffer from the pangs of abortion and child-birth.

66. If the delivery be natural and free from mishaps, planetary influence makes the child sick and causes much anxiety to the parents. Subsequently when it grows up to youth, without profiting by the instruction given from the fifth to the sixteenth year, and turns out a stupid young man that is another source of uneasiness. Similarly after being initiated into the rites of the sacred thread, to continue in ignorance of self, as to remain unmarried after having learnt the *Shastras* are all sources of grief to them.

67. Then again, after having settled in marriage life to turn into the paths of immorality and vice causes much uneasiness, likewise does his poverty. On the other hand, if he grows rich and dies, the parents suffer intensely, so that actually there is no end of their sufferings [commencing with gestation till the period of his death].

68. [What has been said in respect to son, applies equally to wife, riches and the rest. They are faulty too, so that the pupil] abandons all affection for them and knowing to a certainty his individual Self to be the seat of supreme affection is ever and anon engaged in discovering him.

69. [So far then applies to the pupil. Now in regard to his adversary, the theosophist's reply that "your dear will make you cry" is thus being fully set forth]. A dissentient person fond of dispute never abandons the view or side he takes from his animosity to a knower of Self. Such a one either inherits hell or is made to pass through successive re-births in the several grades of animal existence, experiencing grief at the separation of the female partner by death, and

getting what it had no liking for. Hence the above answer "your dear will make you cry" is virtually a curse:

70. [For] a knower of BRAHMA is BRAHMA,* therefore is he ISWARA; and what escapes his lips must verily come to pass, so that dissenter surely suffers from the curse of the theosophist.

---

* A theosophist is BRAHMA, because the *Sruti* says, "A knower of BRAHMA is BRAHMA," and for his own experience of oneness with It. He is ISWARA, or Lord; because excepting BRAHMA there is no other ISWARA. Or, as ISWARA the predicated intelligence of *Maya* for the knowledge of his identity with all selves is their collective aggregate and free, so in a theosophist for a similar knowledge of his identity with all selves he is their collective aggregate and free; and like the discovery of uncovered BRAHMA to ISWARA, the predicated intelligence of *Maya*, in the form of his own self, it happens to a theosophist too. Thus then for a similar identity of quality also, a knower of BRAHMA is ISWARA. For example, a certain king and his queen had two sons, of whom the eldest inherited the whole state and ascended the throne, the youngest for his stupidity had to turn into a servant. Now between the brothers the difference in condition was extreme; subsequently the youngest took the injustice done to him to heart, and wanted to share the ancestral property equally; justice was on his side, and he recovered what was due to him, and was duly installed. In the same way, of the father BRAHMA and mother *Maya* two sons are born called *Jiva* and ISWARA; of them the eldest ISWARA inherited the father's wealth in the form of 'being,' 'intelligence,' and 'bliss;' and the mother's, in the shape of omnipresence, omnipotence and universal control. The youngest, *Jiva*, was deprived of his inheritance from stupidity arising from want of discrimination, and was subjected to experience happiness and misery as a result of works and worship: so that their mutual difference is extreme. Subsequently when he attains the usual means of self-knowledge (discrimination, etc.,) speaks to ISWARA thus;—"I am ISWARA. Thou hast been enjoying the hidden treasure of blissfulness of our common Father,

71. One who worships the witnessing Intelligence, knowing that to be his dearest self. never experiences any pain; as happens to men holding wife, son, and temporal enjoyments dear, when they die or disappear.

72. For his being the subject of supreme affection Self is supremely blissful, and it is but proper so to regard him. As in the *Taiterya* and *Brihadaranyaka Upanishads* :—" From the happiness felt by the emperor of the universe to that pertaining to the position of *Hiranyagarva*, there is commensurate increase of happiness in the proportion as affection is present."

73. But it may be objected, if like knowledge, Self be naturally blissful, then as in all modifications of the intellect, intelligence is said to be present, there should likewise be blissulness.

74 The reply is :—That is not possible. Because, a lamp is a form both of light and heat, but its light only pervades a room; like it, intelligence only is manifested and not blissfulness.

75. Just as the presence of smell, form, taste and touch in the same substance is recognised by the senses—one only by each—smell by means of the nose; form, eye; taste, tongue; and touch, skin; so of the two—intelligence and bliss —intelligence alone is manifested.

76. If it be alleged, Intelligence and bliss are not separate

---

and after dividing the maternal property turnest me into a beggar asking me " To give all this to thee," and pointing the sanctioned works which I am to perform and the prohibited works which I am not to perform, thus veritably reducing me to the position of a servant so far as obedience to the *Vedas* is concerned; but now by the help of *Guru*, I will snatch from thee, the present fund of blissfulness, inasmuch as I have done away with our associate-created-difference of visibility and invisibility, etc., and joined intelligence with intelligence for they are one." In this manner does a theosophist become BRAHMA.

and distinct, but smell, form, etc., are mutually distinct; then the question is, whether that non-distinction of Intelligence and bliss exists in the witness (Self), or elsewhere—in the modifications of associate ? [This is for the dissenter to answer.]

77. If the first view be admitted, then look at the identity of smell, etc., in the same flower too. And if you hold smell, form, taste and touch are distinct (for the presence of distinction in the several senses through which they are cognized), you should likewise admit a distinction between Intelligence and bliss, for a difference in the modification of the intellect caused by the active and good qualities of the mind.

78. When as a result of meritorious work, the mind has assumed the modification of good quality, a person then discovers intelligence and bliss are identical; because the modification of good quality is pure and faultless (transparent). But the modification of active quality is impure, and that is why the part representing bliss remains covered and hidden as if under a sheath.

79. Just as a sour fruit eaten with salt has its acidity covered, so from the modifiction of active quality blissfulness is covered.*

---

* Just as in bewilderment or confusion of the mind, subjects —situated near, and visible are not discovered, so from its active modification, the mind fails to take cognition of felicity. Or for his being the subject of excessive love, the felicity of Self, manifested always, is only ordinary; but when it is reflected in the modification of the mental function, then it is intensified. Just as a looking glass receives the reflection of a person but does not give a faithful image, so are the modifications produced from the active and dark qualities capable of receiving the reflection of intelligence only and not bliss, for which it is not discovered. Like the removal of acidity from an unripe and sour mango by means of salt, the felicity naturally present in Self is removed by the modifications of the mental function stirred up by activity and ignorance.

80. If it be asked, even admitting the supreme blissfulness of Self to be due to excessive love for him, without mental restraint *(Yoga)* what would be the result? [No emancipation would result from the knowledge that blissfulness of Self is owing to excessive affection which all individuals have for him; and that he is quite distinct from son, wife, physical body, and the other four sheaths; or as they are otherwise called, things 'dear,' 'worthless,' and 'hateful.' Such discrimination is not enough, something more is needed and that is 'visible knowledge' of Self. Such is the purport of the contention which his antagonist asks the *Siddhanti* to solve.]

81. [And he replies.]—I say the same result follows discrimination of Self as is produced from *Yoga*. Visible knowledge follows equally in the former as in the latter. [To be more explicit, mental restraint has already been pointed out in the preceeding section to be the means for the rising of knowledge, so the present consideration of Self—primary, secondary and unreal—and discriminating him from the five sheaths foodful and the rest, is alike productive of gnosis.]

82. Of them (*Yoga* and discrimination) as a source of knowledge where is the authority? The *Gita* says "Whatever position a person attains to, from the discrimination of Self from not-self, is equally attained by the *Yogi*." [So that the result is equal in both.]

83. To some qualified persons practice of *Yoga* is difficult; to others again, discrimination of Self from not-self is impossible; knowing this, SREE KRISHNA pointed out these two separate paths for the acquisition of knowledge.

84. Thus then, as the *Gita* speaks of equality of result following the practice of mental restraint and discrimination of Self, how can ye dissenter hold the first to be superior? Then again, so far as desire and hate are concerned, neither a *Yogi* nor a person of discrimination is subject to them.

85. One who knows Self to be very dear, has no more

desire for temporal enjoyment, hence he has no ardent desire; and as he has no enemy, he has no hate in him.

86. If you contend, discriminate persons are seen to express their hate; the reply is, it holds equally true with a *Yogi*. In short, whatever causes pain to the body, etc., from the sting of a scorpion to the injury caused by tigers and other wild animals, are equally objects of hate both in a *Yogi* as well as a man of discrimination. And if during such conduct, you cease to recognise the discrimination of the latter, I may as well cease to call the former a *Yogi*.

87. If you say, that inasmuch as a person of discrimination sees the objective world, which a *Yogi* does not, therefore is the latter superior. The reply is, in ordinary practice this material world is equally dealt with by both. If you say, there is no cognition of phenomena in *Yoga*; it holds equally true when the person is in his discriminating mood.

88. And that imperception of phenomena will be spoken of, in the following section. It is faultless.

89. One who experiences in his person the blissfulness of Self, and takes no heed of this vast material expanse, in short sees them not, if such a theosophist, be your *Yogi*, may you be content, and grow in years.

90. [The purport of the work is thus briefly declared.]——*Atmananda* forms the second chapter of the treatise *Brahmananda* containing five chapters. It is written for the benefit of qualified persons of dull intellect; and it treats on the natural blissfulness of each individual self situated most intrinsically.

SECTION XIII.

(c) *Adwaitananda or the Felicity of Non-Duality.*

[IN the first chapter (corresponding to Sect. XI) felicity has been declared to be threefold, *viz.*, that proceeding from the cognition of BRAHMA, self-knowledge, and temporal enjoyment; to them has been added in the preceeding treatise another variety, to wit, self-happiness (*Atmananda*): to prevent any misapprehension as to its antagonism to the first three forms, the author thus opens the present work :—]

What has already been spoken of as felicity proceeding from (*Yoga*) mental restraint (*Yogananda*) is no other but self-happiness. Just as happiness derived from the cognition of BRAHMA is due to the practice of *Yoga*, for which it is called *Yogananda*; and for its being unassociated, self-happiness (*nijananda*); so with the view of declaring the desirability of knowing the felicity of BRAHMA by a separate consideration of the three forms of Self—secondary, unreal and primary—the word '*Atmananda*' has been made use of.] If it be asked, how can self-happiness which is material be identical with the felicity of BRAHMA which is devoid of duality (secondless)? Listen to what follows.

2. Says the *Taiterya Upanishad*:—"From ether to the physical body, all this vast material expanse has been produced from self-happiness, and nothing else; therefore it is secondless and identical with BRAHMA."

3. "This material universe has been produced from happiness, is seated in, and merges into it."* Therefore there

---

* Sexual intercourse is the source of animal life and as its gratification is attended with felicity, it can easily be understood why happiness is said to be the mainspring of phenomena. Death resembles profound sleep, which too, is full of happiness; therefore we find in the text happiness to be the cause of phenomena; they

can be no contention as to its primal cause being Self, and not happiness. If any one be so inclined as to maintain a distinction between happiness and the objective world; the reply is, as the universe is its product, it cannot be distinct from happiness; for the resulting product is never distinct from its cause, as jar from earth.

4. If it be alleged, jar is the product of the potter and they are distinct, so that the above rule does not hold true; the reply is, there are two varieties of causes, instrumental and material; of which the material is non-different from its product. Therefore like earth the material cause (not potter, the instrumental cause,) of jar, this self-happiness (*Atmananda*) is the material (not instrumental) cause of the objective world; for which, they are not distinct from one another.

5. Why is potter not the material cause of jar? Because he is neither the resting place nor the site of its destruction; in short, prior to its production and after it is destroyed, a jar is present in clay only, requiring the aid of a potter with his wheel and turning rod to give form and shape. Since therefore that clay or earth is its resting place, it is said to be the material cause. And like that earth, happiness is the material cause of the universe. As in the, *Sruti*, "These elements have all derived their origin from happiness."

6. This material cause is of three different forms, *viz.* :— (1) Altered condition without change of form and state; (2) Altered condition with change of form and state; and (3) Combination of the units of material cause producing different

---

are seated in it, because everywhere the one predominating idea is how to be happy. Accumulation of wealth, possession of land, property, wife, cattle, son, etc., are all so many means for it, according to popular idea; in death we merge into sleep—a typical condition of happiness.

results (*Arambhaka*).* In respect to substances without form, the second and third do not apply.

7. The *Vaisheshikas* and others who support the doctrine of *arambha* admit other causes than those which produce results as the source from which they are produced: because yarn is seen to produce cloth. Verily yarn is quite distinct from cloth, its product; and their modifications and uses are different; no thread can be worn, but cloth is.

8. When a substance is changed from its former condition into a different form it is called *Parinama*, as curdled milk, jar, and gold respectively, in which their original form and condition are changed.

9. When there is no change of its former condition but a substance is perceived in a different form it is *Vivartta*, as the illusion of snake in rope. And it appears equally to formless substances; as for instance, to ether which has no form, yet perceived blue, resembling a frying pan in appearance.

10. Therefore it is fit to believe that the objective world is but a *Vivartta* of blissfulness; and the force of *Maya* is

---

* When from the relation or connection of the units or parts of the material cause a substance is produced differing in form, then it is called *arambha*; as from the combination of atoms and ether half of jar the result is jar. Altered condition of the material cause is *parinama* as curd is of milk. It will at once be apparent that these indications can only apply to substances which have form and shape, and not elsewhere, where form and shape are wanting; because both in regard to relation, and altered condition, on which *arambha* and *parianama* depend, parts, features or form is necessary. Felicity has neither parts, features, nor form. hence it is quite possible to regard it as the material cause of the universe of the first variety or *Vivartta*; a trite instance of which is the snake in rope. Here the rope is not transformed into snake, but a substance (snake) extremely opposed to the site (rope) and an altered condition of it, is projected on it. Similarly the blue of ether (blue sky) and its convexity are illustrations of *Vivartta*.

the potent cause for such a belief, like things created in a magic performance by the use of chemical re-agents, spells, and charms.

11. But force is not distinct from matter—the atoms of which a body is composed—hence for this absence of distinction as a separate entity, it is unreal. For example, the consuming force of fire is not distinct from fire; nor can it be said that they are identical; for the consuming force is seen at times from the action of chemical re-agents, etc., to be in abeyance, and not manifested. If there be no force on what is the obstacle to act? That is to say, fire which is distinctly seen, cannot possibly have any obstruction, so that if a separate force distinct from fire be not admitted, that obstruction, will have no subject—which is objectionable. Therefore the recognition of a distinct force as the subject of obstruction, separate from the body having that force, is necessary.

12. Force is inferrible from action; so that when in spite of the cause being present, no action results, it is called obstruction. For instance, when a blazing fire does not burn, *Mantras* or sacred formulæ pronounced at the time, are said to be the cause of obstruction.

13. The nature of *Maya* is illustrated by referring to the text of the *Shvetashvataropanishad*:—" A Sage by rigid abstraction and contemplation cognises Self to be no other than BRAHMA. He is naturally self-illuminated but the two forces of ignorance 'envelopment' and 'projection' keep him ever concealed." And " action, knowledge and desire are the various forms of his supreme force."*

* With reference to the causation of phenomena various are the hypotheses prevalent amongst the followers of the different schools. Some say the world has no cause, but against it the objection is, a jar is seen to be produced from clay, and there can be no jar without it; therefore it is against what we see to be a fact. Others assert 'nothing' as the cause; but nothing cannot produce

14. Thus does the *Rigveda* speak of the wonderful force of *Maya*. BASHISTA speaks to the same effect too. For instance, "PARABRAHMA is eternal, full on all sides [completely filling up the four quarters north, south, east and west], secondless and omnipotent. [The first three expletives represent the real Impersonal, and the last the associated or Personal form.]

15. "Whenever that PARABRAHMA is revealed through any modification of the force of *Maya*, the force likewise is manifested in the shape of its products. Oh RAM, in the bodies of *Devas*, men, reptiles, etc., the intelligence of BRAHMA (force in the form of cause of using that intelligence) is seen.

16. "Just as motion is revealed in air, inertia, in stone, in water, its solvent force, and combustion; in fire: [so does the universe (potentially) exist in BRAHMA in its unrevealed state prior to evolution.]*

---

something. A third says 'void'; which is tantamount to ether producing flowers, or reaping a harvest of corn where no seed has been sown. A fourth, atoms; but they are formless and insentient, hence cannot give form and shape to objects. A fifth has time for the primal cause; but even in the presence of time things are not produced always. A sixth asserts nature to be the universal cause, but in the case of sterile women we find the rule broken: for it is the nature of semen to fertilize the ovum yet no conception follows. A seventh fixes it in virtue and vice, which too has faults as it includes one variety of cause producing one set of results and excluding the other. There are others again, who look upon the elements, *Prakriti*, *Purush*, the combination of matter and spirit undergoing change of form and substance, BRAHMA without the *Mayaic* force, and BRAHMA with it, as the All-Cause. Suffice it to say, that with the exception of the last named one, the others are all open to grave objections.

* There are four sorts of destruction (*Pralaya*) :—(*a*) daily, (*b*) occasional, (*c*) material, and (*d*) extreme. Like the light of lamp the dissolution of all substances—their disappearance every moment—or in profound slumber when they are no more seen,

17. "In ether, void is its force; and in things destructible, liability to destruction is the force present. Just as in its egg, a huge snake remains undiscovered, so does the universe in the Supreme Self, remain impressed or exist potentially.

18. "As fruits, leaves, flowers, branches with the ascending and descending stem of a creeper as well as a shady tree are confined within their seeds, so is this wonderful universe present in the Supreme BRAHMA.

19. "From the wonderful influence of time and place some forces are developed from the same BRAHMA; just as several sorts of seeds sown in the ground wait for the proper season and soil to germinate. [To be more explicit; if a handful of all manner of seeds be sown, some only will germinate—those to which the season and soil are both agreeable—others will wait for the proper time to come, or refuse to grow at all, as the soil is unsuited to them; similarly of all the forces centred in BRAHMA, some only—and not all—operate.

---

their disappearance in ignorance is an instance of the first; with the advent of *Brahmā's* night, when everything is destroyed together with the three abodes, such cyclic destruction is called occasional; and when he has completed his span of hundred years, the elements, egoism, and *Mahatatwa* disappear in undifferentiated cosmic matter, it is an instance of material destruction (*Prakriti Pralaya*). The 'extreme' or fourth variety is the result of self-knowledge when everything else excepting BRAHMA appears unreal. In the first three varieties, there is no want of action with material cause; but the products remain in the form of impression in that cause—in short they exist potentionally, and in a subsequent period of time are evoluted again, so that from the ordinary stand-point it does not amount to total destruction of the universe, no matter whether it be revealed or otherwise. In the fourth variety, phenomena together with Ignorance, their material cause, are reduced to non-being, so that to a theosophist, the world does not exist except as an illusion, no matter whether it is in its unrevealed or revealed state.

according to the adaptability of time and locality—circumstances favouring their development, and known by their action.]

20. "RAM, whenever the eternal, manifested and infinite Self, through a modification of the *Mayaic* force assumes the force of intellection, it is called mind."

21. In this way, is the mind first evoluted in the form of *Hiranayagarbha*—the collective aggregate of minds;—next follows the perception of bondage aud emancipation; and next the several abodes contained in the universe; which though imaginary and unreal appear tangible and substantial. If it be asked how can unreal appear substantial? Just as tales concocted for the amusement of children appear real to them and are believed so.

22. The nurse with a view of amusing the children under her charge repeats the following tale:—"In a certain country there resided three handsome princes.

23. "Of whom two have not been born yet, while the third has not been conceived in its mother's womb. All the three brothers were endowed with good qualities, and they lived in a city which existed not.

24. "Their minds were unerring too; as they went out of the city on a certain occasion, they found trees laden with fruits in the ether.

25. "Now they were desirous of sport, and armed as they were with bow and arrows, they give chase to a horned rabbit, killed and partook of the flesh and arrived at a future city where they are living in happiness."

26. "RAM, when the children heard this tale from the nurse, they believed it to be true, for they were too young to exercise any judgment."

27. Similarly the composition of this tangible universe appears real to dull and ignorant persons incapable of judging; and its reality is as firmly implanted in their mind as the reality of the incidents of the above story in the boys.

28. Thus does BASHISTA expound the nature of *Mayaic* force. Its unreality is now being ascertained.

29. *Maya* is distinct both from its product, the world, and its site or receptacle, BRAHMA; just as the force of fire is distinct both from its action or product, sparks, and its seat or receptacle, charcoal: inasmuch as they are visible while the presence of force is only to be inferred from its action or product.

30. A jar with its thickness and round cavity is a product; and earth with its properties sound, form, smell, touch and taste is its receptacle; but the force which produces the jar is distinct from both.*

31. Force has neither thickness, nor roundness of cavity, (properties of the product); nor has it sound, form, smell, touch and taste—properties belonging to the receptacle (earth) —hence it is distinct from both; and for this distinction, it is unthinkable and indescribable.

32. Prior to the production of jar, the force present in earth remained latent, for which it could not then be discovered; with the help of potter, his turning rod and wheel, that force undergoes mutation and is modified into jar.

33. Indiscriminate persons regard the properties of the product (its grossness and round cavity), and those inherent in the cause (sound, form, taste, touch and smell) as identically one, and give the name 'jar' to mark to that oneness.

34. No jar exists prior to a potter's moulding a lump of clay with the help of his stick and wheel, so that to speak of this prior condition of earth as a form of jar, is only an instance of indiscriminate thinking. That jar, is only a subsequent product when its thick form and round cavity are developed; then only is it fit to be called so.

---

* Force has neither thickness nor roundness of cavity like the jar, nor has it the properties,—sound, etc., therefore it is distinct from the product and its receptacle earth, in short, indescribable.

35. A jar is not distinct from earth, inasmuch as it is never found without it; nor is it identical with earth, inasmuch as it is never seen in a lump of clay.

36. Therefore like force, 'jar' is equally indescribable; for which, it is a product of force. If it be asked since 'force' and its 'product' are equally indescribable, what necessity is there for retaining their separate use? The reply is, 'force' is used to express invisibility; while visible condition is expressed by the word 'jar.'

37. To remove misapprehension about the invisibility of *Mayaic* force being subsequently visible it is said :—

In a magical performance, the force of illusion remains invisible till the usual spells, *mantras*, and re-agents are used; subsequent to which, it succeeds in creating charmed fruits, trees, etc.

38. "For their being material, all changed or transformed products are liable to destruction; but their site or receptacle (as earth the receptacle of jar) is real." (*Sruti.*)

39. "'Change' is a mere name, having no reality, inasmuch as excepting its name there is nothing real in jar; but its receptacle earth is real." (*Chhandagya Upanishad.*)

40. Regarding visible products [jar and the rest], their invisible cause, force, and their receptacle, earth, the first two (product and force) for their relation to time (existing in one condition of time and not always in the three) are said to be destructible. But their receptacle, earth, as it exists always in the three conditions of time, is real.

41. Visible products [jar, etc.,] are naturally unreal and discovered so; likewise for their being results of action, they are destructible. And subsequent to production as they are used by name, that also is another cause of their destructibility—[for name and form are subject to destruction.]

42. Moreover, after their destruction, their name only remains in use among, or is pronounced by, men. And for phenomena being ascertained by name [inasmuch as it is

the means of distinguishing one object from another] they are of the same nature as name: for name is pronounced by the tongue which produces sound, and as visible products are distinguished by name, consequently they resemble it.

43. For the disappearance of their actual condition, liability to destruction, and natural resemblance with name—pronounced by the organ of speech, like the elements earth, etc.,—form of visible products is not even partially real. [In short, no part of a jar which is a product of earth, thick with a round cavity, is real. Because the actual condition of earth has undergone modification to produce it; it is destructible; and a product of sound only. "Like the earth" is an exclusive example in regard to the three causes of unreality. Now the inference is:—the product of earth, jar, is fit to be considered unreal (1) for its being a transformed result;—what is not unreal is also not transformed, as for instance, the material cause earth of jar.—(2) Similarly for its destructibility, a jar is unreal;—what is not unreal is indestructible.—(3) Likewise for its being a creation of the organ of speech it resembles sound only in nature, and is unreal; what is not unreal never resembles articulate sound only, as Self.

44. But during the period of action [when a jar is being formed], and both prior to its origin and subsequently, [when it has not been destroyed yet]; earth, for its uniform appearance, preserving its real nature, and indestructibility, is real. Here the inference is, that earth is fit to be regarded real, for its uniform appearance in all the three conditions of time like Self, and preserving its real nature.

45. Now for the contention of the *Vedantin's* antagonist. He asks. If what you have expressed by the three words 'visible,' 'jar,' and 'transformed product' are unreal, how is it that knowledge of earth does not cause their destruction? [Like the destruction of the unreal snake from the knowledge of its site, rope.]

46. It has already been destroyed by the same cause which has removed from you the idea of reality of jar. If it be contended, in the illusory attribution of silver in nacre, the actual nature of *nacre* is only not perceived, but no destruction of its reality is ever seen to follow; then as that is an unassociated illusion, while this is 'associated,' therefore, here destruction of the perception of reality from correct knowledge of site should be regarded as 'destruction' and not imperception, of actual substance.*

---

* There are two sorts of illusions, unassociated and associated; those produced from ignorance only are called 'unassociated,' as the illusion of snake in rope and silver in nacre. Now in regard to these illusions, the instrumental causes are:—(1) Impression of similarity, (2) Defective sight, (3) Defect in the witness, (4) Defect in the subject of demonstration, and (5) Partial (ordinary) knowledge of the site on which illusion is projected or superimposed [portion represented by 'this']; and as they help the ignorance concerning the rope consequently they are "associated." But for a difference in the modification of the period of action, and its prior interval, instrumental causes are divisible into two varieties, *viz.*, from whose contiguity an action is produced, and without which no action results; it is called the instrument modifying the period of action. For example, a pot of water placed close to a wall where the sun's rays have been reflected, and the instrument different from it, is the modification prior to the period of action: as for instance, the wheel and turning rod of a jar. The word "associate" has for its meaning the instrument in the form of modification of the time of action. Such an instrument is wanting in the snake illusion, for which it is "unassociated"; and illusion produced from associate (the aforesaid distinct instrument) together with ignorance is called 'associated': as the reflection of face in mirror, and the reflected shadow of a person standing on the river bank, of trees growing there, or of the blue convex ether, mirage, etc. All of them are caused by the several associates together with ignorance of the site of illusion. Regarding reflection, light and mirror or the contiguity of water are the associates;

47. The reflection of a person's face in water appearing inverted is never really taken for the person; and no one—with or without discrimination—ever believes that face to be real like the person standing on the river bank whose reflection it is.

48. In the same way, notwithstanding the visibility of phenomena, to know their unreality and believe them so, is the certain means of discovering the secondless blissfulness of Self who alone is real; and according to the doctrine of non-duality, such knowledge procures emancipation. If it be said,

---

sunlight and relation of darkness are similar associates in the case of ether reflected in water; in the matter of its panlike shape, contiguity of the earth which is round, is the associate; in mirage, the associates are the sand, and sun's rays glistening on it creating the illusion of water. In this manner, associates are to be considered. In the "unassociated" variety, knowledge of the site of illusion removes the two forces of ignorance,—envelopment and projection, together with its products, so that absence of the imaginary [snake] and the abiding continuance of its site (rope) is the indication of destruction or removal of the snake illusion. In "associated illusions," ignorance with its envelopment are both destroyed and obstructed; but through the influence of the obstacle of ignorance in the shape of associate, there does not follow destruction of the action of its creating or projecting force together with its cause, the same force; but is only removed, prevented or obstructed, and is actually perceived for some time; so that the abiding site continues to the last: or the disappearance of the actuality of the illusory substance is no indication of prevention or obstacle; on the other hand, the certain knowledge of unreality or the absence in all the three conditions of time, is the indication of removal. Thus then, in regard to earth and gold, the respective mistakes of jar and earring and in the case of [egoism too, the illusions are 'associated.' Therefore the ascertainment of their unreality in the manner aforesaid, is the recognised indication of removal and not the absence of actual substance; and necessarily the reality of the site of illusion should certainly then come to be recognised as the remnant of the site.

knowledge of jar as a modification of earth is enough to remove its reality, but it has not been established as such modification or altered condition of earth; then the reply is, since there is no alteration of the appearance of earth in jar, it is therefore an altered condition (*vivartta*) of earth.

49. [To be more explicit :—]

When the original form of the material cause is altered, as curd is of milk, it is called *Parinama*. In *Vivartta* there is no alteration of form in the material cause; as for instance, in an earthen jar and gold earring, their respective material cause, —earth and gold—retains their appearance, and the jar and are ring only altered conditions or modifications.*

50. If it be said, after a jar is broken, its fragments, do not resemble earth in appearance, hence it is proper to speak of it as a modification or altered form of earth; the reply is, after the broken parts are reduced into powder, they resemble earth and not any separate substance: and this is plainly visible. As for gold, it is quite apparent in the earring to require any discussion.

51. To say that the admission of earring and jar as altered conditions without change of substance (gold and earth

---

* What has been said about jar and earring being altered conditions without change of the original substance of earth and gold respectively, is from the ordinary standpoint of common sense; for if subjected to a rigid analysis, it will be evident, that as the *Vedantin* does not recognise anything else but intelligence to be the site (*adhisthan*), consequently earth and gold cannot possibly be the site of jar and earring—for both are unreal; and one unreality cannot be the site of another. On the other hand, as in snake illusion, intelligence associated with the rope is the site on which the snake is projected or created, so is intelligence associated with their respective mate als earth and gold, the site of their products jar and earring; so that the assertion that they (jar, etc.,) are modifications or altered conditions without change of the original substance or material cause (*Vivartta*) is beyond dispute.

respectively) will reduce thickened milk into a similar modification of milk is absurd. Because here the original appearance of milk has been changed, and there is the further possibility of changing it into curd, and neither curd nor thickened milk can be made to assume the original appearance of milk; hence they are altered forms of milk *(Parinama)*. But even after earth and gold have been transformed into jar and earring, there is no disappearance of the original appearance of earth and gold, in their respective products; for which, they are called *Vivartta*.

52. If it be asked, like the two modifications with and without change of original substance or form, why not recognise the theory of *Arambha* in connection with earth and gold? Because in that case, earth and gold will be duplicated. That is to say, according to the supporters of the doctrine of *Arambha* (*Naiyayikas*) the material cause (earth) of jar (its product or action) will assume the shape both of action and cause and thus be duplicated; so that after thus being doubled in the shape of action and cause, the properties will likewise be doubled. And since form, touch, taste, smell, and sound are by them admitted to be distinct both in the cause and its product, consequently it amounts to a duplication of properties.*

---

* For a practical difference between the genus of cause and the genus of effect, a distinction is perceived in them, so that for the same cause being modified into cause and effect, the cause will be duplicated in respect to effect, and when the cause—form and the rest—as well as the properties of the effect—form, touch, smell, taste and sound—should also be doubled (differentiated); but in practice no one says "these are the properties of yarn and these of the cloth its product; nor is such distinction observable. Then again, as in the practical destruction of cause and effect their identity is not established, so to create a distinction in the cause yarn, etc., from want of perception of cloth, does not establish any distinction between cause and effect; on the other hand, their imaginary distinction and natural identity are owing to an indescribable

53. ARUNI speaks of the unreality of phenomena by alluding to the three illustrations of clay, gold and iron (*Chhandogya Upanishad Chat. VI.)*; and as their unreality has been inferentially established, so is the unreality of the objective world which is virtually a product of the elements, and their quintuplication, over and over thought of, that it may continue as a standing impression in the mind.

54. If it be asked what necessity is there to enquire after and ascertain the unreality of effects? To establish knowledge of effects produced from knowledge of cause. To this purpose the sage UDALAKA addresses his pupil Shvetaketu: "As from the knowledge of a lump of clay all earthen objects are known." But how can knowledge of Reality—the cause of phenomena—produce knowledge of their unreality?

55. Reality and unreality both are present in phenomena or effects; therefore knowledge of cause produces knowledge of the complement of reality included in them. Ordinarily speaking, a jar which is a modification of clay—the material cause,—is called 'action,' or 'effect;' its changed portion is unreal, and earth, real; and this knowledge results from knowledge of cause [clay].

56. The complement of unreality imbedded in effects, as it serves no purpose, needs not be known; but knowledge of the complement of reality is alone useful for the purpose of emancipation.

57. For knowledge of cause to produce knowledge of effect is not at all surprising; hence what has already been said in reference to UDALAKA's address to the pupil SHVETAKETU.—"As from a lump of clay all earthen objects are known" cannot excite any wonder. So says his opponent.

58. And the *Vedantin* replies:—So far as persons of discrimination are concerned, it is true indeed. The complement

identity of relation: hence the doctrine of *Arambha* or production of a substance different in form from its material cause, its untenable.

of reality inherent in phenomena resembles the cause, and those who know it are not at all surprised. But how can the wonder of ignorant persons, wanting in discrimination be prevented ?

59. The followers of Naya who regard intimate relation, its want, and the instrumental cause as the three causes ; the advocates of *Sankhya* who look upon change of prior condition as the cause ; an ordinary men unacquainted with the two aforesaid schools of philosophy—all of them—are sure to be astonished from listening "knowledge of one cause produces knowledge of many effects."

60. In order to induce a pupil to ascertain tne identity of the individual and universal spirit which is the subject of non-duality, it has been said in the *Chhandogya Upanishad* (Chapt. VI.),—"From knowledge of one cause all objects are known," and not for a desire of speaking about phenomena.

61. [The above *Sruti* text is now being explained] :—

As from knowledge of one lump of clay all earthen objects are known, so from knowledge of one BRAHMA, the whole universe is known to be Its effect, action or product—[as unreal as the snake in rope].

62. BRAHMA is being, intelligence, and bliss ; but the universe is nominal and non-eternal. This indication of PARABRAHMA occurs in the *Uttar Tapniya Upanishad.*

63. ARUNI speaks of BRAHMA as being or existence, the *Rig Vedic Brahman* demonstrates intelligence, and SANATKUMAR blissfulness only. [ARUNI in his discourse thus addresses the pupil SHVETAKETU endearingly :—"Prior to the evolution of the universe there existed 'being'." (*Chhandogya Upanishad* Chapt. VI.) "Intelligence is the substrate of all." (*Aiterya Upanishad.*) SANATKUMAR in reply to NARAD used the word '*Bhuma*' meaning fullness and bliss]. There are other texts to the same purpose too.

64. Regarding the universe, passages occur in the *Sruti* to shew that it is mere name and form and therefore unreal :—

"The Supreme Self thought of their several forms and gave them names."

65. And "Prior to its evolution, the universe was in an unmanifested condition, subsequently it was manifested in two ways, *viz.*, by name and form." (*Brihadaranyak Upanishada.*) Here 'unmanifested' refers to the indescribable *Mayaic* force inherent in BRAHMA.

66. That *Maya* present in BRAHMA (Itself unchangeable) was modified or transformed into the elements ether and the rest, and the objective universe. *Maya* is nothing else but (*Prakriti*) matter, the universal material cause; and BRAHMA as the receptacle of that (*Maya*) illusion is the Supreme Lord *i. e.*, its controller.

67. The first product of this modification or altered condition of matter is ether; it is existent, manifested and dear—properties derived from the cause,* BRAHMA; and naturally it is void. Now of these two sets of properties those derived from BRAHMA are real, but its individual property is unreal. Why?

68. Because as it did not exist prior to the origin of ether, and will subsequently be destroyed along with it, consequently though manifested so long as ether lasts, it is unreal. How? What did not exist originally and will cease to be in the end, must be taken for the time being it exists, as similarly non-existent.

69. The testimony of the *Gita* goes also to extablish what has just been said. "ARJUN, what are originally unmanifested, manifested in the interval between birth and death, and

* The properties of cause are transmitted to its products; for instance sound is said to belong to ether which is its individual property; water has sound derived from ether, while its own properties are sweet taste, cold feel, etc.; similarly in regard to the three other elements. Therefore the text seeks to create a distinction between the two sets of properties, to shew the complement of reality as also its reverse, present in phenomena.

unmanifested in the end, of such nature are the elements ether, etc." So spoke KRISHNA to ARJUNA.

70. As in all earthen objects (jar, etc.), earth pervades them both in and out, and in all conditions of time; so 'existence,' etc., pervade ether. If it be asked how can 'being' and the rest be inferred apart from ether? The reply is, in the same way as you infer your own self, to be existence, intelligence and bliss.

71. When ether is forgot, say what do you discover in its stead? If you say 'void,' well that is mere sound; for literally it conveys the sense of a receptacle in which that void was existent; but now the void is wanting, consequently its receptacle is the remnant something which is manifested.

72. If it be alleged, this does not settle the question of existence, intelligence and bliss being inferred apart from ether. It is therefore said.—As the receptacle manifesting the absence of ether in it, it is 'being' or 'existence'; and as the subject of indifference it is 'bliss' or 'felicity'; for what is devoid of friendliness or hostility is recognised as felicity.

73. Subjects that are friendly cause gladness of the intellect, as their reverse grief; and absence of both produces blissfulness experienced by one's own self. If it be asked? Why not grief? Because so far as grief is concerned, it is never present in self.*

* Without definite knowledge of happiness in some shape as "this is happiness," its existence is never manifested. Therefore as no happiness can be seen without self who is knowledge, consequently the popular conception of happiness is also of self. What is discovered in connection with a subject is an action of the modification of the mental function; grief never belongs to the nature of self, inasmuch as there are no visible proofs seen to that effect; for instance no one ever experiences "I am unhappy". On the other hand, passages occur in the *Sruti* where self is said to be intelligence and bliss. Moreover every one desires to be happy. Now this popular expression is based on ignorance. For self is happi-

74. Though that happiness of self is fixed and eternal yet as the mind,—its instrument of cognition—is fickle and always changing its site from one object to another, consequently it is but proper to consider both happiness and grief are mental productions.

75. In the same way, is the blissfulness of ether established. Its existence and intelligence require no mention as they are equally admitted [by the *Vedantin* and his opponent]. From air to the physical body, all material objects should be similarly considered to trace the complement of reality and connect it with 'being,' 'intelligence,' and 'bliss.'

76. Motion and touch are the two forms of air; combustion and light of fire; solution, of water; and hardness, of earth. This is certain.

77. Drugs, food grains, and bodies too, have uncommon forms [in their individual virtues]; which should be duly considered.

78. Name and form are as various as they are distinct, but being, intelligence, and bliss are equally seated in them all, so that here there is no contention.*

79. Both name and form are unreal, for they are derivated

---

ness, and a desire for happiness can only be when the individual is in want of it; those who are ignorant of the *Sruti* and have received no instruction on self-knowledge clamour for happiness; they experience felicity by receiving the reflection of intelligence from self, which acting on the mental function creates a relation between happiness and self thus making him the subject of affection and feeling contentment; but this is not found to follow in respect to grief as naturally belonging to self.

* A bubble is neither distinct from, nor one with the sea; nor is it either; so are foam, wave, etc., for which they are said to be indescribable; and as they are born to die, they are unreal in comparison to the sea. Similarly as name and form are indescribable and subject to birth and destruction, they are unreal respecting Brahma.

products ; and liable to destruction. Therefore regard them ... the same light as waves, froth and bubbles are of the sea*—in short, unreal.

80. With the visible knowledge of PARABRAHMA as everlasting intelligence and bliss, name and form appear unreal ; and are shortly afterwards abandoned by those desirous of release.

81. As duality (name and form) come to be disregarded, so does BRAHMA become visible ; and as BRAHMA comes to be visibly known, so is duality (the objective universe) abandoned.

82. From the help of both the above practices (disregard of duality and cognition of BRAHMA), a theosophist for his knowledge of BRAHMA is freed, though he may be alive ; and whatever may be his body.

83. Wise men regard thinking, talking and discussing on BRAHMA so as to help each other to cognise It—in short, to be intent on this one subject—as *Brahmabhyas*.

84. Impression of the reality of this vast material expanse eternally abiding in the mind is removed from long and uninterrupted practice of the aforesaid *Brahmaic* knowledge with affection.

85. Like the force of clay, the *Brahmaic* force *Maya* creates many different effects, which are unreal. And sleep and dreams are illustrations.

86. Just as the force of sleep creates things which are impossible or difficult of being done ; so does the force of *Maya* centred in BRAHMÀ create, preserve, and destroy the universe :

87. Just as in dream, a person sees himself walking in the

---

* Bubbles foam, waves, etc,, are neither distinct form the sea, nor its reverse, nor both ; hence indescribable ; and as they are subject to birth and destruction, they are unreal in regard to the sea ; similarly for name and form being indescribable, and subject to birth and destruction, they are unreal in respect to BRAHMA.

sky (ether), his own head beheaded, (and that dream lasting for a couple of hours appears to have a duration of years); and sees his dead relations, son, etc.

88. There is no rule to settle the consistency or possibility of the things then occuring, but they are seen just as they happen.

89. Since therefore the force of sleep is seen to be possessed with such marvellous power, where is the wonder for the force of *Maya* to have indescribable power?

90. Just as in a person lying down to sleep, it produces dreams of various sorts; so the *Mayaic* force seated in BRAHMA (devoid of action), creates diverse products through change.

91. Ether, air, fire, water, earth, *Brahmá's* egg, the fourteen abodes, together with animate and inanimate objects (such as stone etc.,) are all changed products of *Maya.* Reflection of intelligence in the internal organ inside the body, and its absence, constitute the difference of sentient or animate, and its reverse—insentient or inanimate.

92. The ordinary indication of BRAHMA,—'being' 'intelligence' and 'bliss'—is equally present in both the animate and inanimate: name and form create their individual distinction.

93. As in a cloth, the appearance of trees, beasts, etc., with which it is worked up is unreal, so name and from are unreal respecting BRAHMA. And if they are abandoned (for their unreality), the (remaining) complement of Reality is perceived to be BRAHMA.

94. Just as person standing on the riverbank sees his image reflected in the water which he never confounds for himself, on the other hand fixes his identity with the body standing on the bank; so in the matter of name and form, though visible, the perception of their reality having ceased or been abandoned, self appears as BRAHMA.

95. As thousands and thousands of imaginary substances

(mental creations) though present are discarded alike by all, so are name and form equally fit to be abandoned.

96. As these imaginary products created by the mind last for a short time to be replaced by others; but those which disappear, never re-appear; similarly respecting the cognition of self as BRAHMA and the unreality of phenomena, when they have been once ascertained to be so, the perception of that tdentity of self and BRAHMA receives neither any check nor meets with obstruction; and the duality (phenomena) cease to re-appear:

97. Just as manhood never returns to youth, nor old age to manhood; and as a dead father does not re-appear, nor yesterday come back again.

98. What is the difference between ordinary practice in reference to phenomena liable to destruction every moment, and mental creation? None whatever. Therefore though visible, confide not in the reality of the objective universe.

99. If it be asked, what is the benefit of not conforming to ordinary practice? The reply is, discarding the reality of phenomena makes the intellect assume the modification of BRAHMA; it receives no more obstruction and thus gets firmly seated there. And the ordinary practice [of begging, eating, etc.,] in which theosophists are found to be engaged resemble those performers of popular sports who assume the garb of a tiger, etc., to create diversion in, and not for devouring, the audience.

100. Just as in a current, motion of the water shakes not the stones and pebbles imbedded in the river-bed; so does the ordinary practice of theosophists shake not their non-duality, or the belief of unreality of duality (phenomena).

101. As in a bright mirror, many objects are reflected together with the ether which forms as it were their womb; so in BRAHMA which is eternal, intelligence and bliss, is discovered the infinite ether containing the universe.

102. As without looking in the mirror, things reflected

there are not seen, so without the ascertainment of the everlasting intelligence and bliss of BRAHMA how are name and form to be perceived?

103. After the discovery of BRAHMA in the form of everlasting intelligence and bliss, the intellect is firmly to be concentrated on It, leaving aside phenomena, which (though visible) are mere name and form, and unreal.

104. If that is done, devoid of materiality BRAHMA is established as being, intelligence and bliss; and here all enquirers rest their belief ever afterwards.

105. This third chapter deals on the unreality of phenomena, and the secondless blissfulness which proceeds from such thinking.

SECTION XIV.

(d) On the Felicity produced from Self-knowledeg.

MENTAL restraint, and discrimination of Self as the only reality, producing visible knowledge of BRAHMA and Its blissfulness (in a theosophist), will form the subject of the present treatise.*

2. Like material felicity, happiness proceeding from Self-knowledge is also a modification of the intellect. From a natural distinction in its varieties, it is said to be of four sorts.

3. They are :—

(*a*) Absence of pain or misery.

(*b*) Satiety, or acquisition of all desired enjoyments.

(*c*) Satisfaction produced from the realization or successful accomplishment of what was proper to be done ; and

(*d*). Acquisition of what was fit to have.

4. Misery is of two sorts, according as it relates to present or future existence. Removal of misery relating to the present life is now being set forth after the text of the *Brihadaranyakopanishad.*

---

* It may properly be contended, that as in a previous portion, happiness has been defined to be of three different sorts, the introduction of a fourth variety is quite uncalled for, the more so, as it is said to be a modification of the intellect, like material felicity. Naturally then, its place would be subordinate to, or included in material felicity. Now such a contention does not stand the test of a searching enquiry. For, material felicity has been experienced in all prior re-incarnations (from Brahmá to the lowest insect ; similarly the felicity of profound slumber (*Brahmaic* bliss) and what is derived ftom impressions have been experienced ; but it is reserved for a theosophist to experience the blissfulness proceeding from knowledge ; and as he is beyond the pale of re-birth, he can have no prior impression of it. Thus then it is quite a separate form of happiness without envelopment, full, and with modification of the intellect as its indication.

5 When a person knows the *Atma* to be self and says "This (self) am I," what desire of enjoyment can linger in the body to cause him pain at its remaining ungratified." None whatever. [For that knowledge removes all desire of enjoyment, both present and future].

6. The *Atma* has been spoken of in two ways, *viz.*, the Individual and Supreme Selves. Intelligence present in the physical, subtle and cause-bodies and mistaken with them as identical, is regarded as the agent,—the enjoyer, and called *Jiva* or individual.

7. The Supreme Self is everlasting intelligence and bliss. As the site or substrate of phenomena with name and form, He is mistaken as identically one with them. Discrimination establishes his distinction both from the three aforesaid bodies and material objects.

8. Desire of enjoyment for the gratification of the enjoyer, produces disease which can only affect the three bodies, but not self.

9. Different diseases affecting different individuals owing to a difference in their temperaments have their seat in the physical body. Passions and desires are the diseases of the subtle body; and the seeds (impressions) of disease of both the physical and subtle bodies are seated in the cause body.

10. Consideration of the Supreme Self in the manner pointed out in connection with the "Felicity of non-duality" (*Vide* Section XIII.), leaves no desire of enjoyment. For a theosophist no more confounds phenomena with reality; consequently what more desire can he have?

11. While on the subject of the felicity of Self (Section XII.) the nature of the individual Self has been ascertained, and since there is no enjoyer so far as the three bodies are concerned how then will disease be produced?

12. To think of merit and demerit is the source of pain relating to future existence. But as has already been said, (Section XI. v.5-9.) "no thoughts harass the wise."

13. Just as water touches not the leaves of the lotus, so after gnosis has arisen future works cannot touch a theosophist: [they affect him not, producing neither merit nor de-merit].

14. Like reeds with cotton tufts (*Saccharum spontaneum*) burnt at once by the contact of fire, his accumulated works are burnt by knowledge.

15. As in the *Gita*:—" ARJUN, as a blazing fire consumes the fuel and reduces it into ashes, so does the fire of knowledge reduce all works* into ashes."

16. He who does not believe in his own instrumentality of action " I am a doer of virtue," who has neither inclination for enjoying the fruits of actions, good and bad, nor doubts about them, is no destroyer, though he slays all living creatures in the universe; nor has he to suffer the torments of hell or objective existence hereafter.

17. " Neither matricide, nor parricide, neither theft nor procuring abortion and something equally sinful can destroy his emancipation, and injure the splendour and beauty of his face." (*Chhandogya Upanishad.*)

18. The *Sruti* likewise speaks of the acquisition of all

---

* " All works" have been taken for accumulated works by certain professors, but there are others who hold them to include the accumulated, fructescent and current works. Now, the fructescent are said to be exhausted by actual consummation of their results, so that the view of their being destroyed by knowledge will create an antagonism with the generally received doctrine. Everywhere it is maintained that a difference is found even amongst theosophists, in their present condition; some receiving homage of the high and low; others with difficulty living by means of begging. Some are provided with all comforts, others suffering the usual miseries of a mendicant's life—and this distinction is due to the result of works done in a prior life and which have already commenced to bear fruit. Even *Iswara* is unable to counteract them; they can only be exhausted by actual enjoyment of their results.

desired enjoyments by a theosophist, as it does of his freedom from pain:—"The theosophist attaining all desires is freed from death."

19. "Whether eating, or playing with women; driving a chariot or riding on horse-back, etc., along with his companions, be they wise or ignorant, he remembers not his body, but says that his fructescent works having not yet been exhausted keeps his body alive." (*Chhandogya Upanishad*)

20. "The theosophist attains all desires at once" so says the *Taiterya Upanishad*. Unlike the ignorant, he is no more re-born to enjoy the fruits of works done; but as a result of knowledge, his accumulated works are destroyed, leaving the fructescent to be exhausted by consummation in the present life; but his current (future) works can touch him not [as has already been said.]

21. "With youth, beauty, learning, health, firmness of heart combined an army protecting the whole earth.

22. "Whatever happiness is experienced by such a mighty king endowed with all convinceivable enjoyments and satiated with them is attained by the theosophist too."*

23. Both in that king and in the wise, no desires are left for human enjoyment, so that the attainment of happiness in the form of satiety is equal in them. But in the king it is due to want of desire; while in the wise, discrimination is the source of that absence of desire; so that, cessation of desire procuring satiety is equal in both.

24. Wise men as well as men learned in the *Shastras*, regard temporal enjoyments to be faulty. In the *Maitrayniya Shakha*. Raja Brihadrath speaks disparagingly of them and points out how defective are they.

---

* The word 'too' has a wider range, it includes all manner of happiness and its different grades, beginning with what is enjoyed by *Gandharvas* to that of *Bruhmâ*—all this is equally felt by the theosophist.

25. Defects pertaining to the physical body, mind, and various sorts of material enjoyments are all spoken of by him. Just as no one shows any desire to eat rice-pudding vomited by a dog, so do men of discrimination show no desire for temporal enjoyment.

26. Though, so far as absence of desire is concerned, both the king and theosophist are said to be equal, yet the latter is superior. For the king had to encounter much pain and hardship in the beginning, and is further subject to much anxiety, lest his authority be destroyed at some future period. These are the two defects under which he suffers.

27. They cannot apply to a theosophist for which he is superior to the king. Then again, the king is particularly fond of dancing and music, which the man of discrimination cares not; that is another cause of superiority.

28. There are two sorts of *Gandharvas* :—

Those incarnated in the present *Kalpa* as men and as a particular result of meritorious works who have inherited the condition of a *Gandharva* are called Men-Gandharvas.

29. When for meritorious work done in a prior *Kalpa*, one attains the condition of Gandharva in the beginning of the present *Kalpa*, he is called Deva-Gandharva.

30. Demigods and the spirits of one's departed ancestors eternally live in their own abodes. Those who have attained the condition of a Deva in the beginning of a *Kalpa* are called Ajan-Devatas.

31. Those who have secured an excellent position as a result of the performance of horse-sacrifice in the present *Kalpa* are more honored than Ajan-Devatas, and are called Karma-Devatas.

32. Yama and Agni etc., are the principal Devas; Rudra and Brihaspati are two well-known; Prajapati is called Virat; and Brahma, Threadsoul Hiranyagarbha.

33. From the sovereign exercising universal sway to the Threadsoul Hiranyagarbha, every one is desirous of enjoying

more happiness than what he has; but the blissfulness of self which none can adequately express nor mind conceive of, is superior to them all.

34. Regarding that desire for obtaining superior happinees which king and the rest have, a theosophist heeds not; and as he is perfectly unconcerned and free from desire, he is said to experience it all.

35. Just as he experiences happiness in his own body, for being the witness of the modification of intellect assuming the shape of happiness; so for a similar witness of the same modification of intellect in others too, he enjoys happiness.

36. If it be contended, that as ignorant persons are similar witnesses, they also can be said to enjoy all manner of happiness. That is impossible. For the knowledge that "I am the witness in all intellects seated inside all bodies" is absent in them. As the *Sruti* says:—"Who knows [each individuated self to be Brahma] enjoys all happiness."

37. The theosophist thus sings of his being the all-self as in the text of the Sama Veda:—"I am the food as well as its enjoyer."*

38. Having thus declared the first and second varieties of felicity proceeding from knowledge of self, the remaining two *viz.*, satisfaction from the successful accomplishment of what was proper to be done, and acquisition of the attainable as they have already been discussed in the *Triptidwipa* should be properly studied.

39. Since ample mention has been made of them in the *Triptidwipa* [Sect. vii. ante], the reader is referred to it. For the purpose of clearing the intellect, they are fit to be re-introduced here to ascertain their drift.

---

* He enjoys the blissfulness of heaven quite disinterestedly—without expressing any wish or longing for it, but as the witnessing intelligence prevading everywhere. This is the purport of the *Sruti* text.

40. Prior to knowledge, a theosophist had to perform various works either essential to present or future happiness, or the purpose of emancipation.

41. But subsequent to gnosis, he has nothing proper to do, [no harm can befall him if anything is left undone], for the knowledge of proper and improper has left him, and that produces satiety.

42. Ignorant persons full of grief are actuated by desire, and act as they are influenced by it. Let them continue their everyday practice in connection with their present relationship with son etc.; but as "I am full of Supreme bliss," I have no desire left that can make me conform to this or that practice.

43. Let those desirous of knowledge perform works for the benefit of the future life, but since "I am all the abodes," why am I to undertake works and how practice them?

44. Let professors qualified in them, explain the sacred writings, or give instructions to the *Vedas*, but "I am actionless," therefore not so qualified.

45. "I am the intelligence" desirous neither of sleeping, begging, bathing, etc., nor of doing them, and if they are attributed to me by a spectator what harm can it do me?

46. Just as the seeds of the *Abrus precatorious* piled in a spot mistaken by monkeys for fire cannot burn, so the attribution of ordinary worldly practices cannot make me do them.

47. Let the ignorant betake to 'hearing,' I know the reality, self, what necessity is there for me to hear? Let those infested with doubts have recourse to 'consideration,' but as I am free from them why I am to practice consideration?

48. Let persons holding contrary ideas undertake profound contemplation or deep and repeated thinking. I never mistake the physical body for self, consequently that is not necessary for me.

49. Force of eternal practice as the result of prior impressions make me conform to the ordinary usage and say "I am a man," in spite of the cessation of antagonistic or conflicting ideas.

50. Exhaustion of the fractescent puts an end to practice; but till actions are so destroyed that practice remains unaffected and thousands and thousands of contemplations are of no avail.

51. If you hold diminution of practice to be beneficial for promoting a desire of release, be you engaged in contemplation. As I find practice causing no impediment to self-knowledge why then am I to contemplate?

52. Since I am free from mental distraction, there is no necessity for me to undertake profound meditation for concentrating the mind; both distraction and cencentration are the attributes of changeable mind.

53. "I am the eternal experience"—what experience is distinct from me? None whatever. Therefore what was fit to be done has been done, and what was fit to have, have been gained. This is my certain conviction.

54. I conform neither to popular practice. not what is enjoined in the *Shastras*, nor what is distinct from both. For I am no agent or instrument, but as my fructescent works bid me do, so do I act.

55. Or even if after having discharged what was proper to be done, desire of popular favor makes me conform to the practices enjoined in the *Shastras* what harm can they do me?

56. Let the body be engaged in worshipping Devas, in bathing, cleanliness, and begging, and the organ of speech in recanting the mystic Om or in the study of the Vedanta;

57. No matter, whether my intellect be employed in meditating Vishnu or merging into the felicity of Brahma, as

"I am the witnessing intelligence" I do nothing nor make others do.

58. A theosophist satisfied with the successful accomplishment of what was proper to be done, and again satisfied with the attainment of what was proper to have, constantly reflects in his mind in the following wise :—

59. I have visible cognition of the eternal self therefore I am blessed and blessed. The supreme felicity of Brahma is plainly manifested to me, therefore I am blessed and blessed.

60. Miseries of earth life touch me not, therefore I am blessed. I am successful in having attained my end. The darkness of ignorance has left me, therefore I am blessed and blessec.

61. I have nothing proper left to be done, therefore I am blessed. I have attained the attainable, therefore I am blessed.

62. Verily I am blessed, I am blessed, my satisfaction is incomparable. I am blessed and blessed and twice more blessed.

63. My virtue is excellent, excellent—as it has been bearing many frutis,—and for acquiring that virtue again excellent—I am superior to all.

64. *Brahmananda* contains five chapters of which the present is the fourth; till the felicity produced from self-knowledge has arisen, it is necessary to practice 'hearing,' 'consideration,, and profound 'consideratiou.'

SECTION XV.

Vishayananda or Material Happiness.

THE present treatise has for its subject the ascertainment of material happiness as a part of the felicity of Brahma. What is it like? * It is the means by which Brahmaic felicity is known. On this point the *Sruti* says :—

2. "What is Impartite and essentially one is Brahma that is supreme blissfulness. Other creatures experience a trace only of this Brahmaic felicity."

3. From a difference in its qualities (good, active and dark). modification of the mental function assumes three different forms, to wit: tranquil, active and ignorant. Of them, indifference to, or utter disregard of enjoyment, tranquility of mind or resignation, and generosity or uprightness etc., come under the tranquil modification.

4. Desire and covetousness are the active, as folly and fear are the modifications of ignorance.

5. All these modifications receive the reflection of intelligence from Brahma. Moreover in the tranquil modification besides that reflex intelligence, the blissfulness of Brahma is likewise reflected.

6. As in the *Sruti*:—"The Supreme Self for filling each body with his image came to be reflected." "Like the sun etc."* Now this comparison of Vyas is intended to express the same cause which precludes Jiva from being a part of Brahma, [for It is impartite], reduces him to the condition of the sun's reflection in water.

---

* Just as the reflected face in mirror is a proper and adequate means to know the character or features of the face proper situated on the neck, so the mental perception of reflected felicity of Brahma i. e., *Vishayananda* is an adequate means for the cognition of the Brahmaic felicity manifest in the form of 'being' 'intelligence' and 'bliss.'

7. "That one Universal Self resides in the body of all animated beings, but like the reflection of moon in a tank and jar full of water, He is manifested in one form (Iswara) and manifold forms (Jiva)" [from a relation of associates.]

8. It may be objected that as Brahma is Impartite, therefore to say that in the modifications of the good quality otherwise called 'tranquil,' both intelligence and bliss are manifested; while intelligence is only discovered in the active and dark thus seeking to create a distinction is unsound. To remove such an apprehension the example of moon has been adduced:—Just as the moon reflected in impure and dirty water is dimly seen, and in pure water clearly visible; so is Brahma manifested in two forms [intelligence and bliss and intelligence only] according to different modifications.

9. In the active and ignorant modifications, for the presence of impurity, the blissful portion meets with an impediment; and for a little purity, the portion of Intelligence only is reflected.

10. Just as heat of fire is imparted even to pure water but not light, so in the modifications active and ignorant, intelligence alane is disclosed.

11. Just as in wood, both heat and light [of fire] are developed, so in the modification tranquil of the good quality both bliss and intelligence are developed.

12. How is this regulated? Depending on the nature of substance the above rule has been ascertained to be equal both in the simile and the thing elucidated in it. The proof? According to personal experience, the regulalor is to be made out.

13 In the active and ignorant modifications, no experience of happiness is to be found; in the tranquil variety, some of its modifications are seen to have more, and others less happiness.

14. In desire for house, land, etc., for that desire—a

product of the active quality of the mind—being a modification of the active variety, there can be no happiness.

15. Whether or not temporal enjoyments are productive of happiness, the very doubt is a productive source of pain; and if it be unproductive of happiness, its want of success increases the pain; and when that happiness meets with an impediment it excites anger.

16. If the impediment be of such a nature that it is incapable of being removed, there follows disappointment or dejection; which again, as a product of the dark quality, as also anger, etc., brings forth intense pain, and all hopes of happiness are dissipated.

17. Acquisition of a desired object produces delight—a modification of the tranquil variety—and exceeding happiness is the result; but in connection with the topic of acquisition, there follows little happiness only.

18—19. Indifference to, or utter disregard of material enjoyment is the cause of exceeding happiness, as has already been mentioned in the last section. Similarly happiness experienced from resignation and generosity, after the destruction of anger and covetousness, is due to the reflection of Brahmaic felicity. Regarding modifications of the mental function directed inwards, the blissfulness of Brahma is clearly reflected.

20—21. 'Being,' 'intelligence' and 'bliss' belongs to the nature of Brahma; of which 'being' alone is revealed in inanimate objects, clay, stone, etc., and not the other two, [intelligence and bliss]. In the active and ignorant modifications of the mental function 'being' 'intelligence' both; and in the tranquil 'being,' 'intelligence,' 'bliss' all the three are disclosed. In this way is mixed Brahma [Brahma] with this vast material expanse] spoken of.

22. The unmixed Brahma is to be known only by means of knowledge and mental restraint (*Yoga*); both of which

have already been dwelt upon. Yoga has been treated in Section XI. and knowledge in the two following Sections.

23. 'Non-being' 'insentiency,' and 'pain' are the three characteristic forms of *Maya*; of them non-being relates to things which exist not, as man's horn; ether flowers; and insentiency to inanimate objects wood, stone, etc.

24. In the active and ignorant modifications of the mental function there is pain or misery. In this manner, is matter manifested everywhere. For an absence of distinction between Brahma and this vast material expanse in the tranquil modification the phrase " mixed Brahma" has been made use of to express this mixed condition.

25. This being the nature of Brahma and *Maya* (matter) any qualified person (but with intellect dull) desirous of contemplating Brahma should follow the method here pointed out.—should abandon the non-existing part expressed by the word " man's horn," and meditate on the remaining Brahma ever always without intermission.

26. In stone and wood, etc., name and form both are to be abandoned; only being' is to be thought of. In the active and ignorant modifications after abandoning pain, 'being' and 'intelligence' are to be meditated upon.

27. In the same manner 'being' intelligence' and 'bliss' all three are to be mentally dwelt upon in the modification of the tranquil variety. And these three varieties of meditation are consecutively inferior, middle and superior.

28. Even meditating on " mixed Brahma" is the best for persons of dull intellect [for they are capable of fixing their intellect on the Impersonal method of contemplation]; and this proposition of the *Vedanta* has been spoken of in the present treatise.

29. When the above meditation of the mixed or Personal Form of Brahma has gradually produced indifference to wordly enjoyments and hushed the energy of the modifications of the mental function, then is the individual qualified to medi-

tate on the impression of happiness which is the best of the three aforesaid varieties. These then are the four sorts of meditation.

30. If it be asked whether this resting of the mental function on "impressional felicity" (*vasanananda*) is contemplation? It is not. For the presence of both contemplation. and concentration or mental restraint, it is not contemplation. What is it then? Verily it is Self-knowledge (*Brahma Vidya*). When contemplation produces mental concentration, then is knowledge confirmed.

31. When knowledge of Brahma is confirmed, 'being,' intelligence' and 'bliss' are manifested in the form of One Impartite, and distinction is then done away with; because the associates which are to create distinction have either been restricted or removed.

32. And those difference-creating-associates are the tranquil, active and ignorant modications, as also external objects—stone, wood etc. Concentration of the mind and discrimination removes them.

33. There is no distinction of knower, knowledge and the object to be known, when Brahma has been discovered as the self-manifested, secondless and unassociated Reality.

34. The work *Brahmanda* contains five chapters, of which the present (the last) speaks of temporal happiness. Make your entrance into the felicity of Brahma through this door.

35. For this Brahmaic felicity, let Siva, non-distinct from Vishnu, be always propitious to those who with mind pure and faultless take protection of him; and save them from the over recurring phases of birth and death in this nether sphere of existence.

FINISH.